Pioneering Women

Riddel Hall and Queen's University Belfast

Riddel Hall was founded by Eliza and Isabella Riddel and built in 1915 as a residence for women students at Queen's University. The gatelodge was built in identical style ~ red brick with sandstone dressings.

GATE LODGE · RIDDEL HALL

555/200 Joanna Martin

JOANNA MARTIN 1996

ARCHITECTS W H LYNN — B & P 35073

Pioneering Women

Riddel Hall and Queen's University Belfast

GILLIAN McCLELLAND

with Diana Hadden

ULSTER HISTORICAL FOUNDATION

Ulster Historical Foundation is pleased to acknowledge support for this publication provided by the Belfast Natural History and Philosophical Society, the Environment and Heritage Service, the Esme Mitchell Trust and the Riddel Hall Heritage Association. All contributions are gratefully acknowledged.

First Published 2005
by the Ulster Historical Foundation
12 College Square East, Belfast BT1 6DD
www.ancestryireland.com
www.booksireland.org.uk

Printed by Bath Press
Design by CheahDesign

CONTENTS

Medical and dental students on the bank outside Riddel, spring 1960
E. Murray

FOREWORD

Dr McClelland's history of Riddel Hall is of interest on several counts. It is full of fascinating vignettes and will be read with pleasure by former residents, their children and grandchildren – and perhaps also by their great-grandchildren. Readers will have their own favourites. My own is the young woman who came into residence in 1935, her mother remarking it was a choice between matrimony and medicine and clearly banking on the latter. Quickly her daughter decided on both, although the marriage was cruelly delayed for a decade not only by study but by war and her fiancé becoming a prisoner of the Japanese in February 1942 at the fall of Singapore.

Eliza and Isabella Riddel inherited great wealth and, along with so many of their generation, used it for the benefit of others. At that time their choice of female higher education would have been unusual, but they were building on the work of pioneers such as Margaret Byers and Isabella Tod in Belfast and Anne Jellicoe in Dublin, as well as English women such as Miss Beale of Cheltenham Ladies' College.

The opening of Riddel Hall for female students in 1915 brings the story inevitably into the history of Queen's University. Queen's first admitted women in 1882 and Riddel provided a safe haven for young girls often far from home. The ethos of the Hall reflected the middle-class values of the time, but it recognized that girls might be educated for life beyond marriage and domesticity. Many Riddel women followed careers in medicine or teaching and some managed to combine a profession with a husband and children.

When the Hall closed in 1975 young women (and young men) no longer accepted the values that had governed the lives of their parents and grandparents. They lived in a more liberal (or more libertarian?) and less deferential social milieu. In this history of Riddel Hall we have a microcosm of the transformation in society at large over the relatively short period of sixty years.

Gillian McClelland's text and Diana Hadden's sensitively chosen illustrations have together created a fitting tribute to Riddel Hall and its Pioneering Women.

L.A. Clarkson,
Emeritus Professor of Social History
Queen's University Belfast

Unglazed windows of Riddel Hall porch
Queen's University Belfast

AUTHOR'S ACKNOWLEDGEMENTS

I wish to thank the Riddel Hall Heritage Association for inviting me to write the history of Riddel Hall and for entrusting me with the Hall's records. I am grateful to Lesley Calderwood, Margaret Gowdy, and in particular Diana Hadden, whose faith in the project and tireless energy have made this book possible. I am indebted to the members of Riddel Hall Old Students' Association and Miss Power Steele, Warden from 1944 to 1948, for sharing memories of their experiences in Riddel Hall, and to Martina McKnight for helping me to collate biographical data.

Thanks are also due to the staff of the Public Record Office of Northern Ireland for access to the uncatalogued box of Riddel Hall records; to Nicholas Duffin for his personal records of the Riddel Hall Permanent Committee and to the staff of the Great Hall, Queen's University Belfast, for allowing me access to Riddel Hall records which had survived under their careful supervision.

I am indebted to Dr Diane Urquhart, Dr Myrtle Hill and Dr Margaret Crawford who have read early drafts of the manuscript, and especially to Professor Leslie Clarkson who has read and edited several versions, for their help and advice. Special thanks are due to the Ulster Historical Foundation, in particular Fintan Mullan, for their commitment to this history of Riddel Hall.

Gillian McClelland

'Riddel Afloat', Students' Day 1961
M. Hopkins

ACKNOWLEDGEMENTS

I would like to thank the many people who helped to make this book possible, especially: Lesley Calderwood and Margaret Gowdy who without hesitation joined me in founding the Riddel Hall Heritage Association to enable us to proceed with applications for funds; Gillian McClelland, researcher and author, who was so enthusiastic about Riddel Hall, women and education; Marcus Patton who wrote two short chapters, one in his capacity as conservation architect and one as a previous occupant of the Hall 'after the ladies'; Professor Leslie Clarkson who was supportive and interested from the start, never failed with advice or help in times of need, and kindly agreed to write the foreword; and the members of the Riddel Hall Old Students' Association (RHOSA) for their great interest in the project, their willingness to be interviewed for research purposes and for allowing their reminiscences to be used in the publication. The staff of the Northern Ireland Council for Voluntary Action (NICVA) guided us through organisational issues. Fintan Mullan of the Ulster Historical Foundation provided advice and encouragement in the publication process.

Thanks are due to the following staff of Queen's University Belfast: Ivan Ewart of Media Services for the photographic details of the Hall, and other assistance; the Vice-Chancellor, Professor Peter Gregson; Aine Gibbons; Charles Gray; Shan McAnena, Curator of Art, for access to works of art originally in Riddel Hall and now part of the Collection of Queen's University Belfast; Richard Oldfield and the Great Hall staff for looking after the Riddel archives; David McLean; Gerry Power; Frank Young; also Gwynne Donnell of the Visitors' Centre who had sufficient faith in this project to organise a summer exhibition about Riddel Hall and its women.

Images and illustrations throughout the text have been reproduced with the kind permission of many individuals and institutions: James Allen; Joanna Martin; Carey Ramsay; the Principal of Alexandra College, Dublin; Arts Council of Northern Ireland; Belfast City Council Health and Environmental Services Department (Building Control); Belfast Central Library; The Cheltenham Ladies' College; The Mistress and Fellows, Girton College, Cambridge; Trustees of the National Museums and Galleries of Northern Ireland (Ulster Museum); The National Trust; National Society for the Prevention of Cruelty to Children (NSPCC); Ordnance Survey of Northern Ireland; Public Record Office of

Northern Ireland; members of Riddel Hall Old Students' Association (RHOSA); John Riddel and Son Limited; The Principal and Fellows of Somerville College, Oxford; The Board of Trinity College Dublin; Ulster Society for the Prevention of Cruelty to Animals (USPCA); and the Headmistress of Victoria College Belfast.

Many individuals helped in preparation, production and research, or provided other advice and support, in particular: Pauline Adams, Brian Byrne, Bill Caldwell, Richard Clarke, Nicholas Duffin, Phil Evans, Judith Hughes-Lewis, Aileen Ivory, Gary Jebb, Betty Kerr, Rose Lavery, Pat McLean, Ann McVeigh, Peter Marlow, Nicola Mawhinney, Linda Montgomery, James Morgan, Lesley Morrish, Dean Morrow, Andrew Norton, Ann O'Connor, Kate Perry, Richard Ramsay, Gary Roberts, Rachel Roberts, Robert Watton, Juliet Williams; and especially Sophia Cross who provided invaluable assistance.

Funding was necessary to complete the research and produce a publication with many illustrations, and the following were most generous in their sponsorship:

Awards for All
Development and Alumni Relations, Queen's University Belfast
Esme Mitchell Trust
The Belfast Natural History and Philosophical Society

also many past students of Riddel Hall, with special mention of the following (maiden names in brackets): Frances Arkle (Campbell), Sally Boyd (McManus), Lesley Calderwood (Crozier), Elizabeth Cameron (Elliott), Louise Clowes (Hogg), Joy Coskery (Heenan), Dorothy Dowey (Campbell), Peggy Elliott (Hamilton), Lorna Ferris (Scott), Joan Fry (Crowe), Eileen Gibson (Hill), Margaret Gowdy (Lyons), Gwyneth Grendelmeier (Hutchison), Diana Hadden (Martin), Margaret Haire (Mitchell), Paddy Hayes (McKee), Helen Hood (Lesser), Sara Jamieson, Margaret McCloy (Devenney), Elsie McCune (Archer), Mollie McGeown (Freeland), Roberta Orr (Thompson), Susan Platt (Wallace), Judith Rebbeck (Price), Nessie Redman (Maybin), Sandra Redmond (McMaster), Rae Scott (Buchanan), Ethel Shannon (McRoberts), Doris Stickler (Cole), Moira Taylor (Strawbridge), Vera Williamson (McNeice).

Finally I thank David and the rest of my family who not only put up with this project but actively helped and gave intelligent advice at appropriate moments.

Diana Hadden

INTRODUCTION

It all began with two large leather suitcases.

In 1975 Miss Molly Dawson retired as Warden and Riddel Hall closed. Miss Dawson packed the last remaining important archives into two suitcases and brought them to her new home on the Stranmillis Road. I called to see her from time to time, and, much later, she gave me the two large and heavy suitcases. After a brief look inside at the books and papers, they went up to my attic. But my conscience did not let me forget.

In 2003, three previous Riddel Hall students, Lesley Calderwood, Margaret Gowdy and myself, founded the Riddel Hall Heritage Association with the sole purpose of researching the archives of Riddel Hall and publishing the results. Professor Leslie Clarkson, with his wide knowledge of social and economic history, supported the project from the start, and through him we found Gillian McClelland who with great enthusiasm set to work on the archives; these included papers at the Public Record Office of Northern Ireland and in an old filing cabinet at Queen's University Belfast.

At the start I called this book 'The Riddle of Riddel Hall'. Why did it not survive when similar halls at other universities are still flourishing? Later, when we felt we might know the answer, the riddle for others became, 'Where is it?' Not many seemed to know, not even the students who studied in Stranmillis College next door and walked past the old Riddel Hall gateway every day. This book and the associated exhibition in Queen's University should help to put Riddel again on the map.

But the story of Riddel Hall begins in the mid-nineteenth century with the pioneers who struggled for women to be educated, then to be admitted to university. Queen's College Belfast was one of the first to admit women, earlier than Trinity College Dublin, and far before the universities of Oxford and Cambridge. The Misses Eliza and Isabella Riddel had no chance of any higher education, yet were the first to support the concept in founding Riddel Hall for women students at Queen's. At that time there was no hall of residence, even for men.

Miss Ruth Duffin, the somewhat autocratic first Warden, had a personal mission to educate reluctant Riddel girls in culture and an appreciation of art in all its forms. 'Without a vision the people perish' was one of her firm beliefs. We need her now to answer the final riddle. What lies in the future for Riddel Hall?

Diana Hadden

1

A Riddel Hall Chronicle

Many noble Irish women
Have been honoured in times past,
Two there are of special glory,
The Misses Riddel of Belfast.

Two sisters, rich in this world's wealth,
Still more with heart and wisdom blessed.
They did enduring good by stealth,
And never were by pride possessed.

They saw how women students came
To Queen's from far away: and stayed
In digs, in loneliness, with none
To help, encourage, watch, or aid.

They saw the need, they heard the call,
And looking not for thanks nor praise,
Built and endowed the Riddel Hall,
For women in their student days.[1]

Riddel Hall was founded and endowed by Eliza Riddel (1831-1924) and her sister Isabella (1836-1918) as an independent hall of residence to provide accommodation for 'female Protestant students and teachers of Queen's University Belfast'. From the arrival of its first cohort of students in September 1915, until it closed in June 1975, more than one thousand young women had a 'home from home' during their time at Queen's. At a time when the education of sons was the priority for most families the bequest allowed female students to benefit from facilities well below their real cost. The presence of this safe, monitored environment would now be recognised as empowering for women, as many parents would not have permitted them to attend university if it meant leaving home and living independently. Most students in 1915 were men, which meant that young women were even more isolated as the sexes were discouraged from mixing.

The personal account or 'Chronicle' of Miss Ruth Duffin, the first Warden, recording thirty years of the life of the Hall and written after her retirement in 1943, has been a rich source of information on her 'ideals'. She wanted the account to be continued by her successors, but neither Miss Joyce Power Steele nor Miss Molly Dawson did this. Miss Duffin's records constituted the Warden's reports to her employers, and as such should be recognised as a sanitised version of Hall life. Miss Dawson's written records such as annual addresses to the governors and the monthly minutes of the Permanent Committee became increasingly reflective over the decades. The words of the three wardens entrusted with the running of the Hall provide what might be termed the official history of the imposing red brick building and its successive cohorts of inhabitants. All three wardens conscientiously updated the student records with marriages, birth announcements and career details gleaned painstakingly from letters, Christmas cards, the press and the Queen's Women Graduates' Association (QWGA) magazines. These primary sources are particularly valuable for tracing changing career patterns of this large group of university-educated women from the end of the Great War until the beginning of the twenty-first century, and to reconstruct a picture of life in Riddel Hall from 1915 to 1975.

The official accounts have been enhanced – and occasionally modified – by interviews with former students for whom life in Riddel Hall resulted in lifelong memories and enduring friendships. Oral history is a valuable way of augmenting the written records with the memories of students who made it their home, although it has its dangers. When they talk about their lives, people are likely to embroider, exaggerate or get things wrong, although the thrust of what they say remains true.[2]

Reminiscences allow hidden characters to emerge: two less obviously powerful members of staff have been identified in this way. They both served the Hall for more than twenty-five years. The much-loved Matron, Miss Boyd, and the head parlour maid, Lily Gaston, are central characters who left no written records. Past students remember their overall experiences in similar ways but have very different impressions of personalities. Miss Duffin and her successors thought of the staff and residents of the Hall as a family and, as in all families, siblings' memories and the actual experiences of their parents differ. The rise and fall of Riddel Hall's fortunes are closely related to the change in status of the family in society.

The members of the Riddel Hall Old Students' Association (RHOSA) have kept in contact with their peers and the Hall since graduation, and have been happy to contribute their recollections of life in the Hall. No one admits to a negative experience in Riddel Hall, although some recall that there were a few girls who left after only a term. They appear to have been very much in the minority. The overwhelming memory was that their stay in Riddel was a special time between childhood and adult life. It was a place where they were part of a 'nurturing community' of women and, perhaps most significantly, made lifelong friends.

Over the sixty years of Riddel Hall's existence the position of women and the career opportunities available to them changed significantly, as did social and economic conditions. Its residents were not a representative sample or cross-

Miss Duffin, seated left, after she retired, in a family group outside Summerhill
Carey Ramsay

section of society, but the Riddel bequest contributed in its way to the development of a society where educational ability became valued more than background, gender or wealth. For young women who gained the necessary academic qualifications to enter the University, but whose parents were in reduced circumstances, bursaries permitted them to stay in the Hall either free or at a reduced rate of fees. In this way Riddel Hall can be viewed as a microcosm of a society undergoing dramatic cultural change and this book aims to put its story and the experiences of its residents into the wider context.

When the Hall opened in 1915 the Great War was in its early phase, and although women had not yet gained the parliamentary vote, the British suffrage movement had suspended its campaign for the duration of the war. Higher education for women was still in its infancy; the first five women to graduate from Queen's College Belfast had done so in 1884.

Between 1881 and the 1911 census the percentage of Irish women defined in the census as 'indefinite and unproductive' (i.e. not in employment) fell from 80 percent to less than 70 percent. There was an increase of 5,561 females in the 'liberal and learned professions' – schoolmistress, nun, hospital-certificated nurse

Early photograph of Queen's staff and students. The number of students and the presence of eight women suggests the occasion was Graduation 1886. Queen's College Belfast was the first university college in Ireland to admit women
Queen's University Belfast

and midwife – between 1901 and 1911, but this figure was artificially inflated since nurses, previously categorised as domestics, were now included.[3] Nevertheless, 26 percent of the Irish female workforce were in this category, although in Belfast only 4 percent of the female workforce were in the professional class (many of these women were teachers), compared with 73 percent in industry, reflecting the strong manufacturing base of the city.[4] In those professions not seen as an extension of women's 'natural' role of mother and carer, women had made few gains. In Belfast in 1911 there were only six women doctors (there were only thirty-three qualified women doctors and sixty-eight female medical students in the whole of Ireland), and no female solicitors or accountants.

The early residents of Riddel Hall were pioneers in achieving their ambitions to become doctors: fourteen of these young women qualified in medicine before 1920. The first female solicitor in Ireland was a Riddel student who qualified in 1926; two of the first cohort of students became lecturers on the staff of Queen's University.

The Home Rule crisis was ongoing when the Hall was founded, and Ireland was partitioned in 1920-21. Twenty-six counties became the Irish Free State and the six northeastern counties remained part of the United Kingdom as Northern Ireland. Throughout the inter-war years, worldwide economic depression, compounded by marriage bars in professional employment, kept women's career options narrow. Most women had to choose either marriage or a career. Winning the vote (for women over thirty years old in 1918, and on equal terms with men in 1928) had led to a belief that equality between the sexes had been achieved. Feminism was largely in retreat.

The Second World War offered some temporary opportunities for women to move outside traditional gender roles, but post-war reconstruction was associated with a return to domesticity for many married women. The introduction of the Welfare State in 1948 would eventually provide more employment options for professional women. The Education Act of 1947 introduced free second level education for all children over the age of eleven and raised the school leaving age to fifteen. This Act created the tri-partite system of grammar, secondary and technical schooling based on academic ability rather than on the ability of parents to pay fees.

The early 1950s were a time of austerity and the trend toward marriage was combined with a 'baby boom' associated with the reassertion of 'domesticity as never before'. By the end of the decade the desire for increased material prosperity was encouraging women to work to improve the lifestyles of their families, but this was still seen as a temporary expedient, not a vocation, and was viewed as unacceptable for the mothers of young children. In 1951 only 26 percent of married women in the United Kingdom were employed outside the home. Nevertheless, young women were benefiting from the expansion in secondary and tertiary education; state scholarships for university education were becoming more widely available throughout the decade. Young women in Britain also benefited from the expansion of university education as a result of the 1963 Robbins' Report, which decried the wastage of female talent and stressed the need for equality between men and women.[5]

In Northern Ireland the Lockwood Report in 1965 extended the Robbins' principles to the Province. The increase in female participation was reflected in Riddel Hall, which had its full complement of students. Indeed, the length of the waiting list led to the governors making plans for expansion.

Throughout most of the period covered by this book young men and women were not legally adults until they were twenty-one years of age. Consequently, the University and the governors of Riddel Hall acted *in loco parentis*. Traditional power relationships and the patriarchal order were largely accepted until the1960s. In this decade amidst 'a seemingly unstoppable demand for sexual and civil rights and disillusionment with political and religious institutions, challenges to the *status quo* were mounted with increasing determination'.[6] In Western Europe and North America many women felt that the time was right to 'claim ownership of their bodies and control over their political and economic destinies'.[7] The availability of the contraceptive pill from 1961 allowed women to make new choices. In 1975 a group of women from Queen's University formed the Northern Ireland Women's Rights Movement, which aimed to 'spread a consciousness of women's oppression and mobilise the greatest number of women on feminist issues'.[8]

The immediate focus of the group was for the extension of British equality legislation to Northern Ireland. In this decade all remaining marriage bars to employment ended, legislation outlawed sex discrimination in employment and equal pay for equal work was introduced. Women finally had won the right to work in any job or profession they chose and were entitled to be paid at the same rate as their male counterparts. Legal equality had been achieved – even if in practice society remained relatively male dominated.

Not only gender and social inequalities, but in Northern Ireland religious inequities were challenged. In the late 1960s there was an increasing awareness of the discriminatory nature of the old Stormont regime. In 1972 the Ulster Unionist Government was suspended and the Province became subject to Direct Rule from Westminster. It was in this atmosphere that the exclusion of Catholic students from the Hall was ended by a successful application to the High Court in 1972. There was also an exclusively Roman Catholic residential hall for girls – Aquinas Hall, on the Malone Road – although this was smaller and its history

Charles Lanyon's original coloured sketch showing his design for Queen's College Belfast. The college opened in 1849, one of three Queen's Colleges of the Queen's University of Ireland, the others being in Cork and Galway
Queen's University Belfast

unrecorded, and it too has closed its doors. Up to that time there were actually more 'official' residential places for women than for men students at Queen's University.

The introduction of grants for all qualifying students also led to a more socially mixed student body. This new financial independence and the centralisation of university applications within the United Kingdom at the end of the 1960s resulted in more young people leaving the Province for their education. The onset of the 'Troubles' in the late 1960s hastened this trend. By the early 1970s it was becoming impossible for the Hall to fill its places with Queen's students alone. Riddel Hall closed in 1975 as it was no longer financially viable and was seen as 'old fashioned' by a new generation of students. The proceeds from the sale of the building were used to construct modern self-catering student accommodation adjacent to the new tower blocks. Bursaries for needy students are still funded by Eliza and Isabella Riddel's endowment and thus the Riddel sisters' generosity continues to assist female students today.

2

Pioneering Women

The only expectation of middle-class girls of Eliza and Isabella Riddel's generation was to learn to be 'ladies'. Ladies were to be imbued with the domestic ideal (this differed from working-class domesticity in that ladies gave orders to servants but did not do domestic chores); the home was to be their domain. Paid work was viewed as demeaning to themselves and a slur on their male providers. The Victorian lady was to be 'accomplished' in social graces, and to conduct herself with modesty and decorum, which would 'render her competitive on the marriage market'.[1] In her spare time, she could engage in 'good works'. The Victorian women's movement began in the 1850s, principally to address the issues of middle-class women's access to education and career opportunities.

These ideals of femininity were reinforced by evangelicalism and influenced Victorian values. It was argued that 'evolution had placed women in the home, and that the dictates of social survival necessitated rigidly defined sex roles and male domination'.[2] Acceptance of these theories influenced educational policy well into the twentieth century. Indeed it was even suggested that mental development would render women completely or partially infertile. It would therefore be detrimental to society to allow female education to advance beyond the most basic level.[3]

Nevertheless, ideologies can be manipulated or changed. Pioneering English campaigners were instrumental in including girls' education in the Taunton Commission on Secondary Education. It reported in 1867 that female secondary education was composed of 'pretentious smatterings'. The commissioners deplored the state of female education, recognised that male and female intellectual abilities were 'essentially the same' and stated that women should be entitled to further education.

In response to this report, the Women's Education Union (WEU) was formed in England by Maria Grey to provide funds for new girls' schools, and within ten years it had educated over 2,800 pupils.[4] Pressure from Emily Davies, the founder of Girton College, Cambridge, leading girls' school principals such as Miss Frances Buss of the North London Collegiate and Miss Dorothea Beale of The Cheltenham Ladies' College, and more than a thousand other teachers, won the right for the formal admission of girls to the Local Examinations of Cambridge University.

This was a momentous victory in England, as prior to this no girls were permitted to sit for public examinations, which were essential passports to a university education. Women were not allowed to attend lectures at Cambridge University with men; sympathetic dons often gave the same lecture twice. It was not until 1948 that women were allowed to take Cambridge degrees. By contrast, Oxford permitted women to take all examinations except medicine in 1894, and finally allowed women to graduate in 1920. Degree courses gradually became more widely available to women in England during the final decade of the nineteenth and the early years of the twentieth century.[5]

Meanwhile in Ireland educational pioneers such as Margaret Byers, who founded the Ladies' Collegiate School (later Victoria College Belfast) in 1859, Isabella Tod of the Belfast Ladies' Institute and Anne Jellicoe, founder of Alexandra College, Dublin, had been fighting their own battles with the Irish educational authorities. These women, who had close connections with English organisations, carried on campaigns appealing to Queen's College Belfast and Trinity College Dublin for the admission of women to university degrees.[6]

These three women were also involved in religious and philanthropic work. They were founder members of the Irish Women's Suffrage Movement, and argued that women, as a consequence of their moral superiority to men, should be educated in order to fulfil their duties to the community, and be empowered by the vote to reform society. Margaret Byers pointed out to her pupils in their school publication in 1893 that education was defective if

Mrs Margaret Byers, founder of the Ladies' Collegiate School in 1859,
and pioneer of education and university admission for women
Victoria College Belfast

It produces women possessed of information, but selfish and devoid of innate and true refinement... There is a loud call at home for the ordinary, common-sense woman who, experienced and capable in home management, can be trusted, as intelligent Christian men are trusted to help in the direction of varied charities and philanthropies so essential for the comfort and improvement of working women and girls, never to speak of hospitals and workhouses in a great and growing city like ours.[7]

Mrs Byers' *Victoria College Magazine* is a useful source of information about women's involvement in social work, both voluntary and professional. It provides evidence of how women were recruited into these activities. The domestic model was commonly employed to justify women's work beyond the home. Women accustomed to 'directing their households and servants', could use these skills in social service. By the end of the century, that same virtue was used to justify their reappearance in the public sphere. The *Belfast Health Journal* stated in 1893 that women had a duty in regard to health:

Ladies' Collegiate School, Lower Crescent, later to become Victoria College Belfast. The opening of this building in August 1874 coincided with the meeting in Belfast of the British Association for the Advancement of Science
Victoria College Belfast

> We know that every household, whether large or small, rich or poor, is guided
> by a woman's head and hand, and in the majority of them its concerns are
> wholly or chiefly managed by her hands... To make the cause of sanitation a
> success our women require – more systematic instruction in the scientific facts
> upon which hygiene is based, access to suitable books and lectures, and the
> popularisation of such knowledge by women among their poorer sisters.[8]

Margaret Byers believed that 'the home is not only the unit of the nation, but the cradle of civilisation'. Thus women's association with the home was perceived to be empowering rather than restricting.

Class was as significant as gender in deciding the type of education a young woman would receive. Isabella Tod, secretary of the Belfast Ladies' Institute, which campaigned to extend higher education to Irish women, pointed out that although 'girls of the lower classes' had schools provided by the state with trained teachers, 'on looking higher all is changed'. For working-class girls the national schools provided an elementary education to fit them for their station in life as domestic servants or respectable wives for working-class men. In contrast for middle- and upper-class girls there were only 'scattered and experimental attempts at anything of the sort'.[9] As it was not considered desirable for the classes to be

Miss Isabella Tod of the Belfast Ladies' Institute campaigned to extend
higher education to Irish women. She, Margaret Byers and Anne Jellicoe
were founder members of the Irish Women's Suffrage Movement

educated together, the educational pioneers' challenge was against gender
difference in educational opportunities and they decried the lack of appropriate
educational provision for women of the middle class.

The Belfast Ladies' Institute was founded in 1867 by six prominent women. Its
aim was to improve the education of women of their own class and as a result to
improve their employment prospects. Significantly, this committee included Ruth
Duffin's grandmother, Mrs Duffin of Strandtown Lodge (née Theodosia
Grimshaw), an active member for thirty years.[10] Professors and physicians from
Queen's College and the Belfast Academical Institution gave lectures. (Another
Duffin connection, Ruth's great-grandfather, William Drennan, was one of the
founders of the Belfast Academical Institution.) The subjects of the lectures
included astronomy, physiology, chemistry and zoology, as well as the more
conventional English language, literature and history. It was 'likely that in offering
these subjects the organisers wanted to destroy the common perception that young
ladies could only expect to acquire the ability to play a little, sing a little, do some
painting on satin or velvet and appear to advantage at a concert or ball'.[11]

The work of the Institute resulted in women gaining access to university
education and, in the first instance, attaining certificates of proficiency. The

request of the Belfast Ladies' Institute for tests was accepted by Queen's College Belfast in 1869 and the first examinations were held the following year. These awards, thanks to the efforts of the Institute, were a passport to a medical education in the London School of Medicine for Women. The first battle had been won, but the war was only starting. In 1873 the Ladies' Institute was unsuccessful in its attempt to gain the right for women to sit for degrees.

The founders of the Ladies' Institute and the Ladies' Collegiate School worked together to ensure that girls would be permitted to sit for the examinations of the Intermediate Board. By the 1870s Miss Tod and Mrs Byers had made contacts with like-minded Irish and English women. Margaret Byers had joined the WEU, which provided the Ladies' Collegiate School with an annual scholarship of £25.[12] The opening of Mrs Byers' new building for the Ladies' Collegiate School in Lower Crescent, Belfast in August 1874 coincided with the meeting in Belfast of the British Association for the Advancement of Science. Speakers at the ceremony included Mrs Maria Grey, President of the WEU, and Lydia Becker, one of the first leaders of the British suffrage movement and an early member of the British Association.

During the British Association's presence in Belfast a meeting of the WEU was held in the new Ladies' Collegiate School. The *Northern Whig* reported that an 'immense number of ladies was present', the subject under discussion being the higher education of women. Dignitaries such as the Countess of Antrim, Lord Waveny, J.P. Corry and Sir Thomas McClure joined Mrs Byers, Miss Tod and Mrs Grey. Dr P.S. Henry, President of Queen's College, vowed that he would 'do anything in his power to improve the education of girls in the province'. In 1875 the College again hosted a public meeting held under the auspices of the WEU and the Belfast Ladies' Institute. Anne Jellicoe and 'other friends of the cause' also took part.[13]

The Irish Society for Promoting the Training and Employment of Educated Women, known as the Queen's Institute, was founded in Dublin in 1861 by Anne Jellicoe. Its aim was to provide an education for 'distressed gentlewomen' and to widen the scope of women's work. This led to the establishment of Alexandra College:

> For the purpose of affording the solid instruction, whose need had been made manifest in the working of the Institute. Out of it arose the Governesses' Association, where teachers found work, and girls found means of becoming teachers; and from both sprang Alexandra school for training teachers and preparing students for the higher classes of college.[14]

Associated with these institutions were cultural and literary societies aiming at the promotion of advanced education for women. A series of Saturday lectures was held in Trinity College Dublin to give women 'some at least of the educational

Anne Mullin, aged 16 yrs, later Mrs Jellicoe, an early pioneer
in Ireland of higher and university education for women
Alexandra College, Dublin

advantages enjoyed by men'.[15] Although Trinity had drawn up tests for the examination of women in 1869, the Board was against admitting them to the College on equal terms with men. From 1880 until 1904 Alexandra College prepared women for the degrees of the Royal University of Ireland, and campaigned to persuade Trinity College to grant degrees to women. The strength of feeling against change can be appreciated in the refusal, in 1895, of the University to accept the arguments contained in the *Movement for the Admission of Women to Trinity College Dublin*. The prevailing attitude was that 'women were devils in skirts'. The College authorities stated forthrightly that, even when chaperoned, it would be left to the discretion of the gate-porter to determine whether, of two women passing through, one was of sufficient age to be a suitable guardian to the other. 'If a female had once passed the gate, it would be practically impossible to watch what buildings or what chambers she might enter, or how long she might remain there.'[16]

Women were eventually admitted to Trinity in 1904. The second Warden of Riddel Hall, Miss Joyce Power Steele was a past pupil of Alexandra College and a Trinity graduate. She remembered that in the early 1930s women entering the College after 6 p.m. had to be chaperoned.

Alexandra College, Dublin
Founded in 1866 by Anne Jellicoe, to enable women to be educated to an equivalent level to men
Alexandra College, Dublin

By 1874 Margaret Byers' pupils had won nearly £3,000 in university prizes. As the maximum sum awarded to any individual was £50, this was a considerable achievement. Miss Tod spoke of the popularity for women of the Queen's Colleges' examinations, which were held in both Belfast and Galway. 'Already they have effected much, but we hope this is only an earnest of what is to come.'[17]

Although private secondary education for boys was provided, for example in the Academical Institution and the Royal Schools, there was no state provision beyond the level of the national school curriculum. The government planned to introduce a fee-paying 'intermediate' system – between a basic education and that of the university.[18] Intermediate education was also financed by funds made available through the disestablishment of the Church of Ireland in 1869.[19]

The 1878 Intermediate Education Act instituted a system whereby schools were financed according to the success of their pupils in examinations. The Act originally referred to boys' education only so Margaret Byers and Isabella Tod organised a delegation to London to pressurise for the inclusion of girls. In this action they had the full support of the Belfast Ladies' Institute and an influential group of Irish men and women in London. Influenced by the 'memorial' delivered by J.P. Corry MP to the Lord Chancellor, Lord Cairns, the Act was changed to include girls. They presented evidence of the successes already achieved by Mrs Byers in her school and so persuaded Lord Cairns that girls must be included in the Act.[20]

This development had enormous implications for female education in Ireland. It provided finance for 'ladies' schools', gave an added incentive to study for teachers and pupils; and perhaps most significantly, it proved that girls could achieve academic excellence and would benefit from higher education. Victoria College was to become the most successful school in Ireland in preparing girls for the Intermediate Examinations.

The 1845 Colleges Bill had established the Queen's University in Ireland and its three constituent colleges in Belfast, Cork and Galway. The intention was to institute non-denominational academic education in Ireland, but the Catholic clergy, and to a lesser extent its laity, argued that the system trained 'the youthful mind in indifferentism to every creed and in practical infidelity'.[21] Their preference was a Catholic university and colleges. Attempts to resolve the differences in opinion on sectarian versus non-denominational education, and the issue of government funding lay behind the Act establishing the Royal University of Ireland in 1879. The Queen's University was disbanded and a newly created Royal University of Ireland became purely an examining body. The three Queen's Colleges were joined by a wide number of institutions that prepared students for its examinations. These were open to both men and women and there was no longer any requirement for a student to be resident in any college or to attend lectures, with the exception of medicine and surgery.[22] While this was helpful for women, the facilities available to them to prepare for examinations were not comparable to those available to men. In 1882 the Belfast Ladies' Institute again approached the Queen's College Belfast. This time it agreed and the first women were admitted to arts classes during the session 1882-3; Queen's College Belfast became the first university in Ireland to admit women. The following year women were admitted to science classes, but it was not until the end of 1889, with the enrolment of women in the medical faculty, that they were able to attend all classes. Dr Elizabeth Bell became the first woman to qualify in medicine in

Ireland, and eventually included the care of residents of Riddel Hall in her medical practice. Women were not eligible for college scholarships until 1895 when the necessary changes were made to the original college charter.[23] The strength of feeling against the admission of women to the old Queen's University in Ireland was summed up in a sardonic speech given by the Reverend William Park to the Victoria College students and parents on prize day 1891.

> If in the old Queen's University, which is unfortunately gone, a young lady had presented herself for examination they [staff and students] would have been so struck with wonder and horror that the pens would have dropped out of their hands, and they would have expected a policeman to carry the intruder away to an asylum or some other suitable abode.[24]

Victoria College ensured that women were qualified for the examinations of the Royal University of Ireland. For over twenty years after the opening of Queen's College Belfast to women their number remained small and Victoria College continued to be the main source of university education for women in Ulster until 1908. Between 1891 and 1900 only nineteen women graduated from Queen's College compared with ninety-five from Victoria College.

3

Students and Suffragettes

In 1908 the Irish Universities Act abolished the Royal University of Ireland and created in its place two new institutions. One was the federal National University of Ireland, incorporating the former Queen's Colleges in Cork and Galway and the Catholic University founded in Dublin in 1852. The other was an independent Queen's University of Belfast that replaced the old Queen's College. The Senate of Queen's University Belfast controlled its own appointments and policies and granted its own degrees. In 1908-9 there were eighty-seven women out of Queen's University's total student body of 456.[1] The new university was relatively progressive in admitting female students; in 1911 there were only 280 female university students in the whole of Ireland. Indeed only 13,600 females were involved in secondary level education and less than 1 percent of women aged 17-24 were still in full time education.[2]

By the outbreak of the Great War in 1914 women were becoming more visible in Queen's. There were two women members of the Senate, one of whom was Eliza Riddel. She was on the Voluntary Aid Detachment (VAD) committee with Dr Marion Andrews. University regulations demanded that 'all women students

Early women graduates. At times of fierce discussion in the Debating Society and struggles for equality, these pioneering university women did not seem to fit the description of 'sweet girl graduates'
Victoria College Belfast

are required to attend the classes and to qualify themselves in the subjects of ambulance work, sick nursing, invalid cookery and hygiene, unless excused for good and sufficient reason by the committee of discipline'. This obligation was withdrawn after the father of a student objected.[3]

The Great War was raging at this time and women students were expected to play their part not only as a condition of university life, but by joining the Women Students' Red Cross Training Corps.

> The object is to provide the women students of the university with thorough training in First Aid and emergency nursing and such other work as would enable them to be of use in civil emergencies or in case of war to take charge of the wounded during transit and in rest and evacuation stations.[4]

Women were also enthusiastic members of the Debating Society. At 'Ladies' Night' on 27 January 1915 the motion for debate was 'That men should receive higher wages than women for the same work'. Almost sixty years passed before equality legislation fully resolved that question.

The early residents of Riddel Hall had grown up at a time of radical suffragette activity. The militant Women's Social and Political Union (WSPU) founded in 1903 and the Irish Women's Suffrage Federation (IWSF), an umbrella association representing several smaller groups formed in 1909, were both active in Belfast prior to the Great War. Female students were interested in the suffrage movement. In the January 1914 issue of the Students' Representative Council magazine, *QCB*, an article entitled 'Acute Epidemic Suffragitis' was published. The desire for votes for women was sardonically described as a disease and its symptoms, treatment and prognosis were fully described.

Acute Epidemic Suffragitis

An acute specific fever characterised by its virulence, and by the fact that it is confined to the female sex. ETIOLOGY – Whites suffer more than blacks; and the disease is commoner in towns. Apparently the organism possesses great resistance. It has even survived the application of water charged with CO_2 from a hose – in fact, this appears rather to intensify the inflammation, giving rise to the so-called 'aggravated-female' form. INFLUENCE OF SEX – The disease is confined to the female sex. AGE INCIDENCE – Seventeen to forty-five is the most susceptible period. CLINICAL FEATURES – Stages of incubation variable. The disease has been contracted in public meetings; a heated atmosphere would seem to favour its propagation. SIGNS AND SYMPTOMS – Patients show a tendency to 'recurring utterances'. In one recorded outbreak of epidemic suffragitis among an 'educated' class of young women, the sufferers herded together in a certain recently-erected building, and invited some 300 men to come and be inoculated. It has been suggested that these peculiar manifestations may have been due to overwork and consequent nerve strain superimposed on the original infection, and in support of this theory the writer has been informed that some of the cases had subsequently to take a rest cure for some days. MORBID ANATOMY – There is evidently some lesion of the central nervous system, for patients exhibit violent spasmodic movements, hysterical in type, and several cases have come under our notice in which the hands went into a condition of tetanic contraction if permitted to come in contact with the hair of the male scalp. These facts, together with the mania for destroying unguarded property and letters, go far towards proving that the disease is really a degenerative or retrograde change – whether in the pyramidal tracts or in the higher cerebral centres is still an open question, though many authorities incline to the latter view. DIAGNOSIS – Generally the appearance (*facies Suffragetica*) is quite unmistakable, but some cases do not show the characteristic cast of countenance, and these are often the most intractable, and resist all methods of treatment. PALPATION – Often gives a negative result; tenderness can never be elicited. COURSE AND TERMINATION – During the active inflammatory stage patients will carry with them (often concealed) a small weapon or hammer. The crisis of the disease is reached when sufferers are found to be retailing copies of *The Suffragette* – the appearance of these is absolutely pathognomonic of the disease. PROGNOSIS – Although it is generally said that the course of the disease is progressively downwards, yet each case must be considered on its own merits. In our extensive experience of this class of case, we have seen several instances where prospects of becoming 'the better half' have produced a complete and permanent cure. TREATMENT – It is improbable that a male practitioner will be called to see a case of this kind professionally. The liberal treatment at present lavished on these patients cannot be said to have given very satisfactory results. A modification of this, the *felis musque* treatment, has not proved very successful in George Lloyd's hands. We would suggest change of air and environment. In severe cases a prolonged sojourn in Spitzbergen would probably prove beneficial. FEES – For laboratory treatment *en masse* – gratis; for treating cases at patient's own residence, £5 (this may, however, be remitted under certain circumstances.[5]

Some of the references in this article suggest that suffragettes known to the author were engaged in civil disorder activities such as smashing windows and the destruction of property. A mansion at Whiteabbey belonging to a prominent politician was burned to the ground at this time. The 'liberal' treatment of these women referred to in the article was the unsuccessful policy of Lloyd George's Liberal Government. Suffragettes were arrested for various offences, imprisoned and in many cases went on hunger strike. They were released under the 'Cat and Mouse Act' and rearrested. One of the WSPU members arrested under this Act was treated in prison by Dr Elizabeth Bell. Dorothy Evans attracted 'a concourse of Suffragettes' at a meeting in Queen's in December 1913. *QCB* reported that a Miss Thompson was in the chair for a very rowdy event.[6] The forty suffragettes were outnumbered by 'over two hundred of the sterner sex' and *QCB* described 'a wild scene of pandemonium – detonators boomed, squibs fizzled and crackers exploded, often in dangerous proximity to those on the platform'.[7]

In the academic year 1915-16 female students at Queen's included a very assertive group of young women. *QCB* of January that year reported their protest about the compulsory attendance at 'Hygiene and Sick Nursing' lectures. There was a 'fierce discussion' amongst the 'large and at times vociferous attendance of students who graced the proceedings'. Two Riddel students, Miss Lyon and Miss Curr, were the speakers in favour of the motion 'That the standard of virtue is higher than ever before' at the Literary and Scientific Society ladies' night in 1916. It was reported that 'In the course of the discussion there were some heated interchanges regarding the increase of drinking among women, when several members spoke with a dogmatism, which suggested intimate knowledge'. These

Somerville College, Oxford *c.*1906. The college was founded in 1879 to provide higher education for women, who were not allowed University membership until 1920. Somerville has been a mixed college since 1992
Somerville College, Oxford

young women did not fit into the patronising model used to describe pioneering university women – 'the sweet girl graduates'.[8]

In the academic year in which Riddel Hall opened its doors to the first cohort of students, 1915-16, women made up one third of the student body. This dramatic rise has to be understood in the context of the Great War. Many young men had volunteered for the services. There were 63 women out of a total of 153 in the Arts Faculty, and of 300 medical students, 35 were female. In 1915 the Women Students' Hall was opened. This was not a residential facility but was 'a commodious and well equipped Hall' which contained a reading room, study, sitting room, refreshment rooms and bathrooms; there was also a piano. At this time university education had to be paid for by the students or their parents. Queen's offered only twelve entrance scholarships in the faculties of Medicine, Science and Arts and there was an average of only two scholarships in each county.[9]

Queen's was at the time completely non-residential, unlike some older and wealthier institutions such as Oxford or Cambridge, or the London Free Hospital

School of Medicine for Women. There was a distinct need for accommodation and contemporary newspapers frequently carried advertisements for lodgings. In 1910 at the first meeting of the Convocation of Queen's University Belfast, the newly formed Student Representative Committee requested 'that the committee urge upon the Senate the desirability of erecting halls of residence for students of the university'.[10] Most students enrolled were only seventeen years of age and many came to the city from country districts after several years at boarding school; therefore there was a real need for safe and affordable accommodation. It was many years before the University was able to meet this request, but the generosity of the Misses Riddel made it possible for the women students of Riddel Hall.

Girton College, Cambridge *c.*1900. It was founded in 1869 as a residential higher education college for women, and moved to this (the present) building in 1873. Women were not granted full membership of the University of Cambridge until 1948. Since 1977 Girton has been a mixed college
Girton College, Cambridge

4

The Founding of Riddel Hall

Ruth Duffin wrote in her Chronicle:

> *Riddel Hall, Belfast, was founded and endowed by the Misses Eliza and Isabella Riddel of Beechmount, Falls Road, Belfast in 1913. Miss Eliza Riddel was born in 1831 and died in 1924; her sister was born in 1836 and died in 1918. In appearance they were both plain, and in manners they were very simple and unpretentious. Miss Eliza had a strong sense of humour; in the early days of the Hall I remember her laughing heartily over some of my tales of initial difficulties and contretemps. Miss Isabella was a less forceful character, and generally left the initiative to her sister. They were devoted Unitarians, like so many of the older inhabitants of Belfast, and they united a strong sense of duty with unbounded kindliness.*[1]

Eliza and Isabella Riddel were good representatives of their religious beliefs; Unitarians were characterised by a 'warm concern for all manner of human beings'.[2]

Miss Eliza Riddel, the elder of the two
sisters, was a member of the Senate of
Queen's University from 1912
John Riddel and Son Limited

Miss Duffin remembered that the Misses Riddel,

in spite of their great wealth inherited from their bachelor brothers rather late in life, remained simple in their ways and made no parade of luxury, driving about in their plain one-horse brougham long after motor cars had been adopted by most other people, entertaining but little, and keeping themselves in the background while helping all good causes with open-handed generosity. They were, in fact, typical of the best side of the Victorian age – of unswerving integrity, and with a strong sense of responsibilities entailed by the possession of great wealth.

Other beneficiaries of the sisters' generosity were the Royal Victoria Hospital, the Belfast Hospital for Sick Children, the Belfast Maternity Hospital, the Midnight Mission, the Society for Providing Nurses for the Sick Poor and their congregation's Domestic Mission for the Poor of Belfast.

Eliza and Isabella Riddel's brother, Samuel, bequeathed to his sisters a total of £432,310 12s 6d in 1903. (At this time a manual worker could live 'comfortably' if he received £1 per week in wages.) This wealth had been accumulated through the hardware business founded in 1803 by their father, John Riddel, at No. 38 Chichester Quay, Belfast. John Riddel was involved in the public life of the growing town of Belfast. He signed petitions to the Sovereign of Belfast (a similar office to the present Lord Mayor) appealing for town meetings on a variety of subjects, including the amendment of the Police Acts and the Repeal of the Act of Union 1801 which united Britain and Ireland following the 1798 Rebellion.

John Riddel's name also appears in connection with the Police Committee, the Library Committee, the Belfast Harp Society and the Committee of the House

Miss Isabella Riddel, the youngest of the family.
She was a less forceful character, generally happy
to leave the initiative to her sister
Queen's University Belfast

John Riddel founded the hardware business
at 38 Chichester Quay in 1803
Reproduced from *In the Service of Ulster: Riddel's of Belfast*

Samuel Riddel inherited the business
from his father
Reproduced from *In the Service of Ulster: Riddel's of Belfast*

of Industry. The latter, founded in 1809, did not intend to give shelter to the poor but to provide them with work and to inculcate 'moral habits', which would, it was hoped, lead to the independence of 'the poor'.[3] John Riddel also took part in the relief of destitution and the fight against the ravages of cholera, a scourge that swept Ireland in the 1830s. He died in 1870.

Samuel Riddel, in turn, was described as a 'man of exceedingly generous disposition, and his hand was practically always in his pocket for one charity or another. At the same time he had the strongest objection to disclosing the amounts he distributed this way, and his name seldom appeared on any advertised list of subscriptions'.[4] During the nineteenth century Belfast was known as 'the city of Good Works'. There was no state welfare provision, except for the workhouses established under the 1838 Poor Law. These institutions were only entered in times of extreme deprivation. The activities of the Riddels were typical of the philanthropic middle-class of their era. Businessmen, merchants and the emerging educated professional classes took their duty towards those less fortunate than themselves very seriously. In the absence of state provision a multitude of charitable associations was required to meet the needs spiritual, physical, educational, moral and nutritional of the industrial working class.

The Riddel sisters did not take an active role in the business. The company employed 225 people in a building of 60,000 square feet. The Chairman from 1903 to 1921 was their cousin, Henry Musgrave, followed by their great-nephew, Major C.G. Duffin, until the mid-1930s. A promotional pamphlet printed in 1935

John Riddel and Son Limited, Ann Street
Carey Ramsay

stated that 'the company was directed by men who regarded the goodwill of the public as their greatest asset. Always they have looked ahead and seen that the way to get goodwill is to sell nothing that will not bring credit to the firm. It is a far-sighted policy and it has been carried out regardless of temporary considerations'.[5]

The Riddels' donation of £35,000 to build and endow a hall of residence for female students of Queen's University Belfast, was not only generous in real terms, but was unusually large at a time when the construction of women's hostels was funded in a 'piecemeal hand-to-mouth way' by ladies' halls committees, local benefactors, voluntary subscriptions and grants from bodies such as the Carnegie or Pfeiffer Trusts. Only Emma Holt, described as the 'fairy godmother' of Liverpool University's Women's Hall donated on such a scale. She was rewarded for her generosity by being awarded an honorary degree in 1928.[6] It is possible

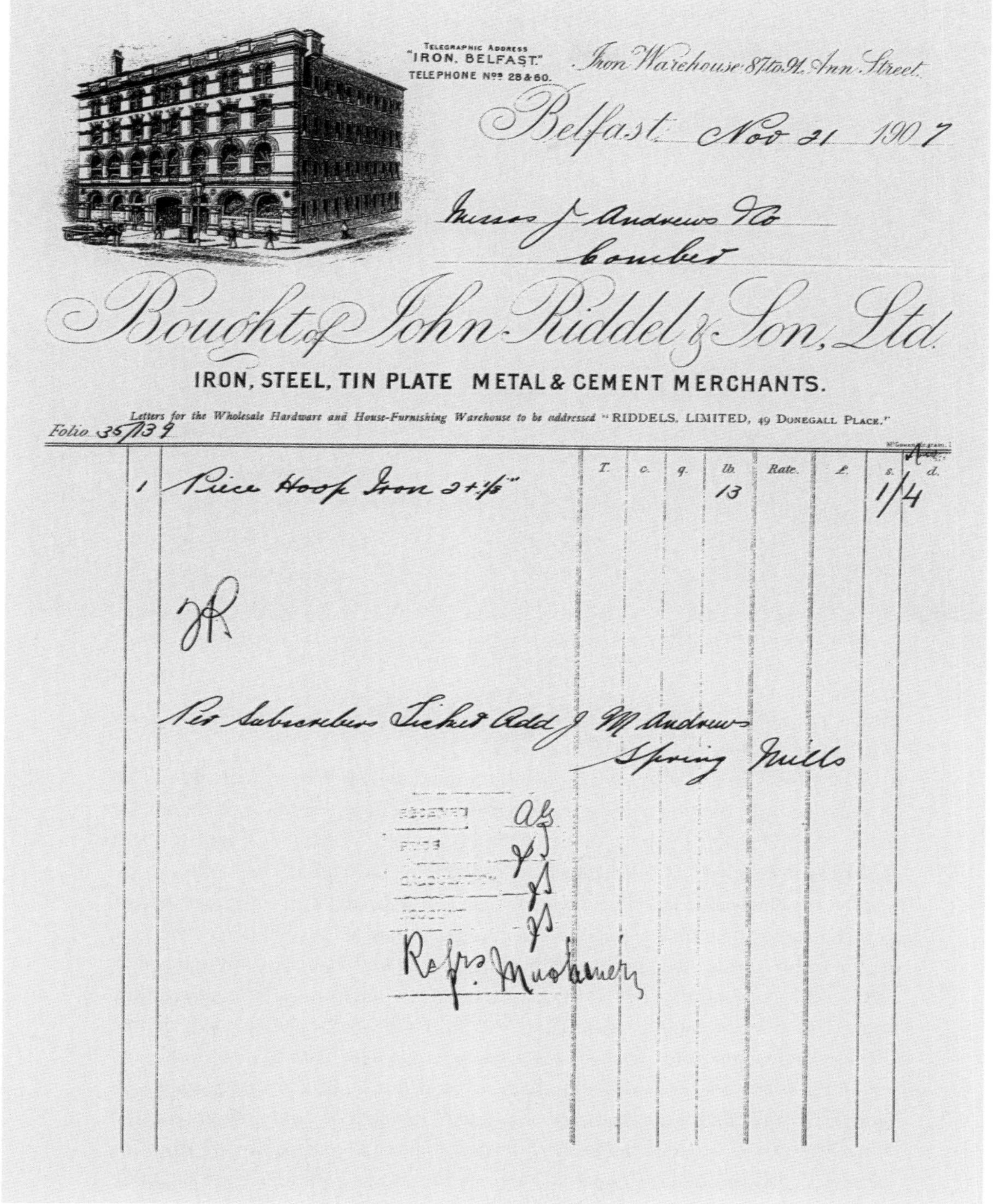

Iron Warehouse 87 to 91 Ann Street.

Belfast Nov 21 1907

Messrs J Andrews No
Comber

Bought of John Riddel & Son, Ltd.

IRON, STEEL, TIN PLATE METAL & CEMENT MERCHANTS.

Letters for the Wholesale Hardware and House-Furnishing Warehouse to be addressed "RIDDELS, LIMITED, 49 Donegall Place."

Folio 35/139

		T.	c.	q.	lb.	Rate.	£.	s.	d.
1	Piece Hoop Iron 2+⅞"				13			1/	4

JR

Per Subscribers Ticket Add J M Andrews
Spring Mills

Received
Priced
Calculation
Added

Refd. Montgomery

Invoice from John Riddel and Son Limited
Carey Ramsay

Beechmount, Belfast. The home of the Riddel family, now Meánscoil Feirste, an Irish-speaking school
National Museums and Galleries Northern Ireland/Ulster Museum

that Eliza Riddel, as 'the most outgoing' of the two sisters was granted a seat on the Senate of Queen's for a similar reason.[7]

The Misses Riddel also gave money for an endowment fund which subsidised student accommodation during the life of the Hall. It still finances bursaries for needy students. They gave a further £15,000 to the Endowment Fund in 1918; Isabella left a further £10,000 and Eliza £20,000 to the Hall in their wills.

Unfortunately we do not have a personal record of the Riddel sisters' motivation for financing a hall of residence. They were elderly women at the time of the bequest; they had apparently lived quiet sheltered lives. They were however involved in several charities with an interest in women's issues and they were related to women such as Mrs Charles Duffin who had been involved in the Belfast Ladies' Institute. They also had connections with members of the Senate of Queen's University. At this time halls of residence in British universities were provided for students for various reasons, some pragmatic, some paternalist and some feminist in origin. The desire to protect vulnerable young women from the perceived dangers of unsupervised lodgings was often a factor. The 'Victorian ideas of chaperonage' were clearly evident. Women educationalists of the time 'were quick to extol the benefits of college life, particularly for female students... Halls of residence provided unparalleled opportunities for women to study: they allowed girls space in which to work without disturbance and where regular hours and regular meals could be guaranteed'.[8] Perhaps all of these factors influenced the sisters or they may simply have wished that young women could enjoy the benefits of university life in the environment of a women's hall of residence.

Riddel Hall was registered as a Limited Company on 3 June 1913 with Henry Musgrave, the last survivor of the five bachelor cousins of the Misses Riddel, as its Chairman. The first

Henry Musgrave 1827-1922, painted on commission by Henrietta Rae *c.*1918, and hangs in the Great Hall of the University
Queen's University Belfast

recorded meeting of the Permanent Committee took place on 5 December 1913. The Musgraves were a wealthy family who owned what Miss Duffin once heard referred to as a 'Principality' in Donegal. The Misses Riddel used to act as hostesses for their cousin at Carrick when shooting parties were entertained. Henry Musgrave was a member of the Senate of Queen's University. Perhaps influenced by the Riddels' generous example, he bequeathed £40,000 in 1922 to provide a hall of residence for male Protestant students of Queen's University. Part of the terrace of seven houses on University Road opposite to the University known as Queen's Elms was purchased and converted for residential use, and became known as Queen's Chambers.

The first Vice-Chairman of the Permanent Committee of Riddel Hall was Sir William Crawford, President of the Linen Merchants' Association and the Central Presbyterian Association. He was also a member of the Senate and Honorary Treasurer of the University.[9] Ruth Duffin recalled that the Permanent Committee was dominated by very elderly men; Henry Musgrave was approaching his nineties, William Crawford, Samuel Dill, R.A. Macrory and Dr Kyle Knox, who always reminded her of 'characters out of Dickens' were also old men. The other founder governors, Misses Eliza and Isabella Riddel, were eighty-two and seventy-

Combined Duffin and

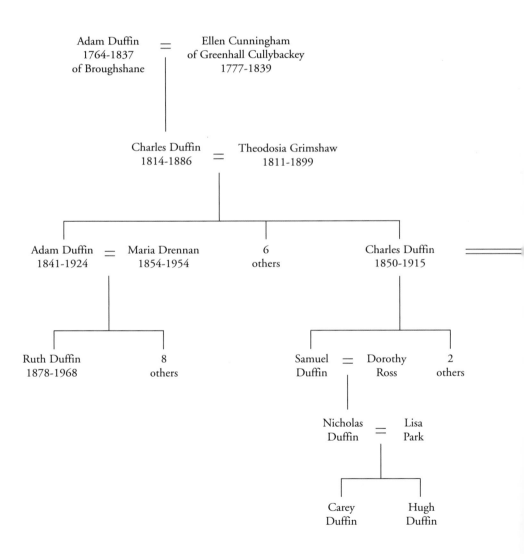

Adam Duffin = Ellen Cunningham
1764-1837 of Greenhall Cullybackey
of Broughshane 1777-1839

Charles Duffin = Theodosia Grimshaw
1814-1886 1811-1899

Adam Duffin = Maria Drennan   6   Charles Duffin =====
1841-1924 1854-1954   others   1850-1915

Ruth Duffin   8   Samuel = Dorothy   2
1878-1968   others   Duffin   Ross   others

Nicholas = Lisa
Duffin   Park

Carey   Hugh
Duffin   Duffin

Riddel Family Trees

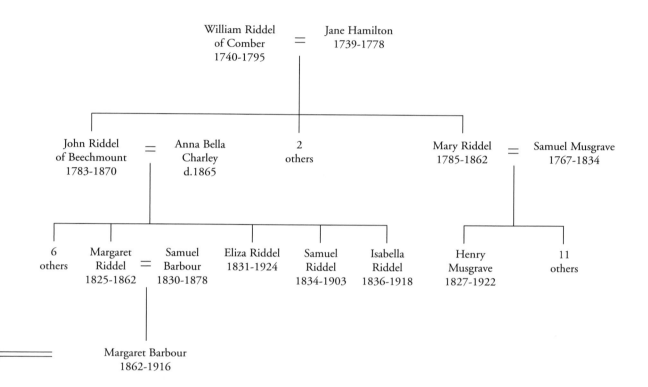

seven years old, Mrs Charles Duffin (their niece) was, at fifty-three years old, as Ruth Duffin wrote, 'young in comparison'. Sir Samuel Dill, Professor of Greek from 1890 to 1923, was one of the most distinguished scholars of the Arts Faculty of Queen's.[10] Other members were Samuel Barbour Duffin (son of Mrs Charles Duffin), and Robert and George Macrory, the Riddels' solicitors.

There were also governors, qualified by virtue of their positions: the Vice-Chancellor of Queen's University, the Church of Ireland Bishop of Down, Connor and Dromore, and the minister of the First Presbyterian Church, Rosemary Street, Belfast, the congregation to which the Riddel family belonged. Other representative governors were the Lord Mayor of Belfast, the Moderator of the General Assembly of the Presbyterian Church in Ireland, and the Chairman of the Belfast Harbour Board. The incumbents of these positions could only serve if they were Protestants and were willing to act. There were also to be ten elected ordinary governors, five 'ladies' and 'five gentlemen'. Finally there were to be five elected 'lady graduate governors' who were graduates of Queen's University of at least three years' standing who had been 'at least three terms in residence at the Hall'. Two of the first five lady governors were Marion Andrews and Elizabeth Bell, who were two of the earliest women to qualify in medicine in Ireland. Another was Miss F.W. Rea who was one of the earliest women lecturers in Queen's. She is described in verse, patronisingly, in *QCB*.[11]

> While in the Chemistry lecture hall
> From 12-1 each day
> She reigns as Queen of Metals
> That damsel fair Miss Rea.

The primary objects of the company were:[12]

(1) To take over from Henry Musgrave, Sir William Crawford, and George Crawford Macrory, a sum of £35,000, which has been deposited with them by Eliza and Isabella Riddel, or the investments representing the same, for the objects of the Corporation.

(2) To found, establish and maintain in or near the city of Belfast, one or more Hostels or Houses of Residence for female Protestant students of and teachers in the Queen's University Belfast.

(3) To provide board, lodging and attendance, and other necessaries and conveniences for students and teachers resident at such hostel or hostels, and to afford to such students tutorial assistance and facilities for study and cultivation.

(4) If thought desirable to assist needy and deserving students resident at any such hostel, by affording to them all or any of the advantages of the hostel, either gratuitously or on reduced terms, or by the granting of bursaries.

Henry Musgrave and others gave money to the University to found a hostel for men students.
Queen's Chambers, in four of the houses of the terrace opposite Queen's, opened in 1936
Queen's University Belfast

Property in Belfast at the time cost only a fraction of £35,000: for example, a 'Double Villa on the Holywood Road', a middle-class area, was for sale at £295. A terraced house in Dunluce Avenue, Lisburn Road, described as a 'desirable residence' with two reception rooms and four bedrooms could be rented at £24 plus taxes per annum.[13]

The contract for building the Hall was made with Henry Laverty and Sons. The architect was W.H. Lynn working in conjunction with S.P. Close and Son. Laverty and Lynn were builder and architect respectively of the new building programme at Queen's commenced in 1911, including the library and student's union (today's School of Music). No doubt they were chosen to ensure a degree of harmony between University and hall of residence.[14] At the first meeting of the Corporation on 15 December 1913, it was explained how the Misses Riddel's gift of £35,000 was being 'dealt with'. The Hall would be situated on the Stranmillis Road, an area only recently becoming developed. The prestige of the area and the size of the grounds are reflected in the cost – £3,424 10s 6d. By February 1914 the committee had received estimates from several firms for all the requirements of the Hall and the architect had submitted plans for a gate lodge, gates, heating apparatus and plumbing.

An important intention of the company governing Riddel Hall was that 'tutorial assistance' would be available to the residents. The form this might take was not defined and various methods of informal education were provided over the years. From 1916 onward bursaries were available to cover all or part of the residential fees for girls whose families were unable to meet the costs.

The restriction of Riddel Hall to Protestant and female students has to be understood in the context of the times when the Hall was founded. Victorian and Edwardian philanthropists of all religious denominations almost always directed their efforts to serving their own communities, and the idea of a mixed sex hall of residence was unthinkable in this era. Although legally a non-denominational university, students at Queen's were predominantly Protestant until the 1970s. The restriction was removed in 1971 as the denominational (and gender) mix of students was changing, against the background of the changing political climate in Northern Ireland.

For fifty years Riddel offered a safe haven for young women coming to Belfast to study. For thirty of those fifty years it provided the only residential places for female students, until the opening of Aquinas Hall for Roman Catholic students in 1944.[15] By the 1970s the style of living found in Riddel was falling out of fashion and the Hall – sadly – closed.

Aquinas Hall. Originally a private house, opened as a residence for Catholic girls in 1944.
It is now the headquarters of the Arts Council of Northern Ireland
Arts Council of Northern Ireland

5

Miss Ruth Duffin

Miss Ruth Duffin became the first Warden of Riddel Hall in May 1914 at a rate of £2 per week. She set the tone, ethos and tradition for the Hall from its opening in 1915 until its closure in 1975. The appointment was probably influenced by her connections to the Riddel and Musgrave families. Ruth's diaries and letters illustrated her family's philosophical values, which she brought to the Hall and promoted amongst generations of Riddel girls. Her previous occupations provide us with an example of life in which social position determined the nature of education, and an awareness of the limited career opportunities available to middle-class women before the Great War.

Miss Duffin described in her Chronicle how the appointment came about.

> I had been approached in a most informal manner about the Wardenship. Miss
> Violet Kyle Knox, one of the first Ordinary Governors, rang me up on the telephone
> to ask whether, if offered the Wardenship, I would accept it. I have often thought
> that my appointment was an odd one, and I am sure there must have been
> criticism of the fact that the post was not advertised. In fact, there may have been,
> unknown to me, charges of nepotism, as my aunt by marriage, Mrs Charles Duffin,

was a niece of the Miss Riddels and a governor. Earlier in 1914 I had paid a visit to my second cousin, Sir Harry Reichel, Principal of University College, Bangor, N. Wales, and had accepted the post of secretary to him. All I can say with certainty is that there was no pulling of strings on my part, and that the unexpected message from Miss Knox came after I had already accepted the Bangor post. When, however, the chance of a post nearer home arose, I wrote to him, explaining the situation, and he most kindly released me from my engagement.

She had ambivalent feelings about her appointment since she had not been to a university and had no degree. Furthermore,

I was, I think, young for my age, and had never had to exercise any kind of authority, so it will be seen that my qualifications for the post of Warden were not impressive! I sometimes wonder now [1944] how I had the courage to undertake the job, but perhaps ignorance of what it entailed went for something... As far as the elderly members of the Permanent Committee were concerned I do not think any one of them knew anything whatever about the probable needs of a Women Students' Hostel, and I was certainly not qualified to help them! Mr. Musgrave's attitude to what I am sure he would have called the fair sex was courteous, but his ideas on women's intellectual capacities were illustrated in an interview I had with him during which he elaborately explained the meaning of so much per cent. When I intimated that I had grasped his meaning he exclaimed delightedly, 'You're very apt, you're very apt'.

At the time of Ruth Duffin's appointment it was normal practice that wardens were chosen on the basis of education and background. Her family connections were impeccable. Ruth's mother, Maria Drennan, was the daughter of Dr J.S. Drennan, the visiting physician to the Royal Hospital, and a 'far from mediocre Irish poet of the nineteenth century'.[1] She was educated at home and married Adam Duffin in 1876. Adam Duffin was born in 1841, had been educated at Queen's College and trained as a solicitor. Following the death of his father he took over the family business dealing in stocks and shares. The Duffins were involved in numerous charitable societies such as the Society for Providing Nurses for the Sick Poor, and the Joint Committee of Public Health, Town Improvements and Parks. These associations aimed to improve the health and environment of the working class in Belfast. The Duffins were organisers of the Belfast Council for Social Welfare, which had no public funds at its disposal.

Maria and Adam Duffin had nine children in close succession. Ruth, born in 1878, and her six younger sisters were educated in a conventional middle-class fashion with governesses and several German Fräuleins. At the age of sixteen the girls attended Cheltenham Ladies' College as boarders for one year or two to finish their social and academic education, but they were, as they recalled in old age,

Ruth Duffin, from a sketch by Eileen Ayrton. The oldest of seven sisters and two brothers, she became the first Warden of Riddel Hall. She was much influenced by her experiences at The Cheltenham Ladies' College and by Miss Beale
J. Power Steele

'trained for nothing'. The next step in life was to 'come out' into society. Tom Andrews, designer of the Titanic, partnered Ruth's sister Celia at her 'coming out dance'.[2] The sisters followed their mother's example in joining charitable organisations. The three youngest sisters, Emma, Sylvia and Helen, became Voluntary Aid Detachment nurses in the Great War; Emma later succeeded her mother as Honorary Secretary of the Council for Social Welfare.

Ruth Duffin's diaries and letters to her family, while she was at boarding school in England from 1894 to 1896, indicate the extraordinary advances made in female education in her lifetime.[3] Before depositing them in the Public Record Office of Northern Ireland Miss Duffin edited and prefaced them, pointing out that their 'only value lies in that they give a picture of a lost era, for I suppose that no generation in history has seen a more rapid change in the pattern of living'. The documents give a great insight into her personality, which Riddel students were never allowed to see. She was thought of as 'austere', 'aristocratic' and 'strict', but through these documents we can meet 'Ruthie' (all her family used this affectionate name and she signed her letters in this way) as a pleasant and often humorous woman.

Miss Dorothea Beale, pioneer of higher
education and university admission
for women, and founder of
The Cheltenham Ladies' College.
She and Miss Frances Buss of the
North London Collegiate School inspired
the immortal rhyme:

Miss Buss and Miss Beale,
Cupid's darts do not feel.
How different from us,
Miss Beale and Miss Buss!

The Cheltenham Ladies' College

Her Cheltenham experience provided a model for the Riddel Hall community. Several former students particularly remember Miss Duffin as 'an old Cheltenham girl'. Their clearest memories are of her talking about her schooldays at Cheltenham Ladies' College during the formal Riddel evening dinners and reminding them that attending Queen's was an experience denied to her generation.

Cheltenham Ladies' College was opened in 1854 for 'the daughters of Noblemen and Gentlemen'.[4] The College was relatively radical as far as education was concerned but deeply conservative in relation to class-based ideals of femininity. The aim of Cheltenham Ladies' College was to encourage self-development, but this 'collided with deeply ingrained beliefs about family obligations. In spite of their ostensible support of the family, headmistresses were part of the modern male world in their concern to develop individual opportunities over traditional family demands'.[5] The 'Lady Principal', Miss Dorothea Beale was dedicated both to her religious faith and the work of her college. For nearly fifty years, from 1858 to 1906, it was her home and creation of her personality. She half-seriously, half-whimsically, referred to the College as her 'husband'.[6] Possibly Ruth Duffin came to think in the same way about Riddel Hall. A year after leaving school she wrote in her diary, 'I admire Miss Beale very much, more than I could when at college, when her little peculiarities and fussinesses helped to hide how good and great she really is'.[7]

In Ruth's first term at Cheltenham Miss Beale applauded her work: 'Excellent literature and history; the marks are very good, extremely high average for a first term'. Modestly, Ruth wrote to her mother, 'This sounds very conceited, but as I have not a trumpeter at hand, I have to be my own for the present'. She explained that the competition was not too challenging. 'Some of the girls are so dreadfully stupid that they can hardly be counted at all.' This judgement by a young woman who always spoke her mind is not merely intellectual snobbery or false modesty. Many girls of sixteen went to school for the first time to be 'finished' after very poor tuition undertaken by governesses who, despite having the desired social status, were barely educated themselves. Educating young women was an enormous challenge for the College, especially when parents generally did not see the necessity, as daughters were not expected to earn their own living.

Ruth's letters to her mother provide a poignant illustration of the dissonance experienced by a young woman at a time of change. Although pulled by ties of home and family, she wanted the opportunity to study in an academic atmosphere. The College was 'an organic community of nine hundred women'. In 1894 a new wing had been built providing a Cambridge room and an Oxford room for examination classes.[8] In the spring of 1895, which originally was to have been her last term at school, Ruth informed her mother, to whom she wrote almost daily, that she had 'come out top of my class in eight subjects'. She was to have history lectures from an 'Oxford extension' lecturer, and 'Miss Laurie' wanted her to 'take a certificate'. In May that year when Ruth's parents wrote, asking if she would like another year at school, she replied, 'I don't think I would, I would rather be at home'. But the next month, four months after her eighteenth birthday, she wrote,

> I should love to stay for some things, the girls particularly. I am sure the Cambridge would do me a lot of good, on the other hand, I'm sure I can learn things at home and I feel as if I should like to 'come out' now as I am getting quite old. I am sure mamma would like me to be at home too. And there is the expense. I doubt if the good I would get in another year would be worth the money. This year has been, certainly, for I feel broader all round, and I know I have learned a good deal in some ways. On the whole I think I'll go home.

She dreaded the forthcoming history examination, but also the thought of the end of term. Her mother replied,

> Papa and I have been thinking a good deal about you, now we want you to think for yourself. You have got on very well at College and have worked well and it seems to us that it might be rather a pity to cut your career short.

Girls crossing the College Garden *c.*1900. Ruth Duffin attended The Cheltenham Ladies' College from 1894 to 1896, and drew on her experiences there when establishing the ethos of life in Riddel Hall
The Cheltenham Ladies' College

Without consideration it is likely to lead to a good end. If it were a mere question of boarding school I should say you have had a fair share, but might not your staying another year put you in a better position if you have ever to be independent on your own account. I don't mean exactly in the way of certificates for I suppose the Cambridge Local Examinations would not count much above our Intermediate. I mean more that through them you could more clearly climb further on your own account if you worked. Even putting teaching aside if you ever wished to try writing, would not the education and practice be a help? You can form an even better judgement than I can on this point, and if possible I would consult Miss Laurie who must have a pretty fair idea of your abilities and capabilities by this time. Tell her the position also that there are seven girls of you and that we want to do the best for you. Though as parents I do not say that I wish you specially educated for teaching. You might take your BA at home if you wish afterwards in the Royal University. Now, I don't want you to think we are condemning you to a life of toil, far from it, but I feel very little is going on here and it will be so flat without other interests than gaiety. You might as well have another year of companionship and work if you like, I don't want to influence you a bit, I want you to weigh both sides and especially consider if you would reap real advantages from a longer stay. Personally, it will be a great disappointment to me not to have you at home and to lose Olive too. Still, you will only be past nineteen a little when you do return and that is not quite the age of Methuselah.

This correspondence raises several issues pertinent to social change for middle-class women. The Duffins were progressive in their attitude toward education, and in their insistence that the final decision was Ruth's. In subsequent letters she was loath to decide between staying at Cheltenham and coming home, but her mother insisted that the decision must be hers alone. This may be explained by their religious beliefs: Unitarians were known for their 'enthusiastic and active espousal of new ideas in all aspects of life... Unitarian women, therefore, were notable for being educated far beyond the norm'.[9]

Educational reformers experienced an uphill struggle to convince parents that it was economically viable to educate their daughters. Many middle-class parents could not afford the fees for their daughters' education. In Britain in 1898, 80,000 girls over sixteen were at school, but only a fifth of these remained in education after that age.[10] While the prevailing ideology of the time required middle-class women to be dependants of their male relatives, the reality was that sometimes women were forced to become financially independent. The only 'respectable' profession open to them was teaching. Many single women were impoverished and with little education were forced to become governesses. The plight of the governess, highlighted in literature, such as Charlotte Brontë's *Jane Eyre*, was one of the forces behind the mid-nineteenth century women's movement. Teaching rapidly became an overcrowded and underpaid profession. In Ulster at the beginning of the twentieth century there were several thousand schoolmistresses and hundreds of governesses.[11]

Maria Duffin's ambivalent feelings about the changing position of women are expressed in her correspondence with Ruth.

> As I don't want you to turn into a Bee (sic) Grimshaw (who by the way has become editor of a society paper in Dublin) I shall give you a good course of cookery, house keeping and helping me when you do come home, so that you may not turn into a New Woman before my eyes. I don't want you, however, to feel in the future that you had brains and would have worked, and never had the chance, like your mother though for that no-one was to blame but fate.

Bea Grimshaw was Ruth's cousin, who in 1895 was twenty-five years old and living independently in Dublin as a journalist. She was later described as 'the explorer of the South Pacific islands' and wrote travel literature on Borneo and Burma and later settled in Australia.[12] Mrs Duffin did not want Ruth to abandon conventional femininity; she wanted her daughter to have opportunities which had not been available in her youth. At around the age of eighteen young ladies 'came out' into society and attended balls, signifying their availability for marriage. Ruth's grandmother and aunts wanted her to do so in the winter of 1895, but she did not feel ready for this change of status. 'I don't think I should like to. I would still feel so awkward and school-girlish and feel as if I wanted a little more polish still.'

Ruth's mother did not believe that staying at school for an extra year would spoil her daughter's chances of marriage but her diaries and letters indicate that she feared the prospect of becoming an 'old maid'. Following a visit to her aunts in Strandtown Lodge when she was nineteen years old, she recorded that including her own generation there were a total of thirteen Miss Duffins. She wrote in her diary that this was 'a very unlucky number; I hope it does not mean that we are all to be old maids'. Within her extended family marriage was a rather rare occurrence. The great majority of the Duffins, their cousins the Riddels, and their cousins the Musgraves never married. In Ruth's parents' generation, of eight Duffin siblings only three married; in the Riddel family of ten only two married, and the twelve Musgraves all died unmarried.

An unmarried girl was expected to devote her time to the wishes of her family. As servants carried out all serious domestic work, Ruth's time, as her mother pointed out, would be spent on trivia that demanded neither physical nor mental exertion. Mrs Duffin recognised Ruth's academic potential and faced the reality that, as she was one of seven sisters, there would be a drain on family finances if none of them married.

In August 1895, when it had been decided that Ruth should return to Cheltenham for another year, she realised that 'I am very glad indeed. I can hardly imagine that I ever thought of leaving'. She sat the Cambridge Local Examinations in English literature in 1896 and gained two distinctions. She left school that summer; the following year she did a history course by correspondence and travelled to Cheltenham to sit the examination. This did not go so well. On 15 September 1897 Ruth recorded in her diary,

> I had an awfully kind letter from Miss Andrews, Cheltenham, about my exam. I failed in the Cambridge Higher Local history, which was a sad blow. She must have been very much disappointed for she looked for my name among the first class people; I wish she had found it there.

The following year she repeated the exam after some coaching at home, which she found depressing, 'I do hate the thought of going back to that horrid history, though I don't care for being altogether idle even in the holidays'.[13] This time she passed with First Class Honours. This experience may have helped her to be sympathetic later on with students who failed examinations at Queen's. The minutes of meetings with the Permanent Committee show that unless a student failed in all her exams consistently her place in the Hall, and in some cases her bursary, were not at risk.

In Cheltenham there were thirteen boarding houses individually run by housemistresses, which were home to some twenty-five girls for their entire stay. Boarding costs varied from £50 to £90 for the academic year and did not include tuition or extras such as drawing and music lessons. The housemistresses did not teach; many were admirable housekeepers and housemothers giving a life of devoted service to the College.[14] They were chosen by Miss Beale for 'their antecedents and gentility' and played an important motherly role for the girls in their care, contrasting with the more austere, patriarchal position adopted by the headmistress. This model was adopted in Riddel Hall by Miss Duffin and her fondly-remembered housekeeper, Miss Madeline Boyd.

Ruth's letters provide us with a glimpse of the social life in Glenlee, her boarding house. Boarding provided an opportunity for young women to develop confidence in social skills. 'I do think that being at school is good for argument; I read somewhere the other day that girls don't argue about questions the way boys do, but I'm sure we argue all day here, and sometimes on rather difficult subjects.' She enjoyed these intellectual challenges immensely, and excelled in this field.

> The girls here go in for sarcasm a good deal; I don't mean a bit ill-naturedly, but just for the fun of saying cutting things, it is a kind of recognised joke and we all sharpen our wits on it. Mary Weston is much the best at 'squashing', they all say I come next; but I don't think that is at all true.[15]

From her comments about the people she met at 'rather Trollopean dinner parties', it is clear that Ruth was very skilled at 'squashing'. She told her mother, 'at dinner time there is often an argument at Miss Ephon's end of the table that rages furiously for days. Some of the girls are really splendid at defending points; they seem to catch up everything so quickly'.

Miss Beale was often perceived by her pupils as autocratic. In school every aspect of life was rigidly controlled. If a girl spoke in class, she would be 'beckoned to the throne and rebuked; if she walked swinging her arms (like a sailor as Miss Beale phrased it), she would be made to walk the length of the hall under the eyes of the assembled classes'. A former pupil explained that as a result 'we all developed a wonderful walk'. Many former Riddel students recall Miss Duffin's 'ramrod straight' back and perfect deportment. The corridors of Riddel, like those of Cheltenham, were not for running along. Like Riddel, Cheltenham was not remembered for its creature comforts. In February 1895 the cold was so intense that the girls went around 'shivering with cold' in the bedrooms where 'there are no fires, of course!' The boarding house had strict boundaries on appropriate reading matter. 'Some of the girls here have copies of *Jane Eyre*. Mrs Smith found one the other day, and was not pleased at all.' Charlotte Brontë's novel had created a storm of protest when it was first published as it described deep feelings previously unexpressed.

The experience of attending Cheltenham Ladies' College influenced Ruth Duffin profoundly. Many of the lessons she learned there between the ages of sixteen and nineteen stayed with her for life and influenced the ethos and culture of generations of Riddel students. She certainly adopted Miss Beale's philosophy of a broad education.

> I think of some of the miserable starved specimens I have known, fed upon an almost unmixed diet of either classics or mathematics; their physique had suffered, and they had no mental elasticity, their one idea being to win scholarships: they did this, but never flourished at the university, for want of all round culture.[16]

Miss Duffin encouraged Riddel students to mix with fellow residents from other faculties so that friendships would develop between young women who had different academic interests. No one who was in Riddel Hall remembers her insisting that they study intensively; she seems to have left this up to the individual. Ruth Duffin's annual welcoming address focused on gentility and education in its broadest sense; she encouraged the development of wide reading, appreciation of art, culture and the environment.

Ruth Duffin recorded in her 1944 Chronicle that she

> *spent my first grown-up years at home, leading the usual life of a girl of the period, thoroughly enjoying dancing, tennis, hockey, and many other social amusements that came my way, and not at all anxious to start a career! I had learnt a certain amount of secretarial work as half-time secretary to the Lady Factory Inspector in Belfast, having had a few lessons in typing and shorthand. My first job away from home was as secretary to the Guild of Cheltenham Ladies' College, and after that I was six months in Dublin as secretary to the United Irishwomen.*

This rather nonchalant account differs markedly from Ruth's contemporary introspective diaries which expressed her fears that she would never find a useful and fulfilling role in life.

6

Early Days

In April 1915 the Permanent Committee decided that, as the builders had promised the Hall would be completed at the end of July 1915 and be ready for opening on 15 September, it was time to advertise its existence. Printed brochures with a photograph of the Hall on the cover were ready to provide information for prospective students. These were sent out by the University Secretary to local intermediate schools (equivalent to grammar schools today) and prospective students.

> The Hall, which stands in its own grounds of ten acres (including tennis courts and hockey ground) is built on a hill, on sandy soil, and commands a wide view of the surrounding country. It is about ten minutes' walk from the university, and the tram passes the gates. There are forty-two bed-sitting rooms, drawing room, library and music room in addition to ample bathroom and cloakroom accommodation, and a separate flat fitted up for use as a 'sick bay'. There are four students' kitchens, where residents can make tea, etc. or do their own laundry work if desired.[1]

Miss Duffin later recorded in her Chronicle,

in April 1915, when the Great War was raging, I was sent to visit English hostels to get hints for furnishing, etc. I visited Bedford College, London, Westfield College, and subsequently Trinity Hall, Dublin, but I don't remember coming back much wiser than I went.

Throughout her years as Warden Miss Duffin wrote to various halls of residence to find out their fees, house rules and policies on holding conferences in holiday periods, as well as salaries and pension schemes. This was standard practice until the Association of Principals, Wardens and Advisers of University Women Students was formed, which provided a more regular forum for communication and the pooling of experience.[2]

It was the Warden's responsibility to engage staff and domestic servants. In July 1915 she appointed Miss Florence Irwin as Matron at a salary of £70 per annum.

As in the case of the Wardenship, the post was not advertised, but I was asked to look for a Matron. Having been struck for some time by the practical and well-presented household and cookery articles of 'Housewife' in the Northern Whig, I bethought me of writing to [their author], though I did not know who she was. It was a lucky bow drawn at a venture.

The articles were regular contributions to the *Northern Whig*'s Tuesday women's page. Miss Irwin also wrote a regular Saturday column with step-by-step guides to cookery for children – 'simple cookery for little folks'. Florence Irwin wrote these articles for fifty years. Their central feature was frugality. Miss Irwin had been a peripatetic teacher of domestic economy under the Technical Board; she trained at Athol Crescent, Edinburgh, was the first travelling domestic science instructor in Ulster and became known to hundreds of provincial housewives as 'The Cookin' Woman'.[3] When Miss Duffin wrote to her she was acting as a cook in a military hospital at Gilford, Co. Down. Miss Duffin recorded that:

she at once responded to my suggestion that we should meet, and we sat among the long grass and dog daisies at the top of the bank overlooking the ponds and discussed matters, while the workmen hammered at the still unfinished building behind us. I felt convinced that I had hit on the right person, and she agreed to apply for the post. She and I had a busy time choosing kitchen equipment and arranging for the various fitments, cupboards, etc in all the domestic offices, but as we were given a free hand it was quite enjoyable work.

Miss Duffin later recalled that Miss Irwin was 'too impetuous, and used to laugh and say I was acting as a brake; she was generous enough to say that at times the brake was needed'.

Florence Irwin was later appointed as the first Warden of Stranmillis Training College in 1922, a post she held until 1948. She kept up her association with the Hall and was present when her successor, Miss Boyd, celebrated twenty-one years in office. On hearing of Miss Irwin's death, Miss Duffin wrote, 'I missed her vivid personality, her sense of humour and her unfailing interest in Riddel affairs, and lost a most faithful friend'.[4]

Below the housekeeper was the 'lady cook'. Miss Amy Boal was paid £35 per annum and in 1918 she was 'empowered to take on a cookery pupil', who would pay £5 per term for fees and £1 per week for board and lodgings. At the lower end of the hierarchy of the female staff were the domestic servants whose annual wages varied from £20 for the head parlour maid to £14 for the scullery maid. They also received free board and lodgings. Staff members were paid a small retainer for the university holiday periods when the Hall was closed.

There were also menservants, who were responsible for the upkeep of the Hall and grounds. The houseman's wages were 24 shillings a week with 'lodge, light and firing'. William Bailie, the houseman, found it hard to make ends meet as it was reported to the Permanent Committee in June 1916 that he was keeping lodgers at the lodge. They decided 'this could not be permitted and requested Miss Duffin to inform Bailie of their decision'.[5] His wages were not increased and by

The kitchen of Riddel Hall, this would seem extremely spartan today. There was a large range for cooking, and long scrubbed kitchen tables. There were cool pantries and sculleries for washing up, but no refrigerator in the Hall until the 1960s when one was bought from the Jubilee Fund
N. Duffin

1918 a new man was in the position. The gardener was employed at a weekly rate of £1 12s 6d, assisted by a sixteen-year-old gardener's boy at 16 shillings. There was also a fifteen-year-old 'boot boy' who was paid 7 shillings a week to clean the young ladies' shoes. He did not last long, as he was suspected of a number of petty thefts, culminating in stealing and cashing a postal order belonging to a student. Henry Musgrave ensured that he was prosecuted.

In February 1919 Dr Elizabeth Bell was appointed as medical officer to the Hall. She had her own medical practice in Great Victoria Street and was involved in voluntary work with organisations including the Women's National Health Association, the Belfast Babies' Home and Training School, and the Babies' Clubs, which provided subsidised milk for impoverished mothers. She was a medical advisor for the Slainte Health Insurance Society, the Midnight Mission and the Babies' Home at the Grove; she also taught students in the Presbyterian Deaconesses' Home. Other interests were temperance – she supported the Ulster Women's Christian Temperance Association – and the suffrage movement. She was a member of a cross-party suffrage society and was the doctor for suffragette prisoners in Belfast prison during 1914. During the Great War she served in Malta. In the post-war period she served on the Belfast Corporation Child Welfare Scheme and practised as a family doctor; she died in 1934.

Dr Bell took up her duties in the Hall in 1920. 'She proved a firm friend, and a rock of common-sense in her frank and friendly dealings with students' ailments, and I much appreciated the way in which she told me what to note in various illnesses, making me examine ulcerated throats or note a student's general 'type' or constitution.'

Furnishing of the Hall was proving a problem:

> By the 21st of July 1915, we had only arrived at inspecting sample rooms furnished by four different firms. I remember the Committee met in no. 28, and sat on any of the samples available, and subsequently decided to divide the order for students' rooms between two firms, Messrs Thomas, who supplied the light Japanese oak suites, and Messrs Watson, who supplied the dark Jacobean oak type of furniture. (The cost of a bedroom suite from Messrs Thomas was £36) Two of the rooms were 'odd', as we had agreed to retain all four samples. The library, drawing room and dining room were furnished by Messrs Wright and Hunter, and Messrs. Hanna and Browne. The latter charged £10 5/- for two Chesterfield settees and four easy chairs. We made an initial mistake in providing very pretty light cretonnes for the drawing room and also for students' bed-covers and screens. The bright sunlight in the Hall soon faded them, and they were sadly crumpled by their many users, and soon lost their freshness.

Perhaps Miss Duffin's choice of soft furnishings was influenced by the depressing effect her room at Cheltenham had had on her.

Study bedroom, from an early brochure dated 1934. The bed functioned as a sofa during the day
Riddel Hall Archive

Drawing room, from the same brochure. It was a bright and spacious room with a large bay
Riddel Hall Archive

I asked that, instead of contracting for 'suites' for the Warden's rooms, I might be given a sum to spend, and I was allowed £70. This proved to be a very tight fit, and I had to take a carpet that was too small, and do without a hearthrug. Miss Riddel, after seeing the room, and the Matron's, (still more scantily furnished) generously gave us each a Chesterfield sofa.

The list below shows how Miss Duffin spent her allowance and allows us to visualise her apartment in 1915.

Warden's Bedroom		
Thomas bedroom suite	£36	
Bank Buildings toilet set	£ 1	1s
Warden's Sitting room		
Writing table (2nd hand)	£ 4	
Carpet (Hanna and Browne)	£ 7	10s
Coal box		9s 6d
Curb (Hanna and Browne)	£ 1	2s
Firearms		6s 6d
Table (Wright and Hunter) round	£ 3	10s
Chair " " Sheraton	£ 2	1s 6d
" " " "	£ 2	
Wisteria cane chair	£ 2	2s
Armchair (2nd hand)	£ 1	12s
Cretonne	£ 3	1s 6½d
Cushions and covers	£ 3	3s 6d

As it was not until six years after taking up her appointment that the sitting room was wallpapered and the bedroom distempered at a cost of £12 9s 2d, Miss Duffin's rooms must have looked rather spartan.

For the first year the grounds and building remained a 'work-in-progress' as Miss Duffin later recalled. In November:

[I] asked that a hockey ground should be substituted for the proposed croquet ground, and this was agreed to. At this time, and for long after, the grounds were in a state of red sandy chaos, with trucks running on improvised rails carting earth from one place to another. The only trees were the old oak next to the Stranmillis House boundary, and the line of firs along the Stranmillis Road, and a few hawthorns which I only saved with difficulty from the contractor's destructive activities. The 'cutting' leading through the bank beneath the old oak to the terrace above the hockey ground was made subsequently by the Hall gardener, and the lime avenue and the various scattered trees in the grounds were placed at intervals later on. There was an idea that Stranmillis Road would be widened and that our Scotch firs would have to go, so I got permission to plant conifers and other trees to replace them. I made one or two attempts to grow a cedar on the lawn between the

drive and the tennis court, but they did not flourish, and I am afraid it will be a long time before the rather weedy survivor will add dignity to what will then be our ancient buildings. Only a portion of the furniture was ready when the Hall opened; the dining room and library were, I think, complete, but students' rooms were furnished by heterogeneous loans from the contracting firms, and there was great competition from the girls as to who would be fortunate enough to have the new furniture as it was delivered. One load of furniture was 'sunk by enemy action' on its way from Scotland where it was being made. Our china, ordered from Harrods, was not delivered for months, in spite of a fierce and prolonged correspondence, so we used hired stuff – a very expensive business.

Having dealt with the practicalities of equipping and staffing the Hall Miss Duffin was ready for the first cohort of students. The Permanent Committee met on 24 April 1915 and arranged that Miss Duffin and Sir Samuel Dill would 'interview some of the young ladies' at Queen's. In 1922 Miss Duffin provided statistics for the governors on the 155 students and teachers who had resided in Riddel Hall in its first seven years. These showed both the professions of the students' fathers and the degrees for which the young women were reading.

Table 1. Faculties of Riddel students 1915-22

Faculty	*No. of students*
Medicine	80
Arts	33
Science	22
Education	4
Lecturers	4
Commerce	3
Social training & economics	2
Dentistry	1

Source: Warden's report to annual meeting 1922, Riddel Hall Archive QUB

Medical students were the largest single group although only about 10 percent of the 300 students studying medicine in Queen's at this time were female. (This proportion remained fairly constant until the Second World War.) A medical student's stay in the Hall was often five years compared with three or four years for other subjects, so they had more time to establish themselves within the authority structure of Riddel. The Hall was founded for both students and teachers at the University, and there were four lecturers in residence. This figure remained fairly constant throughout the life of the Hall.

In her Chronicle Miss Duffin listed the occupations of the fathers of Riddel students from 1915 to 1924.

Table 2. Occupations of students' fathers

Father's occupation	No. of students
Merchants, shopkeepers, and commercial travellers	43
Farmers, horse dealers etc.	39
Clergymen	17
Doctors	7
Teachers	7
Solicitors	2
Bank managers	2
Postmaster	1
Veterinary surgeon	1

The large proportion of students from farming backgrounds indicated the need for accommodation for young women from rural areas. 'Daughters of the manse' often progressed to higher education despite their lack of resources, as there were about 100 entry 'scholarships open to competition' available to national school pupils each year.[6] Unlike Miss Beale's regime at Cheltenham, the daughters of men engaged in trade were welcome. Their predominance was a reflection of the importance of trade in Belfast society. The cost of educating daughters past the statutory school leaving age resulted in secondary and particularly university education being the preserve of the middle and upper classes. Less than 1 percent of women born around the turn of the twentieth century remained in full-time higher education.

The library at Riddel was a good place to work.
Finola and the Swans by Rosamond Praeger can be seen over the fireplace
N. Duffin

7

Contentious Issues

In her first three years as Warden Miss Duffin not only had to deal with the teething troubles of discipline, and setting of fees, but also wartime shortages of food, and the influenza epidemic of 1918. Fees, rules, coal allowances and food became deeply contentious issues for the first few years of her wardenship.

Miss Duffin met the students for the first time:

> needless to say, with a good deal of trepidation. I knew I should be up for judgement, but I was not prepared for the rather critical, and it seemed to me, suspicious attitude of the students. I had imagined that such a magnificent gift as Riddel Hall would have been greeted with enthusiasm, but at this meeting there was no expression of such a feeling. I was asked if there were to be many rules, they had heard that discipline was to be very strict etc., etc. I replied truthfully that the question of regulations had not yet been considered, but that my own idea would be to begin with the minimum of rules and only add others if they were seen to be necessary. I was not at all favourably impressed by the attitude of the girls, and more than likely their reactions prevented my getting on to terms with them at once. At any rate, I remember feeling chilled and disappointed after my first encounter with the girls I was to deal with. Of course, though I did not know it, some of them were senior medicals, and naturally rather independent after three or four years in 'digs'.

Eileen O. Bartley, a resident in Riddel from 1915 to 1921, wrote many years later that Miss Duffin 'said that, during the first difficult years as Warden, she was somewhat in awe of the senior students but no one would have imagined that such a feeling could exist under the calm, confident and dignified exterior that we saw'.[1] This assertive attitude was not unique to Miss Duffin's students, but part of a wider challenge to Victorian modes of behaviour amongst educated women who 'were in open revolt against their society and often felt little gratitude towards the pioneering women of higher education... The high-minded thinking and dowdy dressing of the lecturers was frankly unappealing and was representative – like the bad food – of limitations, not freedom'. By the second decade of the twentieth century students in England were 'overtly and covertly' breaking their colleges' rules, which were not changed until the end of the Great War. One Newnham College student boasted she had broken all the rules 'except for getting in over the railings at night, and that was not out of respect for the rules, but for my clothes'.[2]

Creating a community of students who would identify with and feel loyalty toward Riddel Hall was an enormous challenge. Although the Permanent Committee was the ultimate authority, on a day-to-day basis she was in control. As Dr Bartley wrote half a century later:

> She handled us very well, treated us as responsible beings and rarely interfered; though she had her own methods of pulling us up. For example, one day a notice appeared on the board to say that there would be an exhibition of interesting objects displayed on the office table the next morning. These objects were to consist of articles found on the ground underneath the windows of the students' rooms. All were invited to attend... To my consternation, among the exhibits was the dead mouse that I had disposed of a few days previously... How that mouse got into my room I have no idea... I decided to get hold of the Hall cat and let her deal with the mouse... Then I had the problem of the disposal of the body. To put it into the waste paper basket never occurred to me, so I just opened the window and dropped it on the ground below. It was the easiest way out and I never thought I should see that mouse again. I won't point the moral but the exhibition did have the desired effect on one student anyway.[3]

Despite her anxieties Miss Duffin appears to have disciplined the majority of students effectively in the same way as her housemistress in Cheltenham did – by force of her personality. The exercise of authority on a day-to-day basis had to be tried experimentally until a balance was found. From the beginning there was a house committee elected by the students themselves. Initially Miss Duffin believed that the girls should be able to discuss issues amongst themselves in private.

The first house rules, subsequently amended many times in the light of experience, were approved on the 28 September 1915. Smoking was not permitted

RIDDEL HALL

HOUSE RULES

1. The internal management and discipline of the Hall is in the hands of the Warden, and Students must conform to all House Rules laid down by her.

2. **Hours.**

WEEK-DAYS.	SUNDAYS.
Breakfast 8	Breakfast 9
Lunch - 12·30—2	Lunch - 1·40
Tea · 3·30—5·30	Tea · 3·30—5·30
Dinner - 7	Supper - 8—9

(Dressing-bell, 6·30. All Students are expected to change their dress for dinner.)

Students are expected to be present every morning at breakfast, except in cases of illness, which should be reported at once. No meals may be served upstairs without an order from the Warden or the Matron. Students may not be absent from dinner unless they are out for the evening.

3. Students make their own beds, and do the light dusting of their rooms. Beds must be made, windows opened, and rooms left ready for the maids by 9 a.m. (10 a.m. on Sundays).

4. Students may not sit in their rooms before 1 p.m., and fires may not be lighted before that hour.

5. **Leave.** Students may not be absent from the Hall after 7 p.m. without leave, the giving of which is in all cases subject to the discretion of the Warden as under :—

(a) Freshers will be granted leave to be out after 7 p.m. only on personal application to the Warden, and for not more than six times in a month.

(b) Any Student wishing to be out after 7 p.m. must, before leaving the Hall, enter her name in the Hall book, giving full particulars of her destination, and must sign it on her return.

(c) Students must in no case be out after 10·30 p.m. without special permission from the Warden, who may grant leave to be out till 11 p.m. for the purpose of attending theatres or concerts. Leave up to 11 p.m. may also be given by the Warden for dances, but, in this case, the Warden must be furnished beforehand with the names of those composing the party, and with a written consent from the parents of the applicant.

(d) Special late leave to be out till after 11 p.m. can only be given for official dances at Queen's University, or in special cases, for dances at private houses, but in the latter case such leave will be granted only if a satisfactory arrangement is made between the Warden and the hostess at least three days beforehand for putting the student up for the night.

In cases of special late leave a key will be given to one member of the party, who will be responsible for returning it to the Warden on the return of the party, and of seeing that all members of the party have returned.

(e) Ordinary late leave must be applied for not later than the morning of the day for which it is required, and any special late leave at least three days beforehand.

Overnight Leave. Anyone wishing to spend a night away from the Hall, except as provided above, must inform the Warden in good time, and invitations may not be accepted without her permission.

N.B.—Anyone who exceeds ordinary or late leave for any reason whatsoever will be deprived of after-dinner leave for a full week. No exceptions will be made to this rule.

6. **Visitors.** Students may receive men visitors in the drawing-room. Fathers or brothers may be taken to students' rooms up to 6·30 p.m. only, and permission must be obtained from the Warden or Matron.

Visitors may be invited to meals in Hall. (For conditions, see Service-room Rules.)

Unless dining in Hall, evening visitors may not be asked until 7·30 p.m., and all visitors must leave by 10·30 p.m.

Visitors may be asked to stay in the Hall, when convenient, on giving not less than 24 hours' notice to the Warden. The minimum charge will be 5/- per day, including all meals. Fire 6d. extra.

7. Smoking is strictly forbidden upstairs, but is permitted in the Library and Drawing-room after 2 p.m.

8. **Laundry.** Students must send to the laundry each week in a bag, with list enclosed :—

| 1 Sheet. | 1 Pillow-case. | 2 Towels. |

The cost of washing these will be deducted from the Student's personal account. Cases of loss or damage should be reported at once.

9. Each Student is provided with the following articles, for which she is responsible :—

1 Bunch of Keys.	Electric Bulb.
1 Tumbler.	Fire-irons and Hearth-brush.
1 Soap Dish.	4 Blankets.
1 Waste Paper Basket.	1 Under Blanket.
1 Duster.	2 Pillows.

Soap and matches will be supplied three times a term.

Pillows, etc., may not be taken out of the rooms.

Nails and pins must on no account be driven into walls or woodwork.

Any article lost, and any damage done to Hall property, must be reported at once, and paid for by the Student concerned.

10. No Hall crockery, knives, plate, etc., may be taken to Students' rooms, under penalty of a fine.

11. Boots should be changed in the ground-floor cloak-room on coming in, and put in numbered pigeon-holes for cleaning. Wet things should be taken to the drying-room below.

12. Students are requested to be most careful to switch off the electric light when leaving the room, even if only for a few minutes. All switches must be off by 11 p.m., when the light is switched off at the main. The light must not be left on in bathrooms and lavatories when not in use. A fine of 6d. will be imposed for lights left burning unnecessarily.

13. Baths may not be taken between 8·30 a.m. and 2·30 p.m.

14. **Fires.** Three-and-a-half scuttlesful of coal per week are supplied to each room. Any coal found in unsuitable receptacles will be confiscated.

15. On returning to the Hall each term, Students are requested to report at once to the Warden or Matron.

Before leaving at the end of term, each Student must have her equipment (Rule 9) checked by the Matron. Keys may not be taken away, but should be left in hall pigeon-holes. At the end of the Summer Term cupboards and drawers must be emptied, and all pictures and ornaments removed.

16. **Extreme quietness is requested upstairs after 9 p.m., and bedroom slippers should be worn after that hour.**

House Rules *c.*1920. These rules covered most aspects of life at Riddel, from times of meals, dressing for dinner, bed making, special permission for absence from the Hall after 7 p.m., men visitors, and times of baths to scuttlefulls of coal
PRONI (D/3119/5/13)

in either the Hall or grounds. This rule was amended in December 1919 in response to a second petition by the students to the Permanent Committee. In the inter-war years smoking was associated with the modern girl, indeed the 'cigarette was central to the modern girl's identity'. Contemporary magazines and society papers, such as *Vogue*, *Eve* and *The Sketch* 'presented [the modern girl] as young, urban, socially and economically independent and compared with her Edwardian counterpart, relatively sophisticated in her dealings with men'. They 'dressed in short skirts or frocks, wore their hair in a bob, shingle or crop, enjoyed freedom of bodily movement and access to public space'.[4]

The rules on the previous page were printed and circulated around 1920.[5] These rules may seem draconian to today's students, but they have to be taken within the context of the time. Other halls of residence had equally strict guidelines for behaviour.

For many years lights were turned off at 11 p.m. at the main switch. This issue was discussed at the last meeting of the informally constructed House Committee in October 1920. Miss Rachel Irwin 'spoke with eloquence on the severe shock rendered by the sudden turning off of the light, and the inconvenience and pain caused by this sudden darkness. The house was loud in its sympathy, and requested that Miss Duffin should be approached on the subject'.[6] Miss Duffin wrote in her Chronicle

> I think it was as a result of this request and of a similar one on November 13th that the system known as 'blinking' was inaugurated, Miss Irwin and I switched the main switches off and on again as a warning that lights would go off in five minutes time... If there are no restrictions, the cost of electricity would be enormous, but I have considerable sympathy for the students who object to having no light in their rooms after a certain hour.

There was a central heating plant, which was used sparingly, and the problem of keeping rooms heated produced similar ill feeling amongst the students. Miss Duffin argued that with three-and-a-half scuttles full of coal per room per week, this was a comparatively trivial matter. In 1921 the students claimed that as the price of coal had gone down they should be entitled to an increased allowance. She remembered

> one student who was a particularly active firebrand (in two senses!!) put her allowance of coal into a suitcase and took it to a shop to be weighed, though as no particular weight was guaranteed to students' rooms, the gesture was rather futile. In my written reply I pointed out that the house had been misinformed as to a reduction in the price of coal.

Early group of students with Miss Duffin 1925
Riddel Hall Archive

The problem of cold bed-sitting rooms was finally resolved in the late 1950s by the installation of electric fires with slot meters.

Providing meals which would satisfy more than forty young women in quality and quantity was a very difficult task. Miss Duffin recognised that

> *food grumbles are almost unavoidable in an institution. From the first, Miss Irwin and I decided that there should be no routine programme of meals, and that monotony should be avoided. We took the attitude that while the choice was an affair for the staff, students should be encouraged to come to us with any complaints as to service, shortages etc. (She and I and our first Lady Cook, Miss Amy Boal, signed the undertaking to keep to the scale of 'voluntary' rations for the Hall, but this was not until 1917.) It may be interesting to note here that the cost of food for the first year worked out at six shillings and six pence per head per week, including a reserve carried forward of 200 dozen eggs in water-glass and 1200 pounds of jam. We had no home grown vegetables at this stage.*

At a house meeting in February 1917, a request was made for a choice of dishes at lunch, and that jam or cheese should be on the table, as some of the girls were 'unable to eat the dishes provided'. Miss Eveline Beattie at the same meeting asked 'that the grumbling about food, which had been going on outside the Hall, should cease. She pointed out that each girl should have the honour of the Hall at heart. The speech was received with applause'. Riddel girls were beginning to feel a pride in belonging to the Hall and recognising that internal problems should be resolved amongst themselves in private.

The students and Miss Duffin expressed their feelings on contentious issues by composing light-hearted poems, the first of which appeared in *QCB* in early 1918:[7]

THE ALPHABET OF THE RIDDEL HALL

A For the Angels that dwell in the Hall, Arts, Science and Medical – there's room for all.

B For the Bell that wakes us at seven, not to mention the books that shut sharp at eleven.

C For Classes we have to attend with hope of obtaining degrees at the end.

D For Dancing, performed after dinner, no one can say we've got any thinner.

E For Exams of which there are plenty, to add to the cares of sweet one-and-twenty.

F For Freshers, with grown up air, ever retiring to put up their hair.

G For Grounds of which we're so fond, enhanced by the beautiful swans in the pond.

H For the Hockey field, two years in the making, only for New Forge hearts would be breaking.

I For the Infirmary so close to the skies, oh may no need for it ever arise.

J For Jokes we so greedily hoard, to use when our names are put upon the board.

K For the Kitchens, so much in demand, with hot buttered toast and tea in your hand.

L For 'Lights Out', we are warned by the blink, and all students to bed, I don't think.

M For the Matron, so courteous and kind, in the latest of recipes never behind.

N For the Needles on 'Knitting Night', some of the comforts are rather a sight.

O For the Oil at midnight in use, when exams come round it's work like the deuce.

P For the Photos and Pictures adorning, our rooms supposed to be dusted each morning.

Q For Queen's of which we all talk, to reach it takes only 10 minutes' walk.

R For the Rations to which all adhere, at the memory of feasts we all shed a tear.

S Stands for the Students, who hasten to lunch and find soup and sago, but nothing to munch.

T Stands for Tennis at which we all play, and lectures are cut on a very fine day.

U For the Undergrads, who are so stupid, reading tea leaves to find little cupid.

V For the Visitors, who early and late hop off the tram as it passes the gate.

W For the Warden, who tries to conceal the shocks and sensations she's likely to feel.

X Stands for 'late tea' when by lectures detained, few were the fragments that ever remained.

Y For the Years over wretched books spent, surely for this beauty never was meant.

Z For the Zeal with which this began, and now that it's ended I hope it will scan.

BOCCHE

It is interesting to note that in this affectionate poem food is mentioned in more verses than any other single issue. Lights were also mentioned twice. The 'hoarding of jokes' and the 'names on the board' refer to the rota system where each resident had to sit in turn at the Warden's table and make 'polite conversation'.

Miss Duffin's Chronicle mentions another instance when poetic licence was used to express the students' unhappiness with the food provided. On one occasion an anonymous set of verses appeared on the notice board. The poem is particularly amusing in the light of some of Miss Irwin's columns in the *Northern Whig*. The most economical of her dishes were her eggless milk puddings, described under the heading of 'cheap and nourishing puddings in wartime'. The prime example was 'cookie pudding'. Miss Irwin pointed out that 'stale cookies and barmbrack, especially if they have been toasted and buttered are very often wasted'. She wrote in 1915, 'for cookie pudding. It does not matter how stale they are, whether they have been toasted and buttered, it is excellent in any case'. It is almost certain that they had this and other similar delicacies at Riddel.

Miss Duffin responded to the poem with her usual sense of humour, by putting up her own poem on the notice board entitled:

RETALIATION (NOT BY OLIVER GOLDSMITH)

If Halls were run by students,
Oh, wouldn't it be fine?
We'd have ten breakfast dishes
All hot from 8-9
We'd have a four-course luncheon
From 10 o'clock till 3,
And soon as that was finished
We'd all sit down to tea
With bread and jam and BUTTER!
And cake of several kinds,
For forty different people
Have forty different minds
We'd have hot joints for dinner,
And always throw away
Whatever wasn't eaten
Not use it up next day.
Economy is vulgar,
And all should have their say
In choosing dainty dishes
According to their wishes –
BUT I WONDER WHO WOULD PAY!

Food remained a contentious issue for several years; Miss Duffin remembered a house meeting on 3 November 1919 where:

> the vexed question of students' teas was discussed. At the outset students' teas were served in the dining room, but it was soon found that some students came in so late the maids could not get the dinner tables laid in time. Then it was arranged to have a 'late tea' in one of the students' kitchens, with a maid in attendance. This was unsatisfactory, so rations were left in each student's room. As no-one remembered to give warning if they were going to be out, this led to a hopeless waste of food. Ultimately, after much trial and error, the present system was instituted, each student providing her own tea-things and being responsible for washing them up, and calling at the service hatch for rations on coming in.

The question of waste of food in students' kitchens was always cropping up at meetings and one student suggested as a remedy that Riddel Hall should 'indulge in a pig'. The pig never became a resident. The waste of bread especially was a perennial problem; the daily excess was weighed by Miss Duffin and the Permanent Committee was appalled.

Miss Duffin regarded the Permanent Committee as the ultimate disciplinary authority. On one occasion in particular when twenty-six students, including Miss Molly Dawson, later to become the last Warden of the Hall, signed a petition about 'the quality and quantity' of their lunches, Miss Duffin brought it before this august body. The students had not expected this, as her Chronicle records.

> This was such an unexpected development that some of the students indignantly said that they would have worded the remonstrance in different terms, if they had known! The Committee inspected the menu book, and subsequently interviewed the petitioners in the library. Professor Henry, monocle in eye, questioned some of the malcontents, and when one girl said she had had no lunch that day because the dish was Irish stew, he appropriately 'settled her hash' and the Committee came to the conclusion that there were no grounds for complaint.

The setting of fees was a particularly difficult matter. Annual expenditure during the first year was a little over £2,000. On this basis it was decided to charge 10 shillings per week for board and to have charges for the rooms varying from 3s 6d to 7s 6d per week. These fees subsequently proved to be too low, but Sir Samuel Dill, who was rather pessimistic by nature, insisted 'that if they were higher we should have no residents, and that the Misses Riddel would be supremely disappointed if the Hall did not fulfil its purpose'.

It was very difficult to set fees at a consistent figure in wartime. The prices of goods were constantly changing and Miss Irwin was wrestling with the problem

All meals were served in the dining room, and most girls walked up from Queen's for lunch. There were constant battles about food, both quantity and content, and the question of dressing for dinner
N. Duffin

of keeping food costs down and satisfying the demands of the students. The weekly cost of food per person almost doubled between 1916 and 1919. In May 1916 the fees were raised. Every time there was an increase in fees at least one family gave notice that they could not pay. In many instances Miss Duffin appealed to the Permanent Committee, who frequently agreed to accept a lower sum when evidence of hardship was proven. This assistance was part of the Riddel bequest and a system of bursaries was instituted to assist needy students. Nevertheless in June a protest signed by thirty-two students pointed out:

> Knowing that it is possible to live in lodgings on lower terms, we do not feel justified, under present circumstances, in asking our parents to incur the increased expense. We realise that the Committee has endeavoured to meet this difficulty by the arrangement for admitting some students at reduced fees, but we feel that the new scheme which involved each student making a separate arrangement with the Warden, would place individuals in an invidious position, and would be likely to lead to friction and complications. Knowing that the object of the Hall is to enable women students of Queen's University to enjoy the advantages of a Hostel at the same terms as they could live in lodgings, we have ventured to bring this matter again before your notice.

Notwithstanding, the Permanent Committee's decision to raise the fees was not reversed as the books were not balancing. Costs, particularly the rates, were higher than expected and income tax at six shillings to the pound had to be paid on the interest from endowments. Amongst those objecting to the price rises were Catherine Hunter and May Lyon who became teachers, Eileen O. Bartley, later a lecturer in Bacteriology at Queen's University and Winifred Hadden, later a medical practitioner. All went on to be lady graduate governors of the Hall.

Raising fees was not enough to cover expenditure and the situation did not improve. In 1918 a deficit of more than £384 was recorded. Fees were again raised in October 1919; the term fee became £6 10s and the weekly fee £1 1s. This caused another protest at what Miss Duffin remembered as a

> very prolonged and obstreperous House Meeting on the 3rd November 1919. The perennial troublemakers, Miss Sinton and Miss Anderson, led the offensive. Miss Sinton said she did not understand the increase in fees. She understood that in a community one should be able to save 30% on the cost of living; she felt she could live in lodgings for a smaller sum than 35 shillings. No one seems to have pointed out that the amenities provided in 'digs' were hardly comparable with those in the Hall, or that there were ten acres of ground to be kept up! Miss Moore did say that the whole question raised was the result of the ignorance of everyone at the meeting. Miss Anderson proposed that the cost of the upkeep of the Hall should be explained fully to the students. Miss Moore thought that the financial affairs of any institution were usually considered a private matter, and commented adversely on the practice of discussing Riddel affairs in tramcars and the University buildings. Miss Sinton wished that something might be done, as in these days of democracy students should not be ruled from Olympia.

Almost thirty years later Miss Duffin recalled

> I used to dread seeing little knots of girls evidently discussing some matter in the corridors. Miss Irwin said she could always sense the atmosphere when trouble was in the wind! I did not always attend house meetings at this time, feeling that the girls should have an opportunity for talking things over 'on their own'. But later I found it wiser to have meetings summoned with more formality, and I took the chair myself – less democratic, I suppose, but it worked better in practice.

From January 1921 the new system for house meetings came into being: a roll was kept and rules drawn up. Miss Duffin herself wrote them up 'as a preface to the new minute book'. Each student had a vote and the election was held at the beginning of term to choose the Chairman and Secretary. The House Committee was thus given authority over the residents 'in all matters concerning the students'. On taking office each member had to sign a declaration that 'it is my purpose without fear or favour, in all things to uphold the honour and further the welfare of the community of Riddel Hall'.

West view of the Hall
N. Duffin

Members of the House Committee were the acknowledged 'leaders of the house'. The first extant minute book, begun in 1920 and written by Miss Duffin herself, lays out their powers and responsibilities. Their primary function was disciplinary and they were told that

> They should not be afraid to exert the authority vested in them by the Warden and by the House, nor to express their opinion if they consider the members are not acting in the best interests of the House as a whole. They also owe loyalty to the Warden and should let her know at once if there is anything going on which is not desirable for the welfare of the House, and with which they themselves are not competent to deal. The Warden will always be glad to discuss matters with the House Committee, but she will give the answers to resolutions in writing, unless the secretary in handing over the minutes expresses the wish of the House Committee to discuss them, or unless she herself considers it advisable to summon them or to answer the House in person. In accordance with House Rule No.1, the Warden's decision in matters of management and discipline is final, in accordance with the authority given to her by the Governors, but she will never refuse to allow the House Committee to lay any matter before the Permanent Committee, if the House so desires.

These instructions clearly illustrate the hierarchical structure of the Hall. They show how under Miss Duffin's direction it was to develop into a democratic community with a corporate identity, which however could only exist within strict limits. The experiment of permitting the students to create their own community had not been a success so the Warden had to take a more authoritarian stance. Miss Duffin found to her relief that the new form of House Committee 'heralded a more peaceful era in Riddel history'.

There were a few resignations from the committee following these changes, which prevented 'irresponsible malcontents' from calling meetings whenever they wished to air a grievance. Two medical students, Dorothy Sinton and Rachel Irwin, almost certainly among the malcontents, seemed to work together to create havoc. For example, initially it was decided to stop using the system of proportional representation to elect members of the committee. However Miss Irwin proposed that it be retained in house elections and Miss Sinton seconded the motion. The meeting ended with the resignations of Miss Anderson, Miss Sinton and Miss Irwin; all were the frequent instigators of student protests. At the last meeting of the 1920-21 session Miss Sinton proposed several facetious motions, seconded by Miss Roden, including introducing a book in which students had to enter 'the day and time when she indulged in the luxury' of a bath. After some discussion Miss Sinton 'begged to withdraw her proposal'.

Miss Duffin remembered the difficulties some twenty-five years later.

> As may be gathered, this was a rather difficult time in the history of the Hall, as there were a few troublesome people who seemed to think that decisions on all questions affecting students should be arrived at by a majority vote of the students themselves. I suppose anyone who has had to deal with communities must have been struck by the trouble, which can be caused by even one or two malcontents who become a storm-centre. It is also noteworthy that when these same malcontents have outlived their 'growing pains' they often turn out exceedingly well. They are generally girls with some force of character and capacity for thinking for themselves, but with not sufficient experience of life to have a sound judgement. And, oh, they can be a thorn in a Warden's flesh.

Riddel's group of 'irresponsible malcontents' went on to establish worthwhile careers. Dorothy Sinton became a 'very popular' and 'hard working' medical missionary in charge of a women's hospital in the Irish Presbyterian Mission Station at Kirin, Manchuria. Dorothy Anderson stayed in Riddel from October 1916 until 1921, the year she qualified as a doctor. She responded to a 'circular letter' from Miss Duffin in 1927 telling her about a reunion of old students. She hoped 'that the Hall is flourishing', but explained that she would be unable to attend as she was practising in Rapallo, Italy. Rachel Irwin left in July 1921; she must have found 'digs' as her family home was in Broughshane. Dr Irwin qualified in medicine in 1923; in 1925 she was 'helping temporarily in the Irish Presbyterian Men's Hospital, Moukden' before moving to Fakumen, Manchuria. She ran 'her own hospital and carried on medical work in a big district single-handed'. She had re-opened a hospital previously closed since 1915. In 1931 she was with Dorothy Sinton in Kirin. During the Second World War the missionaries were evacuated and she went to Melbourne, Australia.

The student records show that six of the early medical graduates from Riddel Hall went on to become medical missionaries. From the 1870s onward women aspiring to develop medical careers often spoke of answering 'God's Call'. The opportunity to practise medicine presented itself in the form of missionary work in India and China. Margaret Byers was especially committed to this form of 'women's work for women'. She inspired many of her pupils from Victoria College to volunteer for the mission field.[8] Although she died in 1912 the encouragement toward missionary service remained in the College for many years. The calling was also supported by the University. In 1890 the President of Queen's College Belfast was

> happy to think that from the very early days I have been in favour of the practice of medicine being open to women; and my Indian experiences have deepened the strength of my convictions on the point... Indeed, already several eminent female practitioners are established in the principal Indian cities and have been everywhere welcomed with acclamation.[9]

On 22 November 1921 an article about Riddel Hall entitled 'Finest British Hostel' appeared in the *Belfast Telegraph*, written by Miss Irwin, by 'permission of the Governors'. There were only thirty-nine students in the Hall that year, so the article may have been a form of advertising, but it aroused some negative publicity. Miss Irwin portrayed Riddel in a poetic way, writing of 'the marvels of this hostel'. She described students' rooms. 'A red tiled fireplace with "basket" grate completes the arrangements for making the room all that a bed-sitting room should be, and when pictures, flowers, photos etc., are added, and a bright fire burning in the hearth, cosy and comfortable it may well be termed.' At this time, Miss Duffin later recalled, the rooms were still distempered and 'had been left with the original plaster untouched'. The 'cosy rooms' must, in reality, have looked rather bleak, and protests by students about skimpy coal allowances cast doubt on the notion of 'bright fires'.

Miss Duffin admitted that Miss Irwin's article 'unfortunately gave rise to a rather unpleasant newspaper correspondence'. Someone calling himself or herself 'Bon

Two girls in their study bedroom. Still an open grate! Coal allowances were a problem
Riddel Hall Archive

Ami' complained of high fees, saying 'surely this is a matter for the Governors to enquire into, and in the interest of the public demand an explanation; otherwise they will find that the object of the Misses Riddel will soon be defeated'. The writer argued that equivalent hostels were less expensive than Riddel.

On 26 November one of the governors, Henry Seaver, wrote to the *Belfast Telegraph* explaining that the interest yielded by the Endowment Fund was absorbed by rates and income tax, consequently the whole cost of running the Hall had to be met by students' fees. The financial information demanded by the 'malcontents' in 1919 had now been placed in the public domain rather than kept within the community of the Hall. This was not the end of the newspaper correspondence. The cost of residence in the Hall would exclude the daughters of 'Paterfamilias', who had a large family and 'moderate means'. This correspondent argued that 'it is self-evident that Riddel Hall is only suited for the well-to-do, and not for those for whom it was intended at the opening'.[10]

Miss Duffin's annual report for 1921-2 admitted that 'the Hall was not so full as usual last year, partly owing to the higher fees, and partly due to the fact that business and farming were not so flourishing as during the war years, and consequently there were fewer women students at the university'. Northern Ireland's main industries underwent significant decline throughout the 1920s;

economic recession was exacerbated by the Wall Street Crash of 1929, and the unemployment rate of insured workers rose to 28 percent.[11] In times of hardship further education was favoured for sons rather than daughters. The Hall's capacity was fifty students: in the first term there were forty-eight regular and two temporary students, in the second and third terms there were forty-three in total. However, there is no record of ex-students wishing to put their point of view in writing to the press.

On 17 December 1921 the *Belfast Telegraph*, 'Bystander' stated:

> I believe that the women students in Riddel Hall have little say on matters affecting them as a whole. Surely life in a hostel should promote all-round development. Are social duties the only requirements of a woman passing straight from a university to a position of responsibility?[12]

Riddel's management was accused of not running a democratic establishment. This was not entirely justified; there was a certain level of democracy through the House Committee. The Hall's records demonstrate that the accusation that it was failing to provide society with young educated women, equipped for their role in vocational and public life is totally without substance. Riddel students went on to forge worthwhile careers in medicine, teaching, social service and the law. Miss Duffin's annual addresses to the students provide much evidence, supported by past students, that she consciously set out to make Riddel Hall a base where students had a broad 'liberal' education, with a focus on manners and culture. By treating the Hall as a microcosm of life she ensured that the young women in her charge had practical experience in the duties and benefits of citizenship.

Many, if not most of her students appreciated Miss Duffin's devotion. One young woman even owed her life to the Warden's unselfish care. In November 1918 Miss Duffin was forced to close the Hall as a precaution against the spread of the influenza epidemic 'which swept the world and killed thousands of people'; the eventual death toll was counted in millions. Miss Irwin had been taken ill. The Warden had been left with seven patients and no nurse to assist her. One student, Amy Moore, said she felt unwell on the morning that the others left. Miss Duffin remembered:

> *She had a very slight temperature, and as she lived in Mayo, I detained her. When I went round my patients that evening her temperature had risen to 105.6. I had never heard of such a high temperature and with shaking knees I rushed to the telephone to get in touch with a doctor. (We had no official doctor at the time.) I tried one after another, but not one could come, so in desperation I asked one for directions. He prescribed a tepid sponge and castor oil. I could feel the heat rising from the patient as I sponged her down, and my heart sank. Numbers were dying;*

four masters and several boys had died at the Methodist College. I felt helpless,
frightened, especially as I had no one to take on night work. However, after a day
or two my patient did well and had no complications.

Amy Moore recovered, went on to follow a postgraduate course in economic
history and was voted Head of House the following year. She, perhaps, was
motivated to repay Miss Duffin for saving her life, and defended the management
of the Hall at difficult times. She joined the teaching profession, later becoming
headmistress of a private school for girls in England.

While tending her patients on the evening of 11 November there was, in Miss
Duffin's words,

a tremendous hullabaloo from the maids, and on going out from a patient's room
to rebuke them, I found them all out on a balcony cheering. The news of the
Armistice had come through; the War was over.

Two students, Dorothy and May Entrican, sisters who stayed in Riddel in the early
1920s, corresponded with Miss Duffin. Dorothy served as a medical missionary
to China with the London Missionary Society. In her seven-page letter of 1931 she
sent Miss Duffin 'a small book-marker with my love', and gave her a detailed story
of its origins. She described her garden in China adding, 'you would love it... Will
you write and let me know how Riddel Hall is when you have time? You know
how I am always eager for news'. May went on to do a Diploma in Education, and
teach in schools in England and Wales. She wrote in 1943:

Someone sent me a notice of your resignation from the post of warden of
Riddel Hall. I shall be sorry not to think of you there. The days we lived at
Riddel were very pleasant ones and I enjoyed everything about the Hall... I do
hope that you will enjoy a good rest when you are at home; a change from
having to see that everyone and everything was in order! I thought, for a short
time, of sending in an application myself, but I have no special qualifications
for the post, and should probably have not an atom of chance of being
appointed... Although it's a long time since I was at Riddel, I would like to
thank you for everything that you did for us there, and to say again how glad
I am to have been there.

These are typical of many letters received by Miss Duffin. The large majority of
Riddel girls remembered their Warden with respect and affection. Phyllis Kerr, in
the Hall from 1927 to 1931, an award-winning writer of poetry and Personal
Secretary to the Prime Minister of Northern Ireland in 1945, wrote to Miss
Duffin, 'you have no idea how much I have loved that time, and how happy I was
in the Hall'.

8

Warden and Matron

From the nineteenth century onward residential university colleges modelled themselves on the mid-Victorian family. Miss Duffin kept and annotated an article in *The Spectator*:

> A College is in its nature a family; and like all families it has its discipline – a regular way of life, which, for the sake of the servants as well as the members, has to follow regular hours. The discipline of a family is made by father and mother; and there seems to be no reason why the discipline of the College should not be made by master and tutor. The wise master and tutor, remembering that the members of the family are 'of a larger growth', will do well to consult the leaders among the undergraduates about the rules of the family life; and in the writer's experience such consultation is as natural and regular as it should be in any family.[1]

She consciously followed these guidelines in running Riddel Hall. Old students pointed out that Miss Duffin took on the austere, authoritative paternal role. She is remembered by students in the 1930s as being, as Nessie Maybin expressed it, 'a ship in full sail, she was a tall woman, a very big woman with a big frame'. Elizabeth Mills and Eleanor Wilson agreed that 'we were scared of her – we held her in great respect'. She had 'a real presence'.

Annie Roden, one of the more challenging students resident in the Hall during the Great War, reflected in 1968 when she was 69 years old, 'I was re-reading an epistle I once had from the warden when I was at RH... Miss Duffin was such a very delightful person in her role of Miss Duffin, but she really did consider the students worth less than the dust. Still we had a good time'.[2]

Molly Dawson, a student from 1929 to 1933, expressed a different view. 'Behind the sometimes-stern exterior, there was always, as I have cause to know, a great kindness in time of trouble, a lively sense of humour and a real interest in her students, which extended far beyond their years in the Hall. I doubt if she ever knew how much she was held in affection and regard by so many of her old students.'[3]

The public and private personae only conflicted when brought together, for instance when she invited friends and acquaintances to dinner. Some students in residence in the late 1930s particularly recall the visits of R.M. Henry, Professor of Latin at Queen's, a 'member of many learned societies... a picturesque figure, with his black hat and flowing cape... a scholar and a wit... who was a nominee for the presidency of Eire in 1938'.[4] One old student said 'we thought Miss Duffin had a crush on him'.

Miss Duffin maintained her contacts with the literary world throughout her lifetime. She met William Butler Yeats several times and his sisters Elizabeth and Lily, who ran the Cuala Press in Dublin that published some of Ruth's poems. Ruth and Celia were jointly awarded a medal in a competition organised by the Royal Dublin Society (of which one of the judges was W.B. Yeats) for *Escape*. (This is the name of a poem in a small book of poems of the same name, by Celia and Ruth Duffin.) Elizabeth Yeats regularly visited Riddel Hall and stayed at Summerhill, Mount Pleasant, adjacent to the Hall, the Duffin family home from 1924.

In contrast to the authoritative role of the Warden, the Matron typically adopted a softer motherly role. Riddel Hall's staffing policy and the job description indicate that this was deliberate. The Matron was responsible for domestic arrangements, including catering, checking accounts connected with household expenditure and the engaging and supervision of servants. She also comforted the young women when their romances were not running smoothly. The Matron's position provides an interesting case study in the emerging field of professional women's work.

In the early years of the twentieth century, paid work became acceptable for middle- and upper-class women provided it reflected their maternal qualities. A new educated female elite concentrating on a particular kind of professional work began to emerge. Three of the graduates of Bedford College's Hygiene Course went on to have pioneering careers. One of these women was Hilda Martindale, for whom Ruth Duffin worked in Belfast from 1908 to 1909, when she was the first 'Lady Factory Inspector' in Ireland. In 1921 she became Deputy Chief Inspector of Factories, and Director of Women's Establishments of HM Treasury. Another was Maud Holland, one of the first women inspectors under the National Insurance Act; another was Irene Whitworth, Assistant Director of the Welfare and Health Department at the Ministry of Munitions during the Great War.[5]

These careers were, of course, for single women – married women were barred from many professional appointments until the 1970s. The Victorian feminist movement had fought the persistent belief that a woman's natural destiny was to marry; their hope was that a 'new woman' who 'could be a celibate careerist, professionally trained, and financially independent of a husband's economic support', would emerge.[6] Angela Woollacott argues that middle-class status was an essential prerequisite for these new opportunities. 'While theoretically, professional abilities depended upon talent and not class origin, working-class women lacked sufficient educational opportunity to aspire to professional status.'[7]

The roles of Warden and Matron were complementary; the need for 'loyal co-operation' between the two women was highlighted by Miss Duffin's unhappy relationship with Mrs Coates, Miss Irwin's successor, who

Summerhill, Mount Pleasant, was the Duffin family home from 1924. The Duffin sisters were artistic and literary. They were friendly with Elizabeth and Lily Yeats, who came to stay at Summerhill
PRONI (2109/26/1/F)

was unfortunately a misfit, and after a year and a half of hoping for better things,
our relations became so strained, and the morale of the house was so visibly
deteriorating, that I had to ask the committee to give her congé. Those eighteen
months were a very unhappy time for me.[8]

Unfortunately no further explanation on why Mrs Coates was a 'misfit' is given; perhaps it was because she was a married woman who did not wish to live in the Hall. The minutes of the Permanent Committee, of 9 January 1924, state simply that the resignation of Mrs George Coates was accepted. Although she was paid until the end of term, she was asked to leave on 1 March so that her successor 'might be installed some weeks before the Easter vacation'.

Future matrons were appointed on the strength of personal contacts. Within two days of the meeting of 9 January, Miss Margaret Drennan wrote to Miss Duffin applying for the post. She was a native of Limavady, Co. Londonderry; she took the junior and senior Oxford and Cambridge examinations, and then taught at her old school. She entered King's College for Women in 1919 and studied for the three-year University Diploma in Household and Social Science; this included 'theoretical and practical experience in institutional administration'. She did holiday duty at Lady Margaret Hall, Oxford and the Ulster Volunteer Hospital in Belfast where she cooked for 260 patients. The course's final examination subjects were applied chemistry, physiology, hygiene, bacteriology and household work.[9]

Miss Drennan was presently acting as housekeeper for a Doctor Storey in Bournemouth, but 'the work is not at all what I like... the housekeeping has not wide enough scope in itself'.[10] Miss Drennan's testimonials focused on the same central issues as those of future wardens – on education and class status. The Bursar of Lady Margaret Hall wrote, 'she has been very well educated and is in every sense of the word a lady'. Miss Drennan's former headmistress wrote, 'I think very highly of her in every way – she is certainly a gentlewoman and I certainly consider that Margaret is far above the "average matron"'.[11] This letter was dated 19 January 1924. Miss Duffin was anxious not to make another mistake in recruiting her new deputy. Miss Drennan was appointed at the meeting of the Permanent Committee on 1 February, initially for only the summer term, as she had not yet been interviewed.[12] The new Matron 'proved most capable and was very popular with students and a good friend and colleague' to Miss Duffin. Miss Drennan subsequently resigned from her post to marry the Reverend Colin Montgomery, younger brother of Field Marshal Viscount Montgomery, in the summer of 1927. A contemporary newspaper reported that the couple sailed to 'the lonely outpost of Aklavik where Mr Montgomery was to take up his appointment as Canon of the Diocese of the Arctic'.

Miss Drennan's resignation was accepted 'with much regret' and Miss Margaret Roper appointed in her place. Again, this appears to have been on personal recommendation. Her letter of 9 February 1927 stated, 'It was very kind of you to give me the chance of applying for the post of matron at Riddel Hall. It is just the sort of post I have really been wishing for, and I shall be very much obliged if you can obtain the post for me'. Miss Roper had completed a two-year training course at Battersea Polytechnic earning Diplomas in Cookery, Laundry Work and Housewifery. She had been teaching domestic science at a girls' school in Essex for six years and had been house matron for two terms at Duncombe Park, Helmsley, Yorkshire.[13] Miss Roper resigned seven years later 'owing to' her 'approaching marriage'. She left reluctantly, writing, 'I should be very sorry to leave for any other reason'.

Her eventual successor, Miss Madeline Boyd wrote to Miss Duffin

Miss M. Boyd by William Conor
Maddie Boyd was Matron at Riddel Hall for more than 25 years. She was warm-hearted, energetic and loved by all the girls
Queen's University Belfast

on 6 February 1934 saying she 'would like to apply' for the position, having heard from Miss Shearman of Ashleigh House School, Belfast that the post 'might be vacant soon'. She had qualified with the Housekeeper's Certificate from Atholl Crescent College, Edinburgh. The course included training in nursing, and she had a First Aid Certificate. Following her training Miss Boyd went to her old school in Seascale, Cumberland as housemistress in 'the Domestic Science house'. She left this position to return to Ireland. She was a native of Lifford, Co. Donegal where her father had been a general practitioner. At the end of the Great War she worked as a VAD nurse in the Strabane Auxiliary Hospital and had experience as an ambulance driver.[14] In early 1934 she had worked as temporary cook at the Hospital for Sick Children, Falls Road, Belfast, in order to gain experience in catering for large numbers.[15] Another point in her favour was her interest in hockey and tennis. Miss Shearman wrote to Miss Duffin in early March 1934 stating that 'she is really quite an exceptional candidate. First she is a gentlewoman, and so is exceedingly nice to work with as she is not afraid of hard work. She is accustomed to working with girls and young women, and has a great deal of practical common sense and also a great deal of tact'. Miss Boyd sent seven testimonials to Miss Duffin in support of her application. One referee wrote 'I do hope she gets the post, but I suppose there will be a great many in for it and many with more backing'.[16] Three candidates were interviewed by the Permanent Committee in April.

Madeline Boyd stayed in Riddel Hall from 1934 until 1960. She is still remembered by all who knew her as a 'warm', 'motherly' and 'caring' woman. As Mollie McGeown expressed it, 'If you had any problems, Maddie Boyd was the one... she was a good counterpoise to Miss Duffin; she was just what we needed. She didn't strive for the same things; it was a completely different role. She played it extremely well'.

A poem composed for the celebration of Miss Boyd's twenty-one years in the Hall sums up her energy, devotion and warmth.

> MADDIE
> To Riddel Hall in thirty four
> There came a Matron – nay, far more.
> Just hear my tale and you'll agree
> Her equal there could never be.
> From dewy morn till day is done
> She never walks when she can run.
> From North to South: from East to West
> She sees to all and scorns to rest.
> When we were ill she made us well;
> When we were bad she gave us Hell.
> But Maddie's wrath we never heeded
> For she was always there when needed
> To guide, to comfort, to befriend
> To cook, to bottlewash and mend.
> And now we wish all blessings on her
> And light these candles in her honour.[17]

Miss Boyd had high standards about tidiness in students' rooms. She used to make surprise inspections and leave notes for the girls in the dust! She was a 'fresh air fiend', always opening windows. This may have added to the cold in the Hall! She played tennis in the summer term, a 'wizard' with a 'deadly backhand stroke'.[18] She organised tennis tournaments at which the maids came out with jugs of water, orange and lemon for the thirsty competitors.[19]

An amusing anecdote illustrates the difference between Warden and Matron. One evening during the Second World War Margaret Mitchell was busy talking to friends, forgetting that she had been filling a bath (to conform with air raid precautions). Water started dripping through the ceiling and much of the east wing kitchen was flooded. Girls, maids and Matron all mopped up, but Miss Duffin appeared in full evening dress offering a 'face flannel', asking 'would this help?' This is the only occasion that Miss Duffin has appeared as ineffectual. Miss Boyd 'made good fun of it and all hands had tea at the kitchen table'.

9

In Loco Parentis

In 1924 the number of women attending Queen's rose to one third of the student body. Moody and Beckett point out that as they were in a minority there was 'a sense of unity that cut across faculty divisions and added to their influence'.[1] Miss Duffin actively encouraged the cross-faculty mixing in Riddel; she also impressed upon the students the importance of participating in university societies and making use of the Women Students' Hall. In 1925 women were allowed to participate in the annual 'Students' Day' collection and the next year they produced a magazine of their own, *Hall Marked*, which appeared in three annual editions between 1926 and 1928. In 1929 the Women Students' Hall moved from its original cramped quarters at the south end of the original college building to two of the houses in Queen's Elms. For the first time women had accommodation comparable to that of the male students' union for their social activities. In 1926, the students' magazine, *Frav-lio-Queen's*

> noted with sorrow that the Society for the Abolition of Feminine Influence has disintegrated. The promise which it showed in its inception has not been fulfilled. Even the men who filled the highest offices in the Society have fallen from grace. Of course, man is only a frail creature. Under the never relaxing

attack of the women students, the organisation of the Society was shaken...
The fabric of the Society collapsed, the last bulwark of the University men has
gone, and Queen's is once more at the mercy of the women students.[2]

The proclamation of female dominance was somewhat premature. For example
the quota of only 10 percent female admission to the Faculty of Medicine
continued throughout the inter-war years. Many past students point out that
living in Riddel Hall provided them with more opportunity to mix with female
company as male students were greatly in the majority in science and classics
lectures. In the following years, the increase of women students did not keep pace
with the general increase in the student body over this period. In 1934 only a
quarter of Queen's students were female.[3] Women had no strong feeling of
disadvantage due to their sex, as the battles for the vote and admission to higher
education had been won. This contentment with women's position in middle-class
society was a feature of this period; feminism was largely in retreat until the late
1960s.

In Riddel Hall there were many examples of sisters and cousins who shared a
room at a lower rate, negotiated at the discretion of the governors. One 'brilliant'
student of the early 1920s, a Miss Kelly, possessed a scholarship for her university
fees, but had no other form of support. She was permitted to live freely in the Hall
on condition that she paid when she 'gained a post' after graduation. Riddel Hall's
bursary system became formalised in 1926 when a sub-committee of the
governors was established which granted three £30 bursaries for each cohort of
applicants. These were awarded to a tenable number of girls from less well off
families to live in the Hall. In Northern Ireland as a whole the number of
scholarships available through open competition to promising students from the
National School system rose dramatically between 1921 and 1935, from 121 to
719.[4] The Permanent Committee sent a circular to schools in 1927, explaining
Riddel Hall's bursary system and inviting applications from suitably qualified
girls.

By 1926 twenty-six students since the opening of the Hall had paid either
reduced fees, or none. The importance of the Riddel bequest has to be recognised
not only on an individual but a societal level. Some women who would have been
unable to go to Queen's without this assistance have made significant
contributions in their chosen field of expertise.

This is illustrated by the story of one young student.[5] Her father was a linen
finisher earning 55 shillings (£2 15s) per week, the only income of this family of
eight. He was in no position to help his daughter pay her annual university fees of
£25, expenses at the Hall of £55 and the estimated cost of books, clothing etc. of
£20. Her scholarship of £65 went some way to meet this expenditure but still left

a significant shortfall. She was awarded a reduction of fees throughout her three years at the Hall. The reference from her minister in support of her application for a second year bursary would be considered patronising today. 'Her father is an excellent specimen of the working man.' It continued, 'I must express the pleasure with which I have noticed the growing improvement Riddel Hall has made in Miss...' She gained a BSc with First Class Honours in 1930 and a Purser studentship of £108 that led to an MSc the following year; she also obtained the Higher Diploma in Education. She went on to teach in a leading Belfast grammar school and married a clergyman.

The usual procedure to gain a bursary was that a student nominated two referees, usually her minister and headmistress/master, who wrote to the governors with details of the applicant's family circumstances. There was no guarantee of success. One application was turned down apparently because she had 'arrived at the Hall in a motor car'. In 1932 a medical student, from a family of thirteen children, whose widowed mother existed on the profits from a farm of 'mostly bog land', estimated at £5 per annum after expenses, was refused assistance for her first year. Her elder siblings paid her fees and expenses despite incurring financial difficulty as a consequence. The family reapplied for a bursary in 1933, when there may have been more applicants than bursaries, as an examination was set to assist the governors with their decision. An essay entitled 'World Peace' secured a reduction in fees for her second year. This young woman won a Certificate of Distinction in Chemical Physiology that year, and qualified in 1938, taking up a dispensary practice in Co. Fermanagh.

Women who were in Riddel in the 1930s and 1940s still retain a vivid memory of the importance of the Riddel sisters' generosity. Elizabeth Mills' mother had contacted several halls of residence in England and Scotland and concluded that Riddel was the most affordable because of the Endowment Fund, which subsidised the costs. One woman lived in the Hall for her entire student life free of charge. Miss Duffin claimed that once the girls arrived at the Hall everyone was treated equally. Past students were totally unaware of whether others had received a bursary. A new student, who had been at boarding school in England, 'remarked on the absence of cliques and snobbery among the girls, and one of the older ones at once said that snobbery would not be tolerated for a moment if it did put in an appearance'.[6]

The strictly supervised environment enabled many young women to attend university whose parents would not have countenanced their daughters living in 'digs'. Fathers in particular, were 'very keen' to get daughters into Riddel where they would be 'under supervision'. One father, who had lost two children, while encouraging his daughter to study medicine and become independent, was reassured that she was safer in the Hall than in 'digs'. She stayed in Riddel from 1934 to 1937. The majority of parents, happy that their daughters were safe in Miss Duffin's care, found it unnecessary to interfere.

By 1922-3 disciplinary problems appear to have been resolved. Miss Duffin reported to the Annual General Meeting that 'the habit of grumbling, which was at one time rather prevalent, has entirely disappeared'. As conditions in the Hall had not changed, the Warden believed that 'it must have been a fashion, which like other fashions has had its day and fallen into disrepute!' Arriving at the Hall in 1939, Sally McManus remembers that Miss Duffin kept an eye on things, but was always dignified. Perhaps like Mrs Smyth, her old housemistress at Cheltenham, Miss Duffin expected the girls to act like ladies and, under the force of her personality, they did.

Authority over minor disciplinary matters was delegated to the Head of House and in turn to the House Committee. This fitted neatly into the analogy of the family, with elder siblings taking responsibility for their younger sisters. One student in the 1930s took her responsibilities as Head of House very seriously. She regularly reprimanded students for talking in the library, and one particular girl whose boyfriend came into the library every Sunday was scolded publicly. Exercising authority was a skill used later in her wartime experience.[7] More seriously when rare petty thefts had to be investigated a suspect would be identified and watched by the House Committee, and either cleared or found guilty.[8] The governors were informed and they took appropriate action.

In the 1930s freshers had to ask Miss Duffin's permission every time they intended to go out in the evening. The Warden responded to a request from Elizabeth Mills with; 'I did not know you knew anyone here – your people live across the water. Would your parents give permission? Where are you going?' She still remembers 'shaking in my boots' and having to name her escort. Parental involvement was minimal during their time in Riddel. In the late 1930s students could have only four weekends per term away from the Hall; Miss Duffin had to be informed of their impending absence before the previous Tuesday. She did not believe that the experience of being a student could be appreciated on a Monday to Friday basis. There was sometimes a conflict between home and Hall. Mollie McGeown, resident between 1941 and 1946, said that 'Duffie didn't like you to go home at the weekend, but I had only one parent and she wanted me at home'.

Very little escaped Miss Duffin. Her control over the students was augmented by the fact that the front door to the Hall was always kept locked, and the bell answered by the maids. Students who returned to the Hall after 10.30 p.m. were reported to the Warden. Elizabeth Mills still remembers Miss Duffin sitting in her office where the offenders were 'reprimanded for lateness'. Students had to sign the Hall book on going out after dinner with details of where they were going and with whom, but sometimes 'people rebelled' quietly.

Parental authority was delegated to Queen's University as an institution, which acted *in loco parentis* until 1969. The management of Riddel also adopted this concept. Parents delegated their authority to the Warden when their daughters entered the Hall. They were asked to sign a form giving authority to Miss Duffin to permit the girls to stay out overnight provided she was satisfied that the destination was suitable. These forms were still in use in the 1950s.

Miss Duffin always ensured that the rules in Riddel Hall were in step with other university halls. In Oxford, regulations controlled the lives of male and female undergraduates, who had to be in their colleges by 9 p.m.; 'a special police force roamed the streets looking for miscreants'.[9] In 1935 the rules, underlined by Miss Duffin in her own copy, included the following:

> Undergraduates are forbidden to visit a public house, or to use as a bar the lounge, or any room on any licensed premises. A woman undergraduate may not receive into or entertain in her college after the commencement of the Hall dinner, or such other time as may be fixed by her society, a man, whether a member of not, without special leave of the Principal of her society. Men and women undergraduates may not go for motor rides together unless each woman undergraduate has previously obtained leave from the Principal of her society and there are at least two women in the party.[10]

1936

RIDDEL HALL, BELFAST

Form FOR OVERNIGHT LEAVE OF ABSENCE

TO BE SIGNED BY PARENT OR GUARDIAN

(Except when going home, students will not be granted leave unless this form is signed and given to the Warden)

.... *has my permission to be absent*

for one or more nights from Riddel Hall on giving particulars to the Warden

Signed, ...

IF PARENTS OR GUARDIANS WISH TO MAKE ANY SPECIAL CONDITIONS
WITH REGARD TO OVERNIGHT LEAVE, WILL THEY KINDLY DO SO BELOW

Form for leave of absence
Riddel Hall Archive

Women who entered Riddel Hall in the 1930s, especially those who had attended boarding schools, remembered it as a place of 'freedom'. Dorothy Campbell keeps Joanna Martin's picture of Riddel gate lodge in her sitting room today, to remind her of entering these 'gates to freedom' more than seventy years ago.

Elizabeth Mills, resident from 1935 to 1940, pointed out that parents were generally 'very strict' with their daughters, so Riddel presented an opportunity for relative liberty. There was always a small minority who resented the rules.

Some parents carried on a regular correspondence with the Warden if they were at all anxious about their daughters. The mother of Elizabeth Mills explained in 1935 that as her course 'was going to cost a lot of money', the choice was either 'medicine or matrimony – not both'. She hoped that the all-female environment

View of gates and gate lodge, Riddel Hall. Some girls came from such strict homes that they considered these gates to be 'gates of freedom'. The gateway and gate lodge were built earlier than the Hall so were listed before it as historic buildings. The gates and railings were replaced in 2004
D. Hadden

would keep her away from potential suitors. Miss Duffin must have written to Elizabeth's parents informing them of her romance, which began within a month of her arrival at Riddel Hall. Mrs Mills wrote to Miss Duffin:

> Your kind letter has been very much appreciated by my husband and myself. Indeed it has added greatly to our peace of mind – we had known of Elizabeth's friendship with Dr Tom Smiley. But we had hoped that the years of 'justification' following E's hard work would have brought this liking to natural fruition.[11]

The couple suffered many anxious years ahead as Tom Smiley was 'reported missing after the fall of Singapore' and spent the next three and a half years in a Japanese prisoner of war camp. They married in October 1945.

Some students were not prepared to conform. A woman who was mother to one girl and guardian to another staying in the Hall from 1939 to 1942, wrote that 'you have our full consent and co-operation in any restriction you may have to impose – the girls may not agree, but we certainly will!' These two young women appear to have been rather more unconventional than most.[12] Following one incident, which involved an overnight stay in a flat owned by the parents of another Riddel girl, Miss Duffin informed the parents by letter. The girl's mother wrote that she would 'most certainly take steps to put the flat out of bounds'. She continued:

> As to the future, you have my full support in any decision you may make in regard to these late passes. I quite frankly am of the opinion that it is unnecessary for either of the girls to stay out all night. There is quite enough entertainment within the scope of university life for them without seeking anything further afield – and I am much happier when I know that they return to the Hall at night.[13]

It is particularly interesting that this parent went on to write that in an 'exceptional case' her written permission would be required, and reassured Miss Duffin that 'it is hardly fair that this whole responsibility should be yours'. Miss Duffin received eight further letters about these two students from this concerned mother until they left in the early 1940s. Much of this correspondence between parent and Warden was carried out unknown to the students.

> I simply had to say that I had heard from you because otherwise I would not have had any grounds for reproving her... She has not mentioned asking for extra leave in any of her letters, and as far as her movements are concerned she is singularly independent and uncommunicative. I did not implicate you in any way as regards the flat – which is a most delicate subject for you and me.[14]

The girl whose parents owned the flat is recalled by past students who were her contemporaries in the Hall as being the female equivalent of 'a ladies' man', always going out dressed up and having a good time. This young woman was described by the concerned mother as being her adopted daughter's 'beau ideal of all a girl should be and is simply worshipped by her'; her daughter's loyalty to her friend was 'fierce and unswerving'. This role model was also five years her senior and no doubt appeared very glamorous. It was a delicate situation as the families had 'grown up together'. The mother protested that 'while I know that... is sound enough, I cannot help recognising that she is foolishly unconventional in many ways... all this is strictly between ourselves, as you will know'.[15]

The role of Warden with responsibility for about fifty young women must have required a great deal of vigilance, tact, understanding of individual students and knowledge about the standards of behaviour which their parents found acceptable.

Many parents were anxious about their daughters in 1940 when they had to stay in 'digs', due to requisitioning of the Hall by the War Office.[16] This was aborted before the end of the year. The records show that one young woman's father made her relinquish her place in Queen's because the Hall was closed. She accepted a post in the civil service and never returned to university. The father of another student who had completed her first year 'nominated' her for a position in the Northern Bank on discovering that the Hall was closed; her experience of university life also ended abruptly.

The concerned mother felt that 'Digs are all very fine for a while... they are missing the real core of university life – mixing and mingling with others in friendly intercourse. There's simply no comparison with Riddel Hall in any way.'[17]

The governors introduced several schemes to honour the Misses Riddel's desire to provide 'tutorial assistance' to the students. Perhaps inevitably in that era, the earliest classes were on cookery conducted by Miss Irwin; educated young ladies still needed domestic skills. There were also choral lessons and health and beauty sessions. In 1926 Miss Duffin urged the governors to 'appoint a French lady resident to help students of French, and others who are interested'.[18] Perhaps this idea was influenced by her youthful experience of native French and German teachers at home and in Cheltenham. The consultant in this venture was the eccentric Douglas Savory, Professor of French from 1909 to 1940. He would arrive for his morning classes dressed in complete riding gear, excluding spurs, as they made it 'so very difficult to go downstairs'. Following his lecture he was chauffeur driven to the Castlereagh Hills to ride his horse.[19] Professor Savory visited the Director of the *Office Nationale des Universités* in Paris where he looked through the dossiers of more than twenty 'likely candidates' and interviewed a shortlist of three.[20] The first of the residents, Mademoiselle Cavailles from Bordeaux, arrived in October 1926. Her referee wrote to Miss Duffin explaining:

She knows a good deal of French history, geography and literature, and I feel sure she will not be at a loss to interest the students and stimulate their desire to read and learn. Hers is the enthusiastic, not the shy temperament and therefore she does not lack sensitivity, although in a healthy way.[21]

Marie Mouzat, who came to Riddel from October 1929 until June 1930, left a record of her experiences. She organised five classes varying from beginners to advanced, which were held in the evening before dinner. She felt that 'the result cannot certainly be called perfect but rather fairly good'. Twenty-two students attended classes regularly, some 'showing a certain enthusiasm and pleasure', while others asked to be excused as they had too much work to do for other subjects.

Riddel Hall front door and porch, facing south. The porch had unglazed windows at the sides so was a very draughty spot for prolonged goodbyes!
D. Hadden

Mlle Mouzat explained that she 'tried to make the subjects spoken of at the evening classes rather attractive and animated, for I knew some of the students were tired after their day's work'. The subjects included 'French shopping, talks on Paris, Versailles, the French customs, French anecdotes, contemporary literature etc.' The other part of her work was 'to be done at table where the students are supposed to talk French'. This was not so successful as some students, 'owing to their limited knowledge of the language, to their shyness and perhaps also to the fact that I was able to speak English never spoke a word of French'.

The third aspect of Mlle Mouzat's work was to assist Riddel students with their essays and translations; she was available each morning for consultation. This created a difficult situation, as Professor Savory argued that it gave these students an unfair advantage over their peers. Overall she wrote that

> I must not conceal that the work of the French assistant mistress at Riddel Hall is rather difficult to do, the effort being entirely voluntary on the part of the students. I must say some of them have been exceedingly kind and helpful and have certainly done their best for me. After these last months' teaching I have come to the conclusion that a French native can give the Riddel Hall students a great deal of help, especially as far as the improvement of their conversational and colloquial French is concerned.[22]

From the early 1930s German exchange students came to Riddel on the same basis. The inter-war years were generally a time of harmony in Riddel Hall when the aims of the Misses Riddel for a safe, culturally enriching environment for female students were met under the regime of Ruth Duffin. The Warden and Matron took up paternal and maternal roles and the institution worked in a similar way to a large middle-class family, with a degree of democracy provided by the House Committee.

10

A Vision of Culture

Miss Duffin's annual addresses to the young ladies of Riddel Hall illustrate the ideal of middle-class femininity in the inter-war years. This early example is taken from the first house meeting of 1925.

> It is getting more and more difficult every year to find something new to say at the first House Meeting of the session. All the things best worth saying and most important to the welfare of the Hall have been said so often. But modern psychology teaches us that as continual dripping wears the stone, so continual repetition does tend to make an impression and so form a habit. I hope this is so, though I am sometimes tempted to doubt it, and you must forgive me if in my annual speeches I continue my attempts to be the persistent water which will ultimately make an impression on your stony personalities!

It is easy to understand why many of the ex-students remembered Miss Duffin as austere and formidable when this was her welcome to the girls in general and the freshers in particular. Because of her difficulties with the early students she needed to create an impression of authority. She went on to say 'I have no doubt that the spirit of the Hall is a kindlier and happier one than it was initially'. She had a personal mission to educate the young women under her care:

> Without a vision the people perish, Ireland is very sorely in need at this time of a younger generation who will go out as missionaries of beauty, with all their senses heightened and developed to help to make of this country something approaching the perfection of ancient Greece.[1]

Her addresses and reports express her idealism, and the characteristics that she aimed to promote in Riddel students. The raw material with which Miss Duffin was to create her vision of utopia provided her with a difficult challenge. There were many characteristics requiring change in the girls.

> I should say that the principal faults of the girls coming up to the University from North of Ireland schools were of a negative character. They are very loath to assume any responsibility, and are extraordinarily happy-go-lucky in the conduct of their affairs generally, and while they work and are anxious to pass their examinations, among the great majority there is very little desire for any knowledge or culture lying outside their course, and practically no interest in political or social questions which are discussed so eagerly in other universities.[2]

At the beginning of every academic year the Warden gave, as she put it herself, 'good advice judiciously mingled with cakes and coffee' at the first house meeting when all the residents were present. In 1928 she explained her vocation.

> One of the great advantages of community life is the effect that living among others has on character and manners. In a place like this you run up against people with different ideas, people doing different work, coming from different home environments. You have to consider others, to be unselfish, to do things you don't like for the sake of the community at large. And so your character is modified and strengthened. And it is the same with manners. We all know that one of the things most valued in public school life for boys is the finish, the polish, that in some mysterious way boys communicate to each other. I don't know that girls do it quite so much, for they are more individualistic than boys, but I think the Hall should have some of this polishing effect. You have all heard of the 'Oxford manner', I should like to think that some day people might talk of 'Riddel Hall manners', that it might have the effect of rubbing off rough corners, soothing queer idiosyncrasies, and so making you all fitter to take your place in the larger world. For in taking up positions afterwards, manners and 'manner' both count a great deal, and a very small lapse even in mere formalities may give a bad impression.

Hans Iten *On the Lagan, Winter*. This painting, with another by the same artist,
was acquired *c.*1930 for thirty pounds. It was hung in the drawing room
Queen's University Belfast

In pursuit of this goal Ruth Duffin left nothing to chance, and her philosophy for
a cultured life was laid out in her annual homilies. She gave what could be termed
a secular sermon, often taking a particular 'text'. This was usually a Latin motto or
something topical from periodicals such as *The Spectator*, or an address to
university students in other parts of the United Kingdom. She regularly gave
detailed instructions on manners, dress and behaviour at formal dinners,
appreciation of nature, beauty, art and literature. The Hall provided facilities such
as a library, music room and microscope room to encourage this process.

Unlike pioneering academic women such as Miss Beale, her role model in many
ways, Ruth Duffin was interested in fashion – old students remember her as
always being well groomed and elegantly dressed. During the inter-war years there
was a strong association between respectability and the care of the female body.

'Bodily refinement provided a visual clue to respectability and social class. The handy symbols of class... were not just accoutrements such as clothing and interiors, bodily refinement also served as a "handy symbol" of social class and respectability.'[3]

Miss Duffin recalled:

> It is perhaps amusing to note that at this time I seem to have been perturbed at the growing laxity in students' dress, for at a House Meeting on May 16th there is a first mention of the hatless brigade, and it is recorded that 'Miss Duffin did not think it dignified or fitting to go out into the street, even to the post office, bareheaded'. In the same year the Committee authorised me to prepare a leaflet to be sent to parents asking them to see that students were provided with suitable plain clothes for wearing at classes.

The Hall brochure stated that during the day students should wear clothes of a 'plain and serviceable kind' and to change for dinner into 'a simple semi-evening or afternoon frock'. For parties an evening dress was desirable. Dress was always a topical issue. In 1928 Miss Duffin explained that 'good dressing consists chiefly in wearing the right thing at the right time'. For lectures students should wear 'plain clothes' which were 'suitably warm' for winter. She accepted that within limits 'there is plenty of room for individual taste'. The limits were breached by wearing dressing gowns downstairs at any time before 11 p.m. Even more seriously she firmly stated, 'I *don't* want to see slovens in old brocade shoes at breakfast, slipped on because they "came handy".' In May 1935 a student argued that the rule of having to wear stockings at breakfast be abolished. Miss Duffin turned down the request on the grounds that 'it encouraged lazy habits'.[4] But when the war came and with it clothing coupons, she could no long hold the line.

Every 'old student' remembers the chore of dressing for dinner. A bell rang fifteen minutes before the meal was served so that there would be no excuse for not changing. 'Pretty, fresh, but not elaborate clothes' were recommended; 'cardigans and woollies at dinner' could not be allowed. More daunting even was Miss Duffin progressing to dinner 'like an iceberg sailing along in grey voile'. The ritual began with the students who

> foregathered in the drawing room and the people who were on duty had to receive her when she walked in her stately way and walked up with her, she would stand and chat for a minute or two or point out something of interest; it really was ludicrous in some ways but it was awfully impressive. We paraded out of the drawing room right up the hall – a lovely long hall – into the dining room to her table. We all stood until she said grace.[5]

Miss Duffin progressed to dinner 'like an iceberg... in grey voile' from the drawing room (double doors seen at the far end of the hall corridor), past the library, to the dining room (behind observer). The memorial plaque to the Misses Riddel can be seen over the fireplace
PRONI (D/3119/5/7)

A former student, Mollie McGeown, recalled how girls intercepted Miss Duffin at the head of this procession in the hall, to say, 'Excuse me, Miss Duffin, I am going out for the evening'. She remembered sometimes not attending this formal meal and not being dressed for it; simply going out for a walk and slipping quietly back to her room.

Everyone had her allocated place to sit. Freshers had their own table from which they would move by invitation from more senior girls. Miss Duffin strongly encouraged students from different faculties to mix; dinner was a good opportunity to meet others with varying interests. This represented more freedom of choice than a boarding school.

Table manners were another area of concern. Miss Duffin stated firmly that she did not want to see the young ladies of Riddel 'performing curious evolutions with knives and forks at table, or sitting in weird attitudes, or holding cups of tea affectionately in both hands with elbows planted on the table, like some old charwoman preparing for good "crack" in the kitchen'.[6]

She told students that if they must drink at meal time this should be done at the end; she was disturbed to see 'far too many' people 'washing down each mouthful with a sup'; this she decried as both a 'pernicious' and an 'inelegant habit'.[7] The social aspect of the formal meal was paramount. 'Don't sit dumb at table, even if you're tired or worried. It's not fair to your neighbour, and it's your social duty to make things pleasant for other people, who may be equally tired and worried.'

Learning the art of conversation was not left to the girls' own initiative; Miss Duffin took an active role in their individual instruction. A list of four students was placed on the notice board each evening. Mollie McGeown remembered looking at the list in dismay. The girls were chosen by the Head of House to sit at Miss Duffin's table in rotation (approximately once every month), to converse with her on current affairs as individuals, not as a group. The girls were from different years and different faculties to encourage students to mix. They were not with their friends; they got to know many more people. It was intended that each girl should make a 'positive contribution to the talk'. Miss Duffin told a 1936 house meeting that:

> If you can't be a loud speaker at least don't be a mere receiving pit! You can't think how grateful I am to the girls who come to my table and chat or better still, discuss and debate. The negative girl at my table is one of my minor crosses here. Her eye wanders wistfully to other tables, she twirls her spoon or fork aimlessly, she replies yes or no to some questions put by me in desperation to see if I can strike a spark! You see I am letting you into some of the secrets of a warden's life!

Mollie McGeown remembered it was 'a bit terrifying, we had to make intelligent conversation. If we were not avid newspaper readers... we had to think of other things. On the other hand, she was an extremely cultured woman... She liked gardening and flowers, so I had one topic that I knew about'. One of the four had to choose a short poem, which Miss Duffin would read after the meal. This had to be left on the table outside her office before 6 p.m. The inspiration for this practice came from a literary club of which the Warden was a member.[8] Miss Duffin had 'an idle thought or a vision of the night... just suppose if, as a sort of grace after meals, we devoted one minute after dinner to reading aloud a lyric, a sonnet, a beautiful thought in prose, shouldn't we have done something towards developing our sense of beauty?' She argued that this would become one of those 'unique customs that give character to a place'.

After dinner the four girls adjourned to Miss Duffin's sitting room for 'polite conversation'.

William Conor *Children in the Park* ('Ready for Action' in the University catalogue). Conor's studio was on the
Stranmillis Road, opposite the Ulster Museum. He was an occasional visitor at the Hall, and his pictures often hung
in the dining room. This painting was said to have been inspired by seeing Riddel girls with tennis racquets
© William Conor 2005   Queen's University Belfast

I want to say a word about my coffee parties after dinner. As you know I value having you in turn at my table and in my room as a means of getting to know you all personally, but I do not wish you to feel it to be a tax on your time. I therefore take this opportunity of saying that I never expect anyone to stay in my room after eight o'clock. That gives us an hour together, and I do not want to encroach further on your time. This does not mean I expect you to sit with your eyes glued on the clock and so feel you must go at eight if we happen to be having an interesting talk. But it does mean that no one need feel rude or ungracious if she leaves then. On the other hand, as this means that little of your time is taken up, I do expect to have a full table every night. If the people on the list are out, and have forgotten to ask someone to take their place, it is only polite that others should fill the gap. I know it is not meant as a personal insult, nor do I take it as such, but if you put yourself in my place you will realise that one feels that manners are sadly lacking when one is told, 'I couldn't get an exchange', while there are still people at other tables. It is not only to save myself embarrassment that I point this out. It is because I want Riddel Hall girls to have a high standard of manners to anyone, and for the same reason I like to see girls getting up if I come into their rooms, which is a courtesy they owe to any visitor.

The ritual included one of the four asking, 'How do you like your coffee Miss Duffin?' The reply was always 'half and half': the student then poured milk and coffee simultaneously. While conversing in Miss Duffin's room the girls made hearth rugs with thick wool. Sally McManus remembered these being a collective effort. Margaret Mitchell recounted that after around forty-five minutes of 'polite conversation' one of the senior girls, maybe a member of the House Committee, made her excuses – an essay was due; the other three jumped at this opportunity and the ordeal was over.

On Sunday evenings Miss Duffin visited her family in 'Summerhill'. It was as Moira Strawbridge expressed it, 'A free night. We could come down in our pyjamas and our hair in curlers'. Rather than the formal dinner 'we had supper, we could have a guest, even a male guest. Most people went to University Road Church to sing; a whole group of us from Riddel went, it was great fun'.

Sally McManus made a tribute to Miss Duffin's influence, saying that even decades after their time in the Hall past students on meeting a cultured woman would remark 'You'd think she was a Riddel girl!'. Miss Duffin would have been delighted. Moira Strawbridge felt that 'it was as much an education to be at Riddel Hall as to be at Queen's – the two blended together nicely'.

Past students recall the atmosphere in Riddel being warm and welcoming; there was always someone to walk to Queen's with, or people around to chat to. On the other hand if solitude was desired, one's room provided a private space.

Two girls in the drawing room *c*.1962. This room was the scene of meetings, 'hops', formals and general relaxation, as well as the special broadcast by Edward VIII in 1936
PRONI (D/3119/5/7)

'The joyous social round' of life in Riddel Hall was described in an article in the *Belfast Telegraph* of 29 November 1921.[9] This piece recreates the atmosphere of the Hall on social occasions, also warmly recalled by past students.

> The great drawing room provides ample space for social gatherings on a larger scale. It is here that the girls meet for a few moments' chat before dinner, and later on for half-an-hour's dancing before settling down to study. Here parties can be given by the various 'years' or faculties represented in the house. On such occasions the long well-lighted rooms look unusually charming – drawing-room carpets rolled back to leave the shining pitch-pine floor free for dancing, pretty cretonne-covered screens and sofas transforming the wide inner hall into a most picturesque lounge – the library fitted up as supper-room. On Hallowe'en night the residents past and present throng to the annual fancy dress party, at which the good old traditions are kept up: dancing, charades, competitions, and the time-honoured nuts and apples make the evening pass all too quickly.

The members of the House Committee had a social role as gracious hostesses, in addition to disciplinary and organisational duties. At the beginning of the

Riddel memorial plaque by Rosamond Praeger, unveiled in 1926.
It was positioned over the mantelpiece in the hall
© S. Rosamond Praeger 2005   N. Duffin

academic year the House Committee gave an 'official party' to welcome the 'freshers'. In 1922 it was followed by 'at least two others in their honour during the first week'. The two major functions of the year were the Halloween Party and the Riddel Ball – a formal, 'very special' dance usually held in February. Each student gave the name of a male partner to the committee around Christmas time, and an official invitation from the Hall was sent to the young man. Moira Strawbridge remembers that Miss Duffin 'was really very fussy about things'. Eleanor Millar recalled addressing the envelopes, 'Mr so and so'; Miss Duffin pointed out that this was incorrect, and we had to start all over again with, 'So and so, Esquire'. All the furniture in the drawing room was cleared away for the dancing, which followed the 'formal and special' meal in the dining room. Dress was formal, which added to the anticipation and aura of sophistication. There was no alcohol and it was all 'very civilised'.

Some young women held their twenty-first birthday parties in the Hall. The number of guests was restricted, and everyone had to leave by 11 p.m. Elizabeth Mills recalled her party in 1938; her father took the opportunity to travel from their home in England to meet his prospective son-in-law. Mrs Mills telephoned during the evening, and her husband was able to reassure her that 'the inspection of the young man' had gone well!

Riddel students, like other students, attended Queen's 'hops' on Saturday evenings; these provided an opportunity for young women in the 1930s to meet their male counterparts. Although lectures were mixed, contemporary medical students explained that the ten female students (of a total of one hundred) were expected to sit in the front row and not permitted to converse with the men.

University functions were chaperoned by the wives of academic staff; consequently Miss Duffin was confident that her students would be in a properly supervised situation. During the early years of the Second World War a House Committee member was entrusted with the front door key on these occasions. Margaret Mitchell said that Miss Duffin had the 'naïve idea that the one with the key would check everyone, and they would all come home together'! In Miss Duffin's era the young ladies of Riddel Hall did not get involved in Students', or Rag, Day, as it became known. Elizabeth Mills explained that the students wore their undergraduate gowns, but engaging in any pranks was deemed most 'unladylike'.

Good manners were the highest form of beauty, so said Dr T.C. Chao, Dean of the School of Religion, Yenchiang, China. He visited Queen's in 1933. Miss Duffin quoted from his lecture on the ethics and culture of China, focusing on his ideas that life should be lived in accordance with certain rules and 'expressed in beautiful form – in music, in painting, in writing'.[10] She hoped that the students would also develop an appreciation of beauty. This could be in nature, 'art, in buildings, in the details of our home environment, in the arrangement of flowers and in human motion'.

> The Greeks had cultivated their sense of beauty and they left imperishable beauty behind them. Their buildings, their sculptures, have never been surpassed and their sense of beauty of the human form urged them to cultivate physical fitness and physical grace so that they were perhaps the finest race the world has known. And in literature, too, they excelled.[11]

She argued that Ireland, one of the most beautiful countries in the world, was being systematically destroyed by the construction of 'hideous little sordid towns with ugly-ill proportioned houses huddled together'. This was compared with 'the lovely proportions of a Greek temple, where every thing is so exactly and lovingly calculated that no-one who is not blind can look at it without joy'. Miss Duffin explained that in England a focus on material things led to 'havoc being wrought' with the environment. She felt that it was not too late for Ireland, but it soon would be, unless 'the younger generation develop a consciousness about such things'.

> So I want to ask you all to cultivate that love of beauty which made the Greeks immortal – not only the beauty of outward and obvious things, but the beauty which has to be sought and worked for – that we find in fine pictures and good literature. If the university is to do you any good it will arouse and heighten your appreciation of what is worthwhile and if it does not do that, you may be sure that you are missing the chief end of education, no matter how many exams you may pass. If you live resolutely among beautiful things, you will grow to hate the tawdry and meretricious, and your influence will help other people to hate it too.[12]

When funds permitted, the Permanent Committee made grants for pictures. Paintings by Hans Iten were purchased, as were some by Paul Henry, and some former students donated good quality prints. Several 'old girls' said that Miss Duffin was a 'connoisseur' of paintings. Portraits of the Misses Riddel, Miss Duffin and Miss Boyd were all commissioned. Unfortunately the last named was very unhappy with her portrait painted by William Conor because it made her look too severe. In 1929 Miss Duffin pleaded with the governors for 'a few more pictures. Students coming from country places in Ulster have no opportunities of seeing good pictures, and we have many wall spaces that might well be filled'. She organised a small sub-committee which included Rosamond Praeger, a notable Ulster sculptor and President of the Royal Ulster Academy. Her memorial plaque to the Misses Riddel unveiled by Lady Charlemont in November 1926 remains in the Hall today.

'Mens sana in corpore sano' – a healthy mind in a healthy body – was another dictum used by Miss Duffin to illustrate her ideal of education. She believed that the healthy mind would 'reject instinctively all that is small and unworthy' and the best way to acquire such a mind was to 'live with your intellectual superiors'. This could be in 'the shape of professors and teachers or of books and concerts and art galleries'. Miss Duffin went on to say that she would like to: 'urge you as far as possible in your private reading to read what is definitely worthwhile. There are such floods of rubbish being poured out, there is so little time for casual reading, that it is a waste to relax over rubbish'.

To assist in this project and ensure that readers could immerse themselves in the 'good company' of worthwhile literature, the Hall provided a library. Miss Duffin assured the girls that, consequently, 'the second rate' would bore them to tears. In the session of 1927-8 the Vice-Chancellor even visited the Hall to give the girls a 'talk on reading'. The governors occasionally donated books. A set of 'half Morocco' bound *Encyclopædia Britannica* was purchased at the first opportunity that funds were available.[13] The majority were chosen by the students and paid for by occasional grants from the governors.

By 1939 the Library Committee, which included Mollie McGeown, 'a voracious reader', had catalogued the books under the headings of: natural history, autobiography and memoirs, literary criticism, books about Ireland or other countries, travel, religion, philosophy and novels. There were also periodicals, which were especially appreciated by country girls exposed for the first time to such a variety of literature. Moira Strawbridge, a classics student, recalled that

> They had lots of books within the library, and I was dying to read them, but I was too busy working... It was a lovely big library, terribly well kept, with big tables; we didn't have to work in our rooms, we could work downstairs. It was *silence*, of course.

Library book plate
Riddel Hall Archive

She went on to say that it was the 'place where I used to sit with the medicals and put them through their questions before they went down for their orals'. Many residents mentioned the value of this type of supportive environment during their undergraduate careers.

Miss Duffin herself thought that it was 'everyone's bounden duty, especially every woman's bounden duty to cultivate a healthy body'. To achieve this, the regime in the Hall included healthy plain food, bracing exercise on the hockey pitch and tennis court and plenty of early nights (in rooms which were not overheated). The Hall's 'lady' doctors came frequently to give talks to the girls after the first house meeting in October. The cost of health and beauty classes organised in the Hall was subsidised by the governors in 1937.[14]

The students were encouraged to keep up with current affairs not only by the provision of newspapers and periodicals, but also the purchase of a wireless set in 1936. Its use was limited to listening to the news, and 'special programmes', not for fun. For example, Eleanor Wilson, Elizabeth Mills and Nessie Maybin remember the evening in 1936 when they were all allowed to go in to the drawing room to hear the special broadcast of the abdication of Edward VIII. The Prime Minister, Mr Baldwin 'came on' and the King made the announcement that 'I cannot carry out my heavy duties without the woman I love'. 'Several of us were crying.' 'One girl was sitting behind the curtain in the big bay window sobbing her heart out...' Throughout the war the students were encouraged to listen to Churchill's speeches, and the news.

While Miss Duffin aimed to control and improve every aspect of physical and intellectual life of Riddel girls she encouraged them to decide for themselves in spiritual matters. None of the 'Old Girls' remember her insisting or even recommending that they attend any place of worship, however they did so as a matter of course. She encouraged them to think for themselves.

> Remember, too, if you come across problems and doubts in religion, to bring the best of your mind, which is God given, to bear on them, and remember that if you have to throw some beliefs overboard as you go through life – if other people had not done so before you we should still be worshipping sticks and stones.[15]

This advocacy of freedom of religious conscience is very unusual for a woman of her time and may be attributed to her Unitarian background.

The library
PRONI (D/3119/5/7)

11

Citizenship

> An education in excellence from youth on, which makes a man passionately
> desire to be a perfect citizen, and to know how to rule or obey with justice...
> This is the only education that deserves the name. But that other training,
> which aims at money or strength or any other kind of skill apart from reason
> and justice, is mechanical and illiberal and undeserving of the name of
> education.[1]

Like Miss Beale at Cheltenham, Ruth Duffin took the Ancient Greek philosopher
Plato as her inspiration, sharing his definition of education with the students.[2] Her
vision for the Hall was for it to be 'a happy and healthy training-ground for good
citizenship'. She feared her constituency was one that required a great deal of
work. 'I think the independent Ulster character, which has an element of
suspiciousness in it, does not lend itself very readily to a community spirit, or at
any rate it advances very cautiously in that direction.'[3]

At the first house meeting in October each year, Miss Duffin's welcome to new
students focused on their new adult status. 'Those of you who come from school
will enjoy a fuller liberty here, and therefore incur greater responsibilities. You will

be more trusted and less looked after.' She explained that students would miss all the real meaning of university life if they did not learn to be 'if not a perfect citizen, at any rate a good one'. One of the prime functions of Riddel Hall was to train its residents that they 'could not live entirely' for themselves, but were citizens 'of no mean city', with citizens' responsibilities as well as citizens' privileges.

> Let none of you think herself so insignificant that she will not influence other people's lives. Be very sure that if you are unpunctual, untidy, slack, inconsiderate and selfish, you are making it much harder for your fellow students to fight their faults. Just in so much as you are straight in thought and deed, keen on work, keen on play, eager to seize on every opportunity of increasing your knowledge of God's gifts and man's achievements – just so much are you helping other people on the path that leads to true citizenship.

She quoted Charles Kingsley who wrote that 'there are two freedoms; the false, where one is free to do what he likes, and the true, where he is free to do what he ought'. She also referred to Burke who 'tells us the only liberty that is valuable is a liberty connected with order and virtue, but which cannot exist at all without them'.[4] She quoted AE (George Russell):

> Civilisations are externalisations of the soul and a character of races. They are majestic or mean according to the treasure of beauty, imagination, will and thought laid up in the soul of the people. The building up of a civilisation is at once the noblest and the most practical of all enterprises, but it cannot be built up without the same conscious deliberation of purpose as inspired the architect of the Parthenon or of Rheims Cathedral.

She went on to argue, 'Riddel Hall is a microcosm of a state, and we can only make it fine and noble by that conscious deliberation of purpose of which "AE" speaks'. She urged her students 'to feel that each one of you had an ideal for the Hall – not a place to sleep, but a community looking for truth and for beauty... The state depends on you – and on your choice; your ideals, whether you like it or not, are going to form the future'.[5]

This address to the students prefaced the House Committee elections and set out Miss Duffin's agenda for the Hall and her mission to educate her students initially for life in Riddel and by extension for their role in wider society. Every student was encouraged to feel herself as part of the community.

> You should all feel that you are in a very pleasant sense debtors, and that you can only repay that debt to those who are gone by making the fullest and best use of their gift, and by each doing your level best to make the life of the Hall worthy of it, so that no one shall leave it without being in some sense the better for having been here.[6]

Georgina Moutray Kyle *Herring Boats, Ardglass*
This painting was presented to the Hall by Miss Kyle *c*.1930, and was hung in the back hall
© National Museums and Galleries of Northern Ireland 2005
Queen's University Belfast

She argued that the generosity of the Riddel sisters should be reflected and repaid by the 'cultivation of a like spirit to give – if not money – at least the best that is in you to make the Hall an ideal place to live in'. In 1926 she appealed to the students to develop a 'contented happy spirit, taking such turns of fortune as coal strikes with a determination to grin and bear it'. This speech was made in the year the Trades Union Congress called a General Strike of workers in heavy industry as a response to the 'lock out' of the miners by the Coal Board.

Although she did not aspire to reproducing the charitable experiment of the Cheltenham Guild's 'Settlement' in Belfast, Ruth Duffin pointed out that 'the Lord loveth a generous giver'. She expressed her disappointment that 'so little is given to the few collections taken up in the Hall – and yet people seem to have money enough for pictures and amusements'.[7] In 1932, at a time when unemployment was an urgent social problem in Belfast, the students 'adopted' a poor family. Miss Duffin told the governors they 'had heard of a suitable case of a poor widow with seven children through the Belfast Council for Social Welfare'. It is most likely that Ruth's sister Emma, the Voluntary Secretary of the BCSW was the source. She was later awarded an honorary MA from Queen's.[8] The students raised money for this family, which was given through the BCSW, who (in the usual paternalistic charitable manner) made sure that the money was wisely spent: it was augmented by a Christmas hamper and 'occasional presents of food and other necessities'. This was repeated in subsequent years, and in 1935 some students made personal visits to the chosen family and gave toys for the children at Christmas.

Generosity of spirit was also to be shown by giving 'ungrudging and thorough' service to the various committees in the Hall as well as giving 'obedience in order and punctuality' in general. Every member of the community was expected to play her part in disciplining herself and others. 'I ask you to be a little more like public school boys in "ticking each other off".' She quoted 'Father O'Flynn' to inspire the girls to take their part in[9]

> Checking the crazy ones,
> Coaxing on aisy ones,
> Lifting the lazy ones on wid a stick.[10]

The Warden alluded to the early years of the Hall's existence, when girls strove for self-government and made constant complaints. 'There is certainly less stupid grumbling, and less rebellion under the specious guise of a desire for self-government, than there used to be, and yet I am sure I am right when I say that there is more real self-government than when everyone talked about it and held house meetings to demand it.'[11] She went on to say that Riddel girls as 'a community' were 'learning that the only self-government worth having is self-discipline and the subordination of your own desires to the good of the whole'.

In her 1925 address Miss Duffin quoted Canon Woods of Ely, who contended that the ills of society were often due to ignorance and lack of discipline. 'Was it not Bishop Creighton who remarked that though the ape and the tiger within us might die there was plenty of evidence that the donkey still survived'.[12] The Warden's text for 1925 was 'Evil is wrought by want of thinking'. While she 'felt certain' that 'there are very few, if any, of you here that are activated by evil motives', she pointed out that she 'should not like to say that there is a complete absence of the donkey' in the Hall.

> I am going to ask you this year to make an effort to eliminate muddle-headedness and do a little thinking on behalf of the community. I don't want, when I have to scold some of you, to be met by the eternal and quite cheerful reply, 'I didn't think' which most people seem to regard as a perfect excuse, whereas it is the feeblest that was ever invented, and is often worse than the crime it seeks to cover.

The deeply felt principles, which underpinned Ruth Duffin's didactic discourses, influenced her opinion of the international situation of the late 1930s. By October 1938 the British Government under Neville Chamberlain was pursuing a policy of appeasement toward Hitler. Miss Duffin argued, 'we are threatened with disaster, and it is up to each one of us to save civilisation from destruction'. She firmly believed that the world was faced by a 'choice between, on the one hand, a tyranny that forbids a man to think and act for himself, and on the other, spiritual freedom'. Things were not simply black and white. It was possible to admire 'the unity and discipline of the German nation... while deploring the slave mentality that makes them into puppets of their dictator'.[13]

This statement was made through first-hand knowledge of some German students who resided in Riddel. An exchange system had been introduced in 1933 as it was believed that it would be of mutual benefit. Miss Duffin argued that the German girls 'were very much in advance of our own in scholarship, and also with regard to general knowledge they have a wider outlook on world affairs.'

The first German exchange student, Gerda Arnold, arrived at the Hall in 1933, the year Hitler became Reich Chancellor. She was part of a scheme organised by the *Austauschdienst* (a German academic exchange service founded in 1925 originally for US-German exchanges but expanded to cover ten countries. In 1934 the Service's committee compulsorily aligned all its activities to Nazi doctrine. The exchange service ceased its activities in 1943).[14] Gerda Arnold was followed by others in subsequent years. They were carefully chosen students, highly educated, but all inculcated with Nazi doctrines, and while some of them were individually very pleasant, it grew increasingly evident that they were not students pure and simple, but were sent by the Reich with a definite purpose. An immense amount of Nazi propaganda literature, some of it beautifully printed and illustrated, was sent to them by the *Austauschdienst*. Ruth Mayer, who stayed in the Hall from March to June 1938, wrote to Miss Duffin in July: 'I shall have some job of interpreting in August, when I have been asked to come to the National Socialist Party Rally in Nuremberg. There will be quite a number of foreigners who will depend on my interpreting and guiding'.[15]

Miss Duffin was correct in her assessment of these young women. Riddel's exchange students were certainly not representative of the average German woman under Nazism in the late 1930s who 'were extolled as child bearers and keepers of near sacred hearths, well away from desks and decisions. Woe to women who wanted to work... who wanted to be, or remain, legislators, lawyers, or leaders, or independent in action and opinion, or just to have jobs as men did'.[16]

Nessie Maybin, Elizabeth Mills and Eleanor Wilson have a clear memory of these girls and all agreed that it was awkward at times. There was a German girl who used to go off on a Sunday for the whole day and no one ever knew where she was going. The students used to wonder what she was doing and asked each other 'could she be a Nazi?' When a Riddel girl criticised Hitler, her German counterpart was much distressed.

Riddel Hall from the South West
PRONI (D/3119/5/7)

Miss Duffin hoped the visitors learned something from Riddel Hall. She recorded in her Chronicle: *'I remember an unconscious reflection on the Nazi mentality made by one of the students. I had asked her what differences had most struck her between German and Irish ways, and she said, 'Oh, people here are so much kinder'.*

Gerda Arnold wrote to Miss Duffin when she returned to Germany in 1934 expressing her sorrow that due to family responsibilities she could not return for a further year in the Hall. She continued:

> I myself never had the possibility to thank you affectionately for all the kindness you had for me. I think I never told you how much I enjoyed the Hall life and everything there, and that I am very sorry that the time slipped away so quickly. It is very hard for me to express my thanks in English, but I am sure you know what I want to say. I chose a small book, which might interest you, and which perhaps might remind you a little of the afternoons you had time to spend with me.

Miss Duffin spent a great deal of time making the overseas students feel welcome. She had learned German both at home and at school, though she found it difficult, and it is likely she spoke to them in their own language as several of them subsequently wrote letters to her in German.

A Riddel student, Jemima Paul, went to university in Frankfurt in 1935 where she found that 'German universities allow a greater freedom than ours in the choice of subjects and as a consequence the students are more self-reliant and work more independently than we do'. She enjoyed her term in Germany: there was 'marching and drum beating at the slightest provocation'. She heard speeches from Hitler and Goebbels so often that she 'knew all that's going to be said beforehand'. She was impressed by life under the Führer.

> On the whole, however, I must say that there is a great deal to be said for National Socialism as I have spoken with a great many different people about it, and they all seem agreed that it certainly saved Germany from communism, and only just in time. The views on the Jewish question are diverse but as far as I have been able to gather it certainly was a decidedly serious problem in Germany. At Christmas time some of the Jewish shops here were boycotted by fanatic members of the 'Partei'. The boycott was undertaken for the greater part by smaller shopkeepers who suffered from the undercutting of prices by the big Jewish firms.[17]

The last Riddel student to participate in this exchange, a Miss Henderson, left for Germany in the summer of 1938.[18] During the war she worked for the British Foreign Office at Bletchley Park.

In October 1938 Miss Duffin told the students that it was misguided to speak of the Germans or Italians 'as if they were all devils incarnate. Intolerance begets intolerance and leads nowhere'. She then asked the students

> To take definite sides in the struggle that faces us; to make up your minds that as far as in you lies you will uphold truth and justice and freedom and human kindness and sympathy. We cannot overcome evil by force. We can only overcome it by putting positive good in its place, and by returning love for hate, which is the most difficult thing of all, if we feel strongly. Let us make up our minds that war is an unbelievable folly.[19]

As she often did Miss Duffin used Riddel as an analogy for the larger community of the world, pointing out the anarchy that would result if residents fought each other with 'any weapon that came handy before you could decide who was to have each room, or where you were to sit at table, and that to attain your ends it was necessary to call your opponent by every opprobrious epithet you could think of, and speak of her as the incarnation of evil'.[20] She believed that her students would recognise the futility of this situation and realise that in the end 'no one would be a whit the better'.

Gudrun Weiler, the German exchange student who stayed in the Hall from October 1936 to June 1937, corresponded with Miss Duffin. She replied (enclosing photographs) to the Warden's letter of congratulations on the birth of her first child in the summer of 1939. This letter dated 2 August gives us an insight into the perspective of an educated German woman on the eve of the Second World War. Miss Duffin had obviously discussed the situation with her. Her letter provides an interesting legitimisation of Hitler's foreign policy, which broke the terms of the Versailles Treaty.

> You're quite right about the madness of the world today, but I must say that I think England is far too hysterical about things, though I don't think and expect you'll agree with me. Last year in September I also got worked up and so astonished when in Germany everybody kept calm but now I see that it is the right thing. I've got an English newspaper every day and it's funny to see how agitated people in England are while everything's quiet here though we really get to know everything in our newspapers as well, even more than you, because some things aren't put into the English papers. (Honestly, I never saw them in the *Daily Telegraph* at least.) About 'ravening wolves' I think in agitated times there are expressions which aren't too nice but don't you think that also English ministers and prominent people have used worse words about Germany? And about aggression, first of all I think it isn't fair to encircle Germany, but not openly, but who should be the aggressor in the English opinion if not Germany when England tries to get an alliance with every country around Germany. And all about Danzig which is truly a German city which Poland always has tried to ruin economically and in every way. And Hitler had made a really generous offer when he only wanted Danzig back and a road through Poland because if you're honest you must say that it's preposterous having cut Germany in two, it would be funny for the English if they had to pass through French territory going from London to Newcastle, and I think that the English sentiment for the self-determination of nations only serves material interests, or at least sometimes wants, though they said in the 19th century they were the champions of it. And at last I think that just now England should be interested in her own politics in Palestine, Ireland, China etc. About rearmament you must never forget that we should have kept unarmed if the others had disarmed. We had to arm, because we remembered the Ruhr still too well. But you're quite right it's sad and I hope you aren't hurt about my words personally. I just wanted to give you my, and other Germans' opinion and you know I am fond of England and lots of English people and would never like to become an enemy. I really would like again a discussion with you about things because in a letter it's difficult and written words do look different from spoken ones.[21]

Gudrun Weiler wrote. 'It's a pity you aren't coming to Germany to see us, I would have liked you to stay with us and to have shown you Berlin. But perhaps next year?' The war intervened to make it impossible for Miss Duffin to accept her invitation. She seemed to have been very fond of the Warden and 'still liked to remember my very happy time' at Riddel Hall. This was the last news ever received by Miss Duffin from her German student.

12

The War Years

Miss Duffin recorded in her Chronicle:

In December [1937] I note, with some surprise, that I asked whether any measures should be taken for protection against air raids, but the Committee decided to take no action. It shows that Hitler was already beginning to create apprehension. Miss Boyd and I attended Air Raid Protection lectures, mostly about protection against war gasses, and ultimately helped in the task of fitting the citizens with gas-masks.

They, together with two students, qualified as air raid wardens and the committee authorised the equipping of a gas-proof shelter in the basement. Riddel Hall was thus recognised as an Air Raid Protection (ARP) post to deal with seventy people within its precincts, which meant that they were given special equipment and were entitled to a preliminary air raid warning before the general warning. All students were expected to take their turn at ARP duties.[1] During the autumn of 1939 first aid classes were also held in the Hall.[2] Sally McManus recalled that Mrs Estyn Evans recruited students to staff rest centres during air-raids in Bawnmore Hall, Osborne Park, which was within easy walking distance of Riddel Hall. Ruth Duffin remembered:

During the summer preceding the outbreak of war we had to make arrangements for the 'black-out' of the Hall – a colossal task, for none of the landing and staircase windows had ever been curtained, and most of the existing curtains in the rooms had ultimately to be lined to make them really effective screens. Walls had to be plugged to hold curtain poles, and this in itself was a big task. 780 yards of material were bought and made up, 125 windows were dealt with, 64 sets of curtains were lined, and 36 spring blinds put in to screen skylights.

At the first house meeting following the outbreak of war the students were told that it was their duty 'to uphold the home front'; the written records and oral testimonies of contemporary students show that they answered this call. But Hall life was under threat.

In February 1940, the first possibility that the Hall might be requisitioned by the military authorities was raised. I was rung up on the telephone by a staff officer and told that the Hall might be needed as a Military Hospital, but that <u>no one</u>, not even Miss Boyd, was to be told. There were various alarms and excursions, and I cannot remember at what juncture it was that officers in uniform came up and measured the rooms in full view of the students, while I was still told it was a profound secret! A 'secret de Polichinelle', with a vengeance! In March we were told that it was not proposed to requisition the Hall, and we breathed again. On July 8th, however, just after all the staff had gone away for the vacation, I found a requisitioning order, casually left in, taking over the Hall from that date. An emergency committee meeting was held at a few hours' notice, the business arrangements put in the hands of an agent, and Miss Boyd (very busy as a volunteer cook at the military hospital established at the Stranmillis Training College), the temporary houseman (our own man having been called up) and I, were left to cope with making lists, interviewing ATS officers about their requirements, and packing away all furniture and equipment they said they would not need. By dint of hard work we got everything ready, as we were told the ATS might have to move in at short notice, but time passed and nothing happened except that 10 feet walls were built all round the Hall within six feet of the windows. At last, a new General having appeared on the scene who did not approve of requisitioning educational establishments, the Hall was unconditionally restored to us on October 9th 1940, just too late for the autumn term, as the students were established in 'digs' and the staff had taken temporary situations.

The walls were removed in December 1944.

Miss Duffin did not accept the proposed requisition without a fight. She conducted a campaign of letter writing to every authority she thought would be sympathetic to the Hall's students, on the grounds of disruption to their education and the inconvenience to long-serving domestic staff.[3] Miss Duffin also wrote to all the students suggesting that they should meet in 'a club room' occasionally in order to keep the community feeling alive.[4] The Hall was reopened in January

Riddel students with Miss Duffin in the centre, Miss Boyd on her left and Joyce Power Steele on her right, with Margaret Mitchell as Head of House next to her. The photograph shows the large wall that was built when Riddel was requisitioned for use as a military hospital, but never used for that purpose, and 'unconditionally restored' in October 1940, just too late for the academic year

M. Haire

1941, with the walls as a reminder of the requisition. The grounds were used by Queen's University Training Corps on weekday afternoons for military training purposes.[5] Forty-four students took part in the Civil Defence authority's training for firewatchers.[6] Margaret Mitchell remembered that there was drill most Sunday mornings and students were taught how to use hoses. Miss Duffin attempted to cover every risk. Moira Strawbridge recalls that she arranged for all the girls to go to the Royal Victoria Hospital one Friday afternoon in 1941 where they had 'injections to cover every eventuality'.

In April 1941 there were severe air raids on Belfast. Ten incendiary bombs fell in the grounds, and one set fire to the gardener's house. It was dealt with by two soldiers from the military hospital, an ex-policeman, the houseman and 'last but not least, Miss Boyd, who put a saucepan on her head for protection, and did invaluable work' in helping to cope with water supplies etc. Miss Duffin recalled:

> *I shall never forget those spring nights, though we in Ulster had a very short spell of raids compared with other places. Roused from sleep by the hair-raising screeches of the sirens, rising and falling like the moans of some gigantic infernal animal in its agony, we tumbled out of bed in the early morning hours – generally between 1 and 2 o'clock – dressed in haste, and while those on duty stood by their stirrup-pumps and sand bags, the rest of us went to the shelter in the basement, where garden-seats, mats, etc. enabled us to lie down with at least a minimum of comfort.*

Margaret Mitchell recalled there being very little space in this former bicycle shed. More poignantly one evening Lily, the chief parlour maid, appeared with all her worldly goods in a suitcase. In 1941

> *the Governors ordered the whole of the roof-space in the Hall to be treated with fire-resisting paint, another heavy expense, but the roof would have been a difficult problem for women to tackle if incendiaries had penetrated to the very large area under the slates. Upstairs, under the dim 'guide lights' in the corridors, those on duty, wrapped in rugs and blankets, camped out, ready for action, while overhead the planes hummed like huge angry wasps, and the house vibrated to the blast of explosives and the violent anti-aircraft fire of our own guns. Silence would fall at intervals, and then, just as we thought we could relax, another wave of planes would come over. When the high explosives got rather near for comfort we all went down to the shelter, which was fortunately well-protected by the banks of earth on the other side of the open passage. In the middle of the racket, while we were still upstairs, Miss Boyd and Miss Thompson, the lady cook, made tea and carried it round to those on duty. After the worst 'blitz' I went round to Summerhill at 4 a.m. It was a glorious morning, and the birds were singing as if nothing had happened, but the air was full of the smell of burning and the grass was thick with scraps of scorched paper – a kind of infernal 'snow' storm. One could distinguish brown and brittle billheads, bits of ledgers, etc. borne far away from the business houses in the town. Huge areas of the city were laid low, and many familiar landmarks gone.*

On the night of 7-8 April German bombers found Belfast practically unprepared for its major air raid. A raid over the dockside not only caused considerable damage to the Harland & Wolff premises, but also left thirteen people dead. A second air raid on the night of 15-16 April caused considerably more damage. One hundred and eighty German bombers took part in the attack that lasted from just before midnight until 4 a.m. on Easter Tuesday, killing over 900 people. The Civil Defence movement and voluntary organisations such as the ARP units and the Women's Voluntary Service played important roles in the city's defence.[7] The Riddel Hall staff and residents played their part; the pump teams sat up beside their pumps on several nights in succession till 4 a.m., and many of the students spent nights at rest centres all over the city.[8] Miss Duffin was glad to tell the governors that the students on duty 'behaved admirably' and there were 'no signs of fear or hysteria'. One 'Old Student' recalled that most people helped the Women's Volunteer Service delousing children at their centre at Lagan side, (this was close to Riddel Hall) in preparation for evacuation; Miss Duffin was 'rather shocked'. Margaret Mitchell dressed wounds for patients in the Royal Victoria Hospital the night before exams.

Miss Duffin told the Permanent Committee, 'even with the guns going exams loom large!' She recalled that during the raids 'one girl even seized the opportunity to sit under a corridor light and do some work'. Margaret Mitchell said that many girls wrapped themselves in heavy blankets and studied under the pilot lights. In January 1941, for the first time in the history of the Hall, lights had not been switched off at the main switch; however they were, it was emphasised, 'in no circumstance, to be left on after midnight'.[9] This privilege was short lived. At the October house meeting the governors, 'in the national interest decided that all lights must be switched off by 11.30 p.m. and had forbidden the use of candles or oil lamps'. In spite of the interruptions, the examination results did not seem to suffer, and one girl gained a First Class Honours degree in English.[10]

Throughout the war medical students, as Mollie McGeown described, took their turn. They served as

> air raid wardens in the Samaritan Hospital, not that you did anything, or could have done much. You were on the top floor, sleeping there, and you would hear the sirens going off. Presumably if something landed on the roof you would go and get somebody – I don't know what we would have done, but anyway, the theory was that we students, girls, made useful Air Raid Wardens... Others from Riddel did it... I think only medics.

This factory (Milford Clothing Company Ltd.) off the Crumlin Road was destroyed by incendiary devices on the night of Easter Monday-Tuesday 1941
D. Hadden

Margaret Mitchell (left) with another medical student and house doctor
in the Royal Victoria Hospital, wartime 1942
M. Haire

Her lack of confidence is understandable as she was only eighteen years old and in her first year at Queen's. She remembered her mother's anxiety at the time of the major Easter air raids of 1941 knowing her daughter would be close to danger. Moira Strawbridge recalled that a 'devastated' young Jewish student from North Belfast whose family was killed and home destroyed in the bombing was admitted to the Hall, the rule about Riddel being for Protestant students only being relaxed in the circumstances. This brought the horror of war home to the students in a very powerful way. This was not an isolated case. The committee admitted two (one German and one Austrian) Jewish refugees to free places in the Hall.[11] These students 'fully justified' this grant and they were 'of great value to the hall, as they take an interest in cultural activities apart from their university studies'. Trude Seidman took First Class Honours in Modern Languages and was granted a studentship by the University. Many contemporary students remember her as being a lot older than they were and that she was a great pianist. She decided to take an MA by thesis while taking a correspondence course in librarianship, and the committee granted her a free place for a further year. Ilse Glaser also did well academically despite the news that her parents, who resided in Hamburg, were taken to a Nazi concentration camp in 1942; her mother died there.[12]

In Miss Duffin's last year as Warden there was a long waiting list for places in the Hall and the committee decided that senior students whose academic record was unsatisfactory would be asked leave. One student who received what she called her 'walking papers' had a poor academic record; she failed more than half of her examinations. Her mother wrote to Miss Duffin outlining the distinguished war and colonial service of her two sons and elder daughter.

> I wonder if any of the Governors have a family with a better record than mine. Certainly they are no disgrace to Queen's. Here, my experience is people who should go, shield themselves behind the Home Guard and such services. If [——] has been slow they should consider the circumstances. She gave her help during the Blitz going out to Dunmurry at night firewatching all the time etc. Some of your students would not do firewatching and they have more thanks today than she has because they put their work and exams first.[13]

The receipt of this assertive letter did not alter the governors' decision. The student in question had failed four subjects in March 1939 and a further two in June, so her war work was not entirely responsible for her academic difficulties.

The Permanent Committee also thought that 'freshers' should be given priority as they were only seventeen years of age, while senior medical students were twenty-three. One student who had not finished her dental examinations, but had recently married was asked to leave. Some girls lived in the Hall for several years; one third-year student had actually been resident for six years.[14] Life in Riddel had become increasingly popular (difficulty in acquiring 'digs' during wartime may have been a factor) and by 1943 there was a waiting list of more than fifty. Miss Duffin reported that the students 'were anxious that more accommodation should be provided, even at the expense of present amenities'.[15] Some of the large rooms were subsequently converted into dormitories shared by four students.

In May 1942, when she was sixty-five years old, Miss Duffin tendered her resignation as 'she felt a younger warden would be desirable'. The committee had hoped that she would 'retain the post until at least a year after the war ended'. With her characteristic directness she wrote:

> Miss Duffin thanked the Committee and said that that might be a rather long period. She did not wish to embarrass the Committee, but would be willing to retire at any time if a successor could be found and hoped the Committee would be on the look out for a warden in the mean time.[16]

In January 1943 the post was advertised in two of the local papers, the *Northern Whig* and the *Belfast Newsletter*, as well as in the British and Irish 'quality' press.[17] Forty-three letters of enquiry were received and Miss Duffin was 'instructed to follow up references' and prepare a shortlist for the committee. Of only eight candidates that she considered possible, five were deemed suitable only for a matron's position 'having chiefly domestic experience', one 'was too old' and another was in Scotland. The only real contender was Joyce Power Steele, who was a demonstrator in the Physics Department at Queen's, and already resident in Riddel Hall. The Vice-Chancellor pronounced that 'the choice was Miss Power Steele or nobody'; she was interviewed on 19 March 1943 and offered the post.[18] The selection process indicates that there was a strong preference for a younger educated woman who would provide cultural continuity in Miss Duffin's well-established tradition.

At her last house meeting as Warden in May 1943, Miss Duffin gave the students her last 'very useful advice based on her long experience as Warden, and hoped that Miss Power Steele would be as happy in her position as she had been'. Margaret Mitchell, as President of the Hall, paid tribute to Miss Duffin, wished her many happy years of retirement and expressed the wish that she would 'never feel a stranger to the Hall'. The Library Committee proposed that she 'be made a life member of the library'; this motion was carried unanimously.[19] Sixty years on, the former Miss Mitchell remembered presenting Miss Duffin with an opal ring in front of the 'formidable' Board of Governors. She is still not sure whether this occasion or her final medical examinations the following day was the more terrifying!

In her twenty-seven years as Warden, 474 students had benefited from the generosity of the Riddel sisters and Miss Duffin's cultural influence. The words of Moira Strawbridge, as she recalled her almost sixty years later, probably speak for many women. 'Duffie was really marvellous... a great asset to young students starting off, she gave one a great deal of encouragement.'

At the summer graduation ceremony Ruth Duffin was the recipient of the only honorary degree of MA awarded by Queen's University in 1943. This was not only in recognition of her service to the Hall and its students, but also on the merit of her literary accomplishments.[20]

> Professor Llubera, Dean of the Faculty of Arts... said she had been Warden of Riddel Hall for nearly 30 years. Since its inauguration in 1915 she had been responsible for its organisation and development... and had imparted to the Institution her own personality and character. By her attention to the physical and moral welfare of so considerable a number of women students she had rendered signal service to the University. In honouring Miss Duffin the University had in mind not only its particular indebtedness to her educational achievement, but also her wider reputation as a writer of genuine distinction. As befitted a generous and noble heart, Miss Duffin had recorded some elements of her experience in lyrics, of which Ulster could be proud. She had interpreted in elegant verse some of the great themes of Ireland's glorious past. They owed to her also accomplished renderings of French and German poetry.[21]

Miss Duffin's connection with Riddel Hall continued until the early 1960s when she resigned her position as President of Riddel Hall Old Students' Association as she was moving to Newcastle, County Down.

13

Miss Joyce Power Steele

Miss Joyce Power Steele was thirty-three years old, a graduate of Trinity College Dublin, with excellent connections. Her referees included the Archbishop of Dublin, Professor Ditchburn of Trinity and the former Lady Registrar of Trinity College Dublin. She also had an impressive academic record. Following her primary degree in Physics and Chemistry, Miss Power Steele was elected a scholar in 1931. Professor Ditchburn pointed out that as the number of scholarships was small, this was an important distinction and indicates work of a first class standard. In 1932 she was awarded a Fitzgerald scholarship and graduated with an MSc. From 1932 to 1934 she worked with Professor Ditchburn and their research was published in the *Proceedings of the Royal Irish Academy*. For the first of these years she acted as assistant demonstrator in Trinity College Physics Department where she showed herself to be a very competent lecturer.[1] By the mid-1930s Miss Power Steele had decided to become a teacher and entered the Training Department for Secondary Teachers associated with her old school, Alexandra College in Dublin. At the end of this course her reference from the Principal of Alexandra College read that she had gained:

experience in teaching mathematics to pupils aged 15-17, of both pass and honour standard, and nature study and elementary science to girls of 12 to 14 years. Miss Power Steele takes a real interest in teaching. She is anxious to obtain good work even from her backward pupils and is ready to devise ways of appealing to them. She uses her theoretical studies to help her solve some of her classroom problems, and in lectures on the theory and practice of teaching often raises interesting points for discussion.[2]

Miss Power Steele also gained the teaching qualification HDip.Ed and between 1935 and 1938 she taught science and mathematics in Runton Hill School, Norfolk. She combined teaching in both lower and sixth forms where she taught girls who were working for their first MB; she also successfully coached a student for the Newnham College Cambridge entrance examination.[3] Her headmistress at Alexandra College had 'a very high opinion of Miss Power Steele both for her ability and for her personality'. Miss Preston wrote 'she is a gentlewoman, has a bright and pleasant manner in class, and has wide interests'. Professor Ditchburn did not hesitate to recommend her for a teaching post. 'I believe that Miss Power Steele has the strength of character and personality necessary for a successful teacher. I am sure that her enthusiasm for her work and her general influence on the students will be a definite asset.'

Her next move suggests that this highly intelligent woman was not entirely fulfilled by school teaching. She wished to return to Dublin and left her post in England without previously securing a position in Ireland.[4] Before the end of 1938 she was offered a grant from the Medical Research Council of Eire to work on a two-year project to develop a rapid visual test for vitamin A deficiency.[5] The research was published in the *Proceedings of the Royal Irish Academy* and in *The Lancet*.[6] Miss Power Steele did not relinquish teaching completely; she also taught part-time as science mistress at Alexandra College between 1938 and 1940.[7] In November 1940 she was asked by Professor Emeleus of Queen's University to apply for the post of demonstrator in the Physics Department. She wrote to Miss Duffin hoping that there would be a vacancy in the Hall; otherwise she would be unable to take up this opportunity as she had heard that digs were very difficult to obtain in Belfast.[8] Fortunately for both women, Miss Power Steele could be accommodated. She became a resident in January 1941.[9]

Miss Power Steele was Miss Duffin's choice of successor. Miss Duffin had asked her to take over the wardenship, explaining that she had been wishing to retire for some four years, and the Permanent Committee had refused her requests.[10] Her personal characteristics described in her testimonials would certainly have appealed to Miss Duffin. The Headmistress of Runton Hill wrote that 'Miss

Joyce Power Steele (seated at front in dark dress) with Miss Boyd on her right and other members of staff at the side steps of Riddel. Lily Gaston is standing behind Miss Power Steele, third from left
J. Power Steele

Power Steele has a certain cultural background joined to a considerateness for others that make her a very welcome member of the school staff'. She was initially a 'bit appalled', even 'horrified', at the thought of taking over a position requiring 'age and gravitas'. However, on consideration, Miss Power Steele decided 'why not?' Her letter of application, dated 8 February 1943 shows her enthusiasm. She wrote 'I beg to apply for the post of warden of Riddel Hall'. She admitted that although she had no previous experience, 'I have had a unique opportunity of observing it under working conditions both from the point of view of the staff and, to a certain extent, that of the students'.

From March until June of 1943 Miss Duffin and Miss Power Steele appear to have shared the position of Warden; presumably this was a training period for the latter.[11] She told an amusing story that suggested she looked more like a student than a warden. One evening she was rushing into the Hall at the same time as a young man was leaving and he warned, 'you are nearly late – beware of the Warden'. Miss Campbell, a junior lecturer in Latin, who stayed in the Hall from 1944 to 1947 referred to her fondly as 'dear Joyce' and described her as 'the archetype of an Anglo-Irish lady; tall, slim, with patrician features, and the accent characteristic of Trinity College Dublin'.[12]

In her first annual report Miss Power Steele or 'PS', as she was affectionately known by the students, wrote that she was 'very sensible' of the 'honour and of the responsibility' entailed in carrying on 'the great tradition'. She was 'very fearful of doing anything to break down what has been laboriously and faithfully built up'.[13] In October 1943, at her first meeting of the Permanent Committee, Miss Power Steele made a few changes. She gained their permission to raise the servants' wages and the chief parlour maid was given £10 as a wedding present.[14] Some painting of the public rooms of the Hall and her own rooms was sanctioned and she read several proposals made by the House Committee. Miss Power Steele's request on behalf of the House Committee that the library lights be kept on until 1 a.m. was 'unanimously rejected' by the Permanent Committee. However, they sanctioned the use of candles for going to bed after 11.15 p.m., on condition that they were only used 'for the purpose of lighting to bed' and not for reading.[15]

The students were taking full advantage of Miss Duffin's retirement and her successor being more than thirty years her junior. Although former students describe Miss Power Steele as quite formal, Mollie McGeown, who knew all three Riddel wardens, said that '"PS" was a breath of fresh air', with a 'more modern version' of Miss Duffin's austere manner. 'She was certainly not matey, but nothing like as starched. It was an interesting contrast.'

> I had one, maybe two years of her, I found her a huge change. I liked her; and I liked her brisk manner and so on. You could have stood up to her and said what you thought. You really couldn't do that to Duffie: You had to be docile – well mannered and all that. It was totally a different approach. You could say something straight to Miss Power Steele.[16]

Miss Power Steele offered her office in the Hall after 5 p.m. to students who wanted to entertain 'friends'; presumably this applied to male visitors (women friends were already permitted upstairs), and thus offered a greater degree of privacy than afforded in the drawing room and the library where visitors were permitted.[17] She also stated that it was not really necessary to come to her and ask permission for this privilege as she never used the room in the evenings. Mollie McGeown recalls, 'It was easier, you could invite a boyfriend in... I would never have dared to ask Duffie... but not upstairs, that was really verboten!' In 1943 Miss Power Steele also passed on to the Permanent Committee one daring student's entreaty that 'male visitors might be received in students' rooms at certain hours'. That was 'rejected unanimously'. All these new demands must have been too much for one day and a 'discussion on key rules' was postponed for the present.[18]

Miss Power Steele's hand-written speeches prepared for her annual report to the Permanent Committee are interesting not only for what she actually said, but also for those passages which she thought of saying but subsequently crossed out. In October 1943 she intended bringing some members of the House Committee to meet the governors for tea after their meeting.

> I was discussing with the head of house the other day the curious fact that though the governors give unstinted voluntary service to the Hall out of their very valuable time, the students, if they think of them at all, regard them as an alarming and rather ogre-ish ultimate disciplinary body instead of as their generous and kindly benefactors. This may in a way be a good thing but it seems rather ungracious. Even if it should lessen its terrors for the evil doer, I would like the students to have more opportunity of meeting the committee and appreciating what is done for them.[19]

When she arrived at the Hall in 1944 Miss Grace Campbell felt that:

> The gentle figure of Miss Ruth Duffin still brooded over Riddel Hall. References were made to how things were done 'in Miss Duffin's time'. It was thought that Joyce Power Steele's regime was more relaxed, but I was surprised to learn that the students were not permitted to receive men in their rooms at any time of the day. Coming from Oxford, where we could entertain men in our rooms between 2 and 7 p.m. and where we could visit some of the men's colleges up to 9 p.m., I thought the Riddel rule very restrictive.[20]

Six decades later Miss Power Steele recalled that Miss Duffin's presence in her family home next door to Riddel Hall was not oppressive to her; she regarded the recently retired Warden as a friend.[21] In the spring of 1944 the new Warden was given permission by the governors 'to modify' the rules about giving keys to students; ordinary late leave was extended to 11.30 p.m. on Saturday evenings in the summer term. Miss Campbell remembered:

> Joyce also worried when her tenants asked for a key for the front door. I was allowed to take a key to have a duplicate cut, but only from Havlin's then located in Smithfield, and on condition that I did not tell them where it came from. I don't know if Joyce was afraid that wicked students would get hold of a copy of the key, or whether she was afraid of burglars.[22]

Being on Christian name terms with the Warden, even for Queen's staff, was itself an indication of a lessening in formality; Miss Duffin was never referred to as Ruth in any of the records.

The long-standing students' campaign to smoke in their bed-sitting rooms was finally won in May 1944.[23] Smoking in the library had been permitted for several years and many women remember girls, especially medical students, being heavy smokers. Several former students confessed that 'there was a lot of smoking up the

Margaret Mitchell (left) with fellow students in warm coats at a hockey match. These senior girls
knew Joyce Power Steele when she lived in Riddel before becoming Warden
M. Haire

chimneys' prior to the relaxation of this rule and the Head of House was supposed
to discipline those who disobeyed. In November 1945 'after some discussion' it
was agreed that lights in students' rooms were to be available all night, with the
proviso that Miss Power Steele speak to the students explaining that 'economy
must be observed'.[24]

The new order appears to have satisfied the governors as Miss Power Steele's
salary was raised from £200 to £250 per annum. In the new academic year she was
promoted to part-time lecturer in the Physics Department and the Permanent
Committee was satisfied that this would not interfere with her role as warden.[25]
She felt that the two roles could be combined; indeed she believed that by the
1940s there was not enough work involved in the wardenship to constitute a full-
time career.[26] Miss Power Steele's first year in office was a happy one. She wrote 'I
can't adequately express my gratitude for all the kindness shown me by every one
connected with Riddel Hall'.[27] Her appointment appears to have been a very
successful one for all parties and she remembered her time at Riddel very fondly;
'I enjoyed it very much; the atmosphere was friendly and pleasant'.[28]

Miss Power Steele's annual addresses to the students were similar to those of Miss
Duffin. She emphasised the need to guard the 'high tradition of the Hall' built up

principally by the first Warden. Mollie McGeown recalled that 'she carried on quite a lot of the tradition'. The Warden pointed out that Riddel students would all occupy positions of responsibility in the future, as doctors, teachers or parents.

> The Christian religion emphasises the importance of the individual, and a university education develops personality, which enhances all aspects of life. St Paul emphasises this in his words 'whatsoever things are true, whatsoever things are pure, whatsoever things are just, whatsoever things are lovely, whatsoever things are of good report... Our aim should be to select, classify and relate facts, assess values, and learn to discern what is significant in life.[29]

Like Miss Duffin, she felt anxious that students focused too much on examinations and left 'insufficient time for the various cultural influences of university life'.[30] As the students would not make the effort to attend cultural events, Miss Power Steele brought them to Riddel. Both the Music and the English Societies of Queen's met in the drawing room. The organisers of both societies were 'very grateful for what they described enthusiastically as the pleasantest possible room for meeting'.[31] By 1944 the anxiety was that the Hall had little corporate cultural life of its own, although the students were taking an active part in general university activities, supplying eleven office bearers for various societies including the English and Music Societies.[32]

Miss Power Steele continued to bring culture to the students in her own room; in the winter of 1946-7 an audience of ten to twelve girls were 'quite prepared' to argue about modern art with Professor Llubera from the Spanish Department at Queen's. A Mrs Rooney came to discuss 'youth clubs and other things', a Miss Craig talked about China, and on another evening they read a Shaw play. Although the group was not large, Miss Power Steele thought that the students had 'enjoyed themselves'.

The physical aspect of life was not neglected. The hockey pitch and tennis courts were in demand, and on Monday evenings before dinner a 'physical training class' was held in the drawing room by a Miss Schmitz. Twenty-six students attended with great enthusiasm; however Miss Power Steele lamented that 'unfortunately those who need it most are least anxious to go'.[33] The annual tennis tournaments were held in May, and Miss Power Steele recalled some students coming to her with the request that they could use the tennis courts on a Sunday afternoon. She could see no objection, but pointed out that this was permissible only at certain times so that they would not be seen by local churchgoers on their way to morning or evening services. Miss Power Steele recalled that many of the girls had been brought up 'as very strict Presbyterians' who felt this would be breaking the Sabbath.

The ritual of dinner and coffee in the Warden's sitting room continued in Miss Duffin's tradition, the only difference being that two rather than four students took part each evening. Miss Power Steele explained her policy:

> I have a little intelligence test of my own which I apply to all my students. Unfortunately like all intelligence tests it tests other qualities, besides intelligence. Most evenings during term time I have two students to dinner and to coffee with me afterwards. If during the hour's conversation involved I am driven to talking about recent films I reckon the students have failed the test. If I catch them watching the clock I count the examiner has also failed. If the eye on the clock is almost undetectable I reckon they have at least acquired some social grace, if nothing more profound. I take heart from the fact that I have only discussed films twice this term.[34]

At her first annual report she told the Permanent Committee that the students' conduct 'seems to be excellent. Either the rules are scrupulously obeyed or else so cunningly evaded that the evasion has not been detected by me. I hope and believe that the former is true'.

One past student admitted, in confidence, that on the night of 8 May 1945 (Victory in Europe Day) coincidentally the evening that BSc finals ended, some girls actually stayed out all night; she let them in through her bedroom window on the ground floor. Miss Power Steele either didn't know or turned a blind eye in the circumstances. She recalled that the girls were all 'from good homes' and found no evidence of rebellion; indeed she felt that they were rather conservative. For example a group of girls had asked if she minded them playing the piano on Sundays, quickly adding the proviso that they 'would only play hymns'.[35]

The bane of her life was bicycles. The students all had them, and they abandoned them at the front door or the air raid shelter in a heap and not the bicycle shed, as this involved carrying them down the side of the Hall.[36] The House Committee minutes of the time mention this subject unremittingly. Finally one of the office bearers Dill Caldwell was given the task of dealing with 'the perennial bicycle problem'.[37]

In May 1947 Miss Power Steele told the Permanent Committee that she had been appointed Warden of Trinity Hall, Dublin. She was leaving Riddel Hall 'with the greatest regret and sense of loss' after six years of residence,[38] not from any dissatisfaction with her post, but because her elderly parents, who lived in Dublin, wanted her to be near to them.[39] She remembered telling the interview panel at Trinity College Dublin that she had no complaints to make of the Riddel students' behaviour; either they were well behaved or they were good at hiding misdemeanours. She felt that they gave her the post because she was not so naive that she believed implicitly in the goodness of her students.

The shock felt by the students when Miss Power Steele told them she was leaving the Hall is still palpable in the minutes. 'The students were dumbfounded. The president of the house made a few inadequate words of our appreciation of Miss Power Steele.'[40]

At her final house meeting Miss Power Steele said that she much appreciated the gift that the students had presented and the plaque on which they expressed their 'affectionate regards'. She said that these sentiments were 'most warmly returned'. She reassured the students that the newly appointed Warden, Miss Molly Dawson, was 'extremely nice' and they would all 'like her very much'. Miss Dawson was widely travelled, was a fluent French and German speaker and, as she had been an old Riddel student herself; 'she would have the advantage of being able to look at Riddel from the students' point of view'.[41]

Trinity Hall, founded in 1908 as a hall of residence for women students at Trinity College Dublin.
Women were admitted to Trinity College from 1904, many years after Queen's. Joyce Power Steele left
Riddel to become Warden at Trinity Hall, and to be closer to her parents, who were not well
Trinity College Dublin

14

Miss Dawson

Molly Dawson was appointed as Warden in 1948 and aimed to carry on the traditions established by Ruth Duffin. However, the decades in which she occupied the post saw dramatic social and economic change. By 1975 when she retired and the Hall closed, the social order in which she had been 'apprenticed' for her life's work had altered beyond recognition.

Molly Dawson and her sister Norah, whose father was the Secretary of the County Armagh Education Committee, had both been resident in Riddel Hall in the early 1930s. The sisters are remembered as possessing different personalities. Norah was the more outgoing. Molly was very attractive; it seems that the single academic life was her choice. When students invited others into their rooms for impromptu gatherings, Norah was always included. Molly was different. Even as a young woman she was somewhat austere, and could be sharp at times. Both played a role in the House Committee. Molly Dawson was elected as the fifth member of the Amusements Committee in 1931. Norah was on the Library Committee in 1932; she went on to be the County Armagh Librarian in later years.

Molly Dawson graduated with a BA in French and German in 1933. She then went to teach English and attend French and German classes at a Swiss finishing school in Yverdon on Lake Neuchatel for one year. This gave her the 'opportunity of working with students from many different lands'.[1] She shared a room with Fräulein Labutin, with whom she and a young French woman, 'Mademoiselle', who was interested in politics, often discussed current events. We had 'some interesting discussions together. I'm afraid that Herr Hitler comes in for a good deal of abuse and Fräulein has hard work to defend him'. Despite her new, and for the time exceptional, opportunities she looked back wistfully on her time at Riddel Hall.

> I often think of Riddel and the good times I had there, especially since the winter has come and I would give a lot to see an open fire. Often I picture a Sunday afternoon tea party around the drawing room fire and I feel quite homesick on the spot.[2]

At this time there were few opportunities for university-educated women in industry and business. Molly Dawson was typical of 'the new female elite' who became concentrated in teaching posts in the fee-paying schools for middle-class girls established by the English Girls' Public Day School Trust.[3] Between 1918 and 1938 320 students entered Riddel Hall, but only 171 established careers are recorded. Of these, seventy-six became teachers; many of them in England due to a lack of opportunities at home.

From 1935 to 1939 Molly Dawson taught in a girls' boarding school in Swanage, Dorset. She felt 'very lucky to have found such a pleasant post', teaching French and German to senior girls and history and composition to the juniors. Other members of staff were friendly and there was 'no time to feel bored' as, after dining with the Headmistress, listening to the news and having 'our little school gossip it is time for bed'. Miss Dawson was impressed that the pupils seemed 'very well brought up' and were from good families. One girl, Iris Pepys, was a 'direct descendant of the great diarist, Samuel', there were two daughters of Lady Sloggett, and two Irish girls one of whom was a member of the 'very old Blood family'.[4] She made the most of her opportunities.

> Whenever possible during these years I tried to improve my knowledge of my subjects and to profit as far as I could from the long summer vacation. In 1936 I took a course for foreign students in German at Bonn University and in 1937 took a similar course in French at the Sorbonne University of Paris. In 1938 I again spent the summer months in Germany.[5]

Miss M. Dawson by Tom Carr
May (Molly) Dawson was Warden at Riddel from 1948 until it closed in 1975
Queen's University Belfast

On the outbreak of war in 1939 she took up a teaching post in Holme Valley Grammar School, Honley, Yorkshire. As war restricted her summer travel abroad, Miss Dawson took a party of senior girls to a fruit-picking camp in Suffolk in both 1941 and 1942; in subsequent years she assisted in harvest camps in Lincolnshire and Cumberland. This gave her the opportunity of seeing her students from 'quite a different angle'. Miss Dawson also felt that her position as housemistress and form teacher gave her 'the opportunity to gain a good knowledge of girls in the years preparatory to their university course'. Membership of the school's large Old Students' Association for which she organised badminton and tennis teams[6], kept her 'in contact with the modern student'. In 1947 she was a committee member of the Huddersfield branch of the British Federation of University Women and a member of the town's Standing Conference. Miss Dawson spent the first summer after the war in a school in Lausanne. All this experience, together with her own time in the Hall as a student, made her an ideal candidate for the position of Warden.

The post had been widely advertised in the British and Irish Press, and details circulated to British universities in the summer of 1947. However, only four suitable candidates were called for interview. Miss Dawson admitted to the governors that she had no experience of the 'financial duties' of the post. However, she argued that 'these are unlikely to prove too arduous for anyone genuinely interested in the academic and social activities of the students in the Hall.' This lack would be compensated for by the fact that she was 'keenly alive to the advantages offered by Riddel Hall' and her willingness to 'enter fully into the interests and needs of the students'.[7]

The Headmaster of Holme Valley Grammar School stated that she 'sets a high standard and expects it of others' and recommended her 'without reserve' for the post of Warden.[8] The Senior Mistress of the school also held Miss Dawson in high regard.

> She has always been a most valued colleague, giving her services unsparingly to the school. She is an excellent Form Mistress, and gains the confidence of her pupils because she studies them individually and has great insight into the particular problems and idiosyncrasies of each child. Her combination of friendliness and dignity make her very successful with adolescents... I consider her to be an excellent person to be in charge of girls of university age. She is exceptionally attractive in appearance and dresses well. Her voice is pleasing. Her interests are wide. She is obviously the product of a cultured home with high standards of manners and conduct. All these points seem to make her admirably suited to the position of warden.[9]

Miss Dawson was chosen 'unanimously' by the Permanent Committee and took up her position in January 1948. She spent her time both as a student and for the great majority of her career in Riddel Hall, 'I, as man and boy, have spent more than thirty years of my life here'.[10] Her arguably rather sheltered life inevitably shaped her world view, and made it difficult for her to accept the changes that subsequent generations of students demanded. The reminiscences of previous old students provide much evidence for this assessment. One former Riddel student, Susan Wallace, under Miss Dawson's care in the 1950s, thought she did not live in the real world; 'all her friends were literary people; and single'. Some women recalled that she was 'a typical old maid', an old-fashioned 'headmistress'. Miss Dawson thought the students did not take life seriously enough; they were even rather 'silly'. The principal grievance one year was 'the inadequacy of mirrors around the building'. Miss Dawson's reaction was unsympathetic. Instead 'she stirred our consciences with regard to the need for wise giving in the world today, and reminded us of our duty towards movements such as Oxfam'.[11]

Molly Dawson was deeply influenced by Miss Duffin whom she knew not only as Warden but also as a colleague on the committee of the Riddel Hall Old Students' Association (RHOSA), and in the Queen's Women Graduates' Association (QWGA), of which Miss Duffin was an honorary member, from 1948 to 1964. By 1949 the new Warden was a committee member of QWGA. Miss Dawson wrote that her old Warden 'never carped or was critical of the changes' that she made in the Hall and 'age did not blunt her judgement'.[12] The two women were very fond of each other and held each other in high esteem.[13] When Miss Duffin died in June 1968 at the age of ninety-one, Miss Dawson wrote, she 'always appeared ageless, older than her years in middle life and younger in her old age. Looking back I feel it was she who gave to this place its character and standards and her stamp is on much here still today'.[14]

Miss Dawson did not point out, or perhaps was not conscious, that the reason for the continuity was that she did not want to make fundamental change. Mollie McGeown found Miss Dawson to be very similar in essence to Miss Duffin, but in 'an updated version'. A Warden with a different value system and agenda might have transformed any institution in twenty years, especially one where the population was so transitory.

Table 3.   Origin of students in Riddel Hall from outside Northern Ireland 1945-75

Nationality	No. of Students
China	2
England[15]	85
Estonia	1
Germany	8
Gibraltar	1
Guiana	1
India	3
Iran	1
Isle of Man	1
Nigeria	2
Poland	1
Republic of Ireland	5
Scotland	4
Singapore	4
Switzerland	1
Trinidad	10
USA	5
Wales	3

Source: Student records, Riddel hall Archive QUB

The period after the war saw a change in the maturity, and the origins of Riddel students. In the immediate post-war years there were ex-service students who returned to university, having previously left to engage in the war effort. For example Maura Wilson joined the Women's Auxiliary Air Force in 1940 after completing her first year at Queen's; she re-entered the University in October 1947. Dorothea Wilkinson joined the ATS in 1943, interrupting her first year at Queen's, and resumed her studies in 1946. In the post-war era, the composition of the Hall became slightly more mixed. In 1952 the Hall became home to two students from Trinidad and Malaya. From this time onward there were usually six or seven overseas students in the Hall; they were given a warm welcome. It also became more common for past students who had moved to live in England to send their daughters to Riddel and Queen's.

In 1956 the Hall bought a television set. Miss Dawson reassured the governors the residents would 'eventually pay'. The overseas students particularly enjoyed the programmes at weekends when home students were visiting friends and family.[16] This might suggest that overseas students were excluded from community life, but Bree Sawh who came from British Guiana at the end of the 1950s remembers being made very welcome, and invited to the homes of other students 'every weekend'. Bree had stayed at first in the International Hostel of the Young Women's Christian Association (YWCA) in London, trying to find a university place to study medicine. One day she received a telephone call, offering her a place in Belfast. She thought, 'Why not? I'll go anywhere.' She came to Queen's, and has stayed in Northern Ireland ever since. At Riddel she was sheltered from the harsher realities of life in Northern Ireland. She was shocked to find the deep sectarian divide once she went out into general practice: 'We had nothing like that at home'. She was married in the summer of 1958 but kept her place in the Hall until graduation four years later.[17] 'It was traumatic to leave.' In her last year she was elected Head of House. Miss Dawson told the governors:

> For the first time we have an overseas student president of the house, from British Guiana, a medical student in her final year. I should like to put it on record that she was in the best tradition of our presidents and that, in spite of the many derogatory remarks made about the youth of today, the spirit among the seventy two students here was as good as I have known it.[18]

Bree herself said that 'it was a lovely time; it was not like now. Everyone helped each other, it was a community'. Once when the Warden mentioned a health problem to her, Bree diagnosed an ulcer, and soon afterwards Miss Dawson's own doctor confirmed the medical student's diagnosis. 'That put me up high in her estimation'. She felt her role as Head of House was like that of head girl at a boarding school. It included official duties such as laying the wreath at the university war memorial on Remembrance Day. Bree also had a counselling role. 'Some students, if they had a problem, would open up to you; others would be more reserved. The girls were at all different stages in their university careers. It was a nurturing place where everyone cared for each other.'

As Head of House, what she had received, she gave back. 'We had committees; we were well prepared. It was like the old fashioned thing when people did service in the "big house". If you were on the academic side you did your training.' To this she attributed the success of her experience in Riddel. She took people as she found them and they responded positively to her. Coming from an area in South America where there were few facilities for education, she had no opportunity to develop an insular attitude.

The real difficulty for students whose homes were far away was that Riddel was only open during term time, for thirty weeks a year. This was also a problem for medical and dental students with their responsibilities in hospital. Bree Sawh said that one summer when she went to London to work in an orthopaedic hospital

Bree Sawh (front left) with other overseas students at Riddel Hall
Riddel Hall Archive

she stayed in the International Hostel. Another year she and other students from the Hall went to Kent to do hop picking. One of the others, a Chinese girl, had a contact in Kent with whom they were able to stay.

Many of the overseas students kept up a long-term correspondence with Miss Dawson. Their letters provide us with a fascinating account of their travels, careers and family lives. Mary Ekpiken, who was resident in the Hall from 1953 to 1955, was the first Nigerian woman to graduate from Queen's University. She returned home as an Economics graduate to take charge of the employment and statistical section of the Nigerian Civil Service. Her post required her to travel to the United States for research into establishing new industries, as well as training teachers from the United Kingdom and United States to assist in Nigerian educational projects. Another Economics graduate, Vanee Lertdumrikarn from Bangkok, who lived in the Hall from 1957 to 1960, returned to Thailand to work with a development bank. In 1963 she was an economist in the planning section of the National Economic Development Board in connection with the World Bank. Several other Northern Irish and overseas students became teachers, doctors and administrators in newly independent post-colonial states in the 1950s and 1960s.

15

A Story-Book Experience

Riddel life continued much as before under Miss Dawson, but day-to-day activities depended to a large extent on the domestic staff. Traditionally these staff had come from Co. Donegal, as Miss Boyd had recruited them from her home town. Work in Riddel had suited them as they could return during the long vacations to work at home. One of Miss Dawson's first recommendations was to increase the wages of the domestic staff as by 1948 it was becoming increasingly difficult to recruit and retain staff who were prepared to live in the Hall.

Dinner as a ritualised institution carried on in Miss Duffin's tradition. Miss Dawson persisted with the effort to instil good manners into Riddel students. In her address to the house in 1950 she reminded students 'of the importance of maintaining a correct posture at meal times, and of not propping elbows on the table'.[1] She stressed the importance of students and staff taking meals together like a family for keeping the community spirit alive. Former students looking back after forty or fifty years, realised that it was 'a great thing'. They recall with nostalgia impromptu gatherings in the upstairs kitchens, and huddled around each other's bedroom fires. Meeting friends in this way was a favourite aspect of life in Riddel.

In the early 1960s Miss Dawson felt that students were beginning to go home for too many weekends and feared that this would lead to a decline in communal activity. Miss Dawson was possibly being overly pessimistic. Margaret Lyons thought that the Hall never felt empty at weekends; it was when all the relaxation took place. Diana Martin agreed, 'I think people genuinely enjoyed it; you were equally in touch with all the activities in town and at Queen's'. It was an 'Enid Blyton story-book' experience, Rhoda Acheson, a student in the early 1960s, recalls. This image is evidenced in a poem written to celebrate amateurish sport played at the Hall, (to the tune of 'Marching through Georgia').

OPEN AIR

Bring the tennis racquets, girls! We'll have another set,
Slam the ball about the court but not into the net,
Serve, return or volley, that's the game you'll get,
Playing on the tennis courts at Riddel.

Hurrah! Hurrah! It's tennis keeps you fit.
Hurrah! Hurrah! That's the best of it.
Vantage point, then deuce again but finally, it's out,
Playing on the tennis courts at Riddel.

In the wintry weather, hockey is great fun,
Bully off and pass the ball and keep them on the run.
When we play the Edgehill boys we whack them everyone,
Playing on the hockey field at Riddel.

Hurrah! Hurrah! We play a friendly game,
Hurrah! Hurrah! But mind you all the same,
If you try on dirty tricks, you're apt to end up lame,
Playing on the hockey field at Riddel.

Hockey was a feature of life in the Hall on winter Saturday and Wednesday afternoons, as was tennis in the summer term. Throughout the 1950s and early 1960s there was a 'hockey secretary' appointed by Miss Dawson to organise matches. In October 1951, Roberta Thompson, hockey secretary, informed the house that 'Edgehill wanted to arrange hockey matches'.[2] The students were young men preparing for the Methodist ministry. The games continued into the 1960s. Helen Lamptey enquired at the first house meeting in 1961, 'how many would be interested in playing energetic if unorthodox hockey on a Wednesday afternoon?' She took 'care to emphasise for the benefit of the Freshers that we play with Edgehill College boys'.[3] These mixed games became a tradition for many years and were remembered by several students; one girl married one of the future ministers.

Mixed hockey matches at Riddel – not for serious players! Medical and Dental students Autumn 1960
E. Murray

There were different types of hockey players in Riddel. Those who were particularly talented played for Queen's teams, others who were less gifted played on the Hall's pitch. Serious players tended to avoid playing at Riddel as they were likely to get 'silly injuries'. Tennis was played in the summer term at Riddel and at Cherryvale, the university sports ground, which was a considerable distance from the Hall. Many old students remember clearly the energetic cycle to get there.[4]

The recently established student newspaper, *Gown*, sent two male reporters to Riddel Hall in October 1957. Their article suggests that Riddel was perceived as being a pleasant, but rather old fashioned, boarding school. The writers recreated the atmosphere of the Hall.

AS I WAS WALKING DOWN STRANMILLIS ROAD

Riddel Revisited

Some time, about four in the afternoon it was, with the faint crispness of a late, dry October day; the distance slightly whitened and the metal of the motor scooter cold and biting. Rows of rhododendrons, ten acres of grounds from crisp cricket pitchness to the orchard-like grasses between the bare autumn trees that surround the blockish red brick, the Virginia creeper and the still, secluded atmosphere of Riddel. These were the things that you put on paper.

To the door, then, with the great archway, a daylight glimpse into the tiled polish of the hall, and, ring the bell. To the waiting rooms with the first taste of the stag at bay oils in their faded frames; what they call 'relics of oul' dacency' back home. It was here that I perceived the first waft of male trepidation in the all so female air.

Polish and Precision

A slight wait, an interval to straighten the tie and finger the greasy hair, and we were interviewing Miss Dawson in her study. This small room, bare, with roll-top desk, its long table and its aura of official precision, matched well with the slightly girls' public school movements of its owner. This was the first note of hockey sticks and 'taggers', the recurrent theme of The Hall, which hit us most forcibly when we were introduced to the young lady who was to be our guide - she was not Miss Goodwin, she was Goodwin.[5] ... Unlike Chambers [the men's hall of residence] there is no system of faculty allocation, and due to the independent position and size of the endowments, unfortunately, no possibility of expansion. As to rules and regulations, these seem to be all of the hostel-school type: the only ones really affecting the general public being the hours of opening and, more particularly of closing.

Mirror on the Wall

Next Goodwin, in her jeans and scurrying, apologising, guiding, among the chrysanthemums, the lofty ceilings and the ever-present smell of floor polish. To the dining room, its bareness and bright Common-room segregation, we went, then rather shyly and questioningly up the staircase, shades of all those schools one visited in one's youth with the various seconds teams with which one roamed the Province. Startling, odd, at the staircase top, a spark of femininity was a mirror set in the cold bare wall. Eventually, when we had wandered self-consciously, our heels clicking harshly in the silence, we were shown into one of the small bedrooms. I paced the floor. 'Thirty square yards,' I said. There were looks of unbelief and I measured again. I was correct. A rather impersonal room, I thought, but there was one difference about the pictures on the wall here, you could bear to look at them. The paintings on the walls of Riddel were the least horrible part of our visit.

Surprised Femininity

The library was our next stopping off place; the door opened and there was a slow turning of incredulous female eyes, a cluster of surprised femininity before a brisk burning fire. But it was soon over and I retreated to the front door, while scuttling, whispering in the background, the women of Riddel, hockey-clad and school-girlish, watched. As the door closed I made a final attempt to exercise a definite opinion of life up here, a tale of the old student raids or even a breath of scandal, but not a lip was unsealed.

Anyone for Tennis

Back in the cold misty air, I looked over the gravel, the grass, and the winding drive to where the outline of factories was beginning to blot the feeling of anachronism, which the visit had engendered. This, in itself, was unfortunate, for there, between myself and the skyline, were the shorts and whistles of a hockey match. And what a hockey match. The ghosts of the Lower Fourth and the creek of opening tuck boxes may have been there somewhere, for Riddel was playing a local boys' school, with the teams inter-mixed – a Spartan touch that might have disturbed the late Thomas Hughes.

Perhaps we will come back again.
I.J.H. and J.A.

While the patronising male view on women expressed in this article would be unacceptable to many women today, it did not raise even a murmur in the records of the Hall.

Residents of the late 1950s (like those in the 1930s and 1940s) maintained that their parents had been more authoritarian than Riddel's wardens. In the Hall girls who applied for leave simply wrote their names in the 'big book' at the door, and that they were going to Queen's or town. If a student was back before 11 p.m. there was no inquisition. 'We just ticked off our names when we returned, so the last one in would lock the door – there was a great deal of trust that we weren't ticking for anyone else.' Two students who were in Riddel in the 1950s and early 1960s

On the steps outside Riddel
E. Murray

respectively, Thelma Hutchison and Rhoda Acheson, pointed out that this rule could often be used as a 'convenient' excuse to get away at the end of an evening.

In the early 1960s special dispensations to stay out until 11.30 p.m. for the Queen's Hops on Saturday and Wednesday evenings were granted by Miss Dawson. Margaret Lyons thought 'it was unlimited freedom. At home my father and mother wanted to know where I was going; at seventeen I was seldom out after ten, half past ten at the very most'. Diana Martin, before coming to the Hall, thought that 'Riddel might have been an extension of boarding school, where you never would have got out'. For younger ages late dispensations were limited to four per term; students over twenty-one and members of the House Committee were entitled to have a key; a group of girls could have one key with the most senior girl being in charge.

For many Riddel students graduation was not the end of their relationship with the Hall. Most joined RHOSA to keep in contact with their contemporaries, and new generations of Riddel girls. In 1953 Miss Dawson introduced a 'new feature', a combined party for past and present students, through which she aimed to keep Miss Duffin's traditions alive.

> The old students invited the present students to help them revive the Hallow E'en concert which was for many years traditional in the Hall. All the items in the concert were home produced and of a good standard in view of the time available for rehearsal. It was evident that the Hall formed a strong bond between past and present students and in the Hallow E'en games which followed the concert it would have been hard to tell one from the other. As an old student I enjoyed this party and as warden I was glad to feel that there was this body of Old Students still actively interested in our affairs.[6]

One item, entitled 'Broom' probably written for this event, was a tongue-in-cheek critique of the Hall where the windows never kept the elements out. It described 'a blasted hill which is surmounted by a rain-beaten, windswept hall'. Three witches meet to fight against the weather.

> Blows the wind and beats the rain
> Hard against the window pane
> Run for cloths to dry the floor
> Ring them out and start again

The following year RHOSA members invited the students in the Hall to a Guy Fawkes party where the Association members put on a play entitled 'Mad Hatters in Mayfair', described as 'a comedy for women', by Barbara Van Kempen. The students provided the rest of the programme showing 'much originality in the various items, by their skill in dressing up and snappy production'.[7]

16

Demands for Change

As a result of increasing demands for independence and autonomy, the student body and the type of accommodation sought underwent a great deal of change over the period from 1948 to 1975. During Miss Dawson's first years in office some students clamoured for the Hall's rules to be up-dated just as they did when Miss Power Steele took over from Miss Duffin. Miss Dawson's attitude appears to have been that modernisation could not be avoided in the long term, but with some compromise it could be postponed. The House Minute Book shows that the issue of meals led to a degree of conflict. In 1949 the house requested that students have a choice between tea and coffee at lunchtime. Miss Dawson dismissed this idea, telling the house that 'it was good to acquire a taste for things we dislike'.[1]

The first tentative attempt to reduce the number of formal dinners each week had come as early as October 1949. 'A proposal concerning earlier dinner or high tea on Saturdays was also discussed, but no decision was reached.' In May 1950 the house proposed that the formal dinner be held a quarter of an hour earlier 'to avoid undue rushing for students who wish to attend societies at Queen's beginning at 7.30 p.m.' Following a vote in which a large majority was found to be in favour of the alteration, Miss Dawson agreed reluctantly for a trial period, 'on condition that there were no excuses regarding dressing, or leaving dinner early'. Over this period the number of formal meals was frequently under review and in 1953 high tea replaced dinner on Saturday evening. The following year Miss Dawson told the students that she would like to 'see more often a full attendance at dinner, as it is the only opportunity during the day for all to meet together.'[2]

Strong feelings about this issue continued as a feature of relations between the Warden and the students' representatives. On 10 October 1954 the House Committee requested that dinner on Wednesday be replaced by high tea served at 5.30 p.m., as many people wished to go out that evening. Miss Dawson said that she must refer this request to the governors as it meant 'changing time-honoured rules'. The meeting closed with Miss Dawson requesting there should 'be less dissatisfaction in the house, especially about food' and asking students 'for a spirit of co-operation'. The governors accepted the change on condition that formal meals should be retained on four evenings each week.[3]

The first, and only 'extraordinary meeting' of the house was held on 18 October, 'to give the warden an opportunity to explain to the house the decision of the governors regarding the proposals put forward at the house meeting.'[4] The wording of the record suggests there was a distinct level of hostility between house and warden, as does the extreme measure of calling an extra meeting. Miss Dawson pronounced that although high tea would be served on Wednesdays, she 'wished the house to understand that there could be no further concessions in this matter'.

In the 1950s the students felt that the ritual of formal dinner was outdated. Past students remembered the conflict between warden and students. 'It was not approved if you absented yourself.' Elizabeth Lyons recalled she did not always change in the evening. Another, Thelma Hutchison, thought it was all very well 'as long as you didn't meet Miss Dawson's "beady eyes"... She could be sarcastic, saying, "*We* do not behave like that"'. Over Bree Sawh's six-year residence the formality eased somewhat. 'It was one thing we hated; we thought we should wear our everyday clothes. It was very hard to have to change. Sometimes we would just change a top or put on a different dress.'

Students did not like sitting at Miss Dawson's table. 'When it was our turn we said "Oh no!" We couldn't talk the way we used to at our own table in those days.' A further erosion of the number of formal dinners came in 1961, when the students requested that tea be served each evening in the summer term. Miss Dawson judged this as 'a chronic suggestion made by students year after year, and it was a pity to give up one of the things, which was perhaps not fully appreciated now, but only when students have left the Hall'.[5] On this occasion she did not consult the Permanent Committee but accepted that 'the time had come for change'. It was agreed to have tea that term as an experiment. While Miss Dawson saw this as evidence of decline, Mildred Proctor, a postgraduate student who wrote the 'News of the Hall' report for 1966 explained it differently.

> Undergraduate numbers are increasing and as competition becomes more severe academic standards tighten. Perhaps the leisured figures on the Misses Riddel's memorial in the hall never did represent the typical Queen's woman but they do so less than ever in the 1960s. There are very few exam candidates who spend May in the garden idly flicking over the leaves of a text-book. In fact the grind is so intense and begins so early that within the last few months another Riddel institution – formal dinner – has fallen victim to it. Many students, particularly scientists who do most of their work at the university felt that they could not afford to spend three quarters of an hour on a formal meal and regrettably but inevitably it is now only to take place on one evening in the week.[6]

Miss Dawson had not really accepted the changes she had felt forced to concede, and in 1965 she feared for the future.

> There is a constant fight against time and this results in a constant search for short cuts. It is quicker to fetch your own plate at dinner time than to wait for it to be brought to you and quicker still if a ration of potato and vegetable has already been put on the plate, rather than into dishes which have to be passed round later with inevitable delay. It is quicker to throw out a few harmless remarks to your neighbours at table without bothering to find out who they are, where they have come from or what they are reading than to try to integrate and make worthwhile contact with new comers to the Hall... One fights a losing battle to preserve standards. One has to recognise the very real need to get to the university library before all the seats are filled. Bit by bit, another point is conceded and another time-honoured formality goes by the board.[7]

New girls had once sat at their own table for dinner until invited to those of the more senior residents. This system was no longer viable when so many students stayed in the Hall for only a short time. Nevertheless, Rhoda Acheson saw the changes in a positive light, saying that in the early 1960s everyone 'just came in and sat down to dinner in different places each evening, as a result you got to meet more people'.

For some students the main argument was about coming in late. One recalled, 'of all the things we hated was having to come in early'. This was another area of

Riddel Ball Christmas 1960
M. Gowdy

the warden's control, which ultimately was lost. In her first year the new Warden informally relaxed the rule that students should be in by 11 p.m. on a Saturday evening. She 'said that she didn't mind if students were a few minutes late occasionally, for she understood the difficulty in rushing up from the hop, but she would like, if possible, that they should be in by 11.15'.[8] In October 1951 leave was extended until 11.30 p.m. However, Miss Dawson stated firmly on this occasion that 'they must be sure to come in at that time, and not wait' until she came to lock the door. She also gave an increased number of 'late keys' to the more senior students.[9] Bree Sawh remembered that 'to be out past 11o'clock was taboo. I remember the girls climbing up the guttering to get in if they were late. The front door was locked after a certain time'. Some students climbed in windows or threw pebbles up at friends' windows to get in after the door was locked.

Informal 'hops' had been held in the Hall from October 1950, with the dual purpose of raising money for items such as a television set, and providing an alternative to the overcrowded Students' Union on Saturday evenings. These hops were scheduled to end at 11.45 p.m.; Miss Dawson explained the etiquette required for the end of the evening. 'She hoped that, as good hostesses should, we would manoeuvre our partners out before twelve o'clock without giving them the impression of being unwelcome.'

Miss Dawson and Miss Boyd were always present to supervise these informal events, and the annual formal Riddel Ball although the students did the organising. Miss Boyd took care of the catering, while the students coordinated the entertainment and arranged for an inexpensive photographer to come. In the late 1950s Honor Gray was on the Entertainment Committee. Her brother played in a band, and was a useful contact when hiring musicians. Her contemporary in Hall, Thelma Hutchison recalled

> occasional escapades at the 'formal', for we could each invite a partner. One year a couple of the boys rode a motor bicycle through the drawing room and the library. It was a bit like a 'streaker', I think they had pyjamas on just for a jest. Miss Dawson, of course put them out. They did create a stir; the whole idea was to shock her. On another occasion, there was a chap who had a sports car, and some of his friends carried it and deposited it beside the vegetable garden, where it could not easily be moved. They were simple escapades like that.

The House Committee minutes from 1951 to 1957 make no mention of these events. They may have been accepted as fairly innocent fun although they would have been unimaginable in Miss Duffin's time. The 'formal' remembered with such fondness as 'civilised' and 'proper' by students in the inter-war years had begun to show signs of what Miss Dawson, no doubt, perceived as declining standards. In 1958 Miss Dawson abolished the formal for that year and an informal dance was held in its place, to raise funds for a record player.[10]

Another wider university tradition that appealed to Miss Dawson's students was 'Rag, or Students', Day'. Although it had been deemed unladylike in the 1930s by Miss Duffin, the new Warden wrote in 1951:

> Student's Day... arouses great enthusiasm here and reveals powers of creativeness and ingenuity, which one might not otherwise have suspected in certain students. In the summer term there is not much time to spare for the making of costumes but traditionally the evening before is given over to preparation and a dress rehearsal. It is amazing what can be conjured out of the Hall's dustsheets and a few stock properties. The main idea is always to effect a good disguise but many of the costumes show a high degree of originality and ingenuity. Almost all Hall residents, however senior, take part in Rag Day.[11]

In May 1957 Paddy McMaster suggested that Riddel should have a float on Students' Day. Miss Dawson welcomed the idea as very little had been done the previous year.[12] This was Riddel's first official contribution. Thelma Hutchison recalled Paddy McMaster and her sister Barbara, the daughters of a General Practitioner in Broughshane:

Rag Day!
D. Hadden

Riddel girls on parade at the front of Queen's, Rag Day, early 1960s
D. Hadden

They rode horses and had no fear. They had more confidence than the rest of us; they borrowed a long flat lorry. I remember the driver coming; he left it at the front, but it had to be decorated. You couldn't have the mess of it being decorated at the front! That wouldn't be suitable. One of the McMaster girls got into the driver's seat and drove the lorry round to the big yard at the back. So all the mess of decorating it could be done unseen.

Honor Gray remembers the year of the 'Riddel Harem', which won third prize. 'We all wore pyjamas, tied in at the bottom – baggy trousers, and your face covered. The Student's Union lent us the float and we decorated it.' On Rag Day 1961, Riddel's float, 'All at Sea' won first prize.

It was claimed that raids on the Hall by young men on the eve of Rag Day were frequent occurrences. Thelma Hutchison recalled that on Students' Day during the mid-1950s,

it was traditional that the boys from Queen's Elms would try to break into the Hall... actually one of them was quite badly injured trying to climb in through a window and then falling into the basement... I think it was just a heel injury, but it took him a long time to recover from it. They just walked up from Queen's, from their Halls. It was a game really, and a bit of excitement, it was an innocent age. There was never alcohol at Queen's.

Riddel Afloat won first prize on Rag Day 1961
Riddel Hall Archive

Riddel Harem
Riddel Hall Archive

17

Changed Times

The post-war Labour Government came to power as Miss Dawson was taking up the post of Warden of Riddel Hall. It made sweeping social changes and introduced the Welfare State. Even before this, the availability of state scholarships for higher education had led to an increase in the number of students. There were 1,555 students attending Queen's in 1939-40; this had risen significantly to 2,762 in 1948-9. As a consequence Queen's set up a lodgings committee in 1948 'to inquire how the university's responsibility could best be fulfilled'.[1]

Not only were there greater numbers of students, but their social backgrounds had become gradually more varied. The 1947 Education Act raised the school leaving age to fifteen and provided free grammar school education for those who passed the eleven plus examinations.[2] A new tripartite system of grammar, intermediate and technical schools aimed to provide appropriate education for all eleven to fifteen year-olds. The need for this change can be appreciated when we consider that during the 1940s only a very small proportion of the population aged over fourteen years of age remained at school; in 1948 the figure was barely 2 percent[3]. Although both boys and girls were entitled to the education most suited to their academic abilities, education remained strictly gendered and the 'separate curriculum grounded in domestic subjects' for girls was as 'conservative as any advocated during the early part of the century'.[4]

As late as 1951 more than 70 percent of girls of fourteen to seventeen years of age did not remain at school[5], but educational participation continued to rise and by the academic year 1955-6 more than 20,000 pupils in Northern Ireland received state scholarships to attend grammar schools. The number of students in teacher training colleges also doubled at this time.[6]

The effect of the Act on university entry became evident in the mid-1950s. In 1957 there were three times as many young women on Riddel's waiting list as there were places available. There were numerous advance applications from parents whose daughters intended to enter the University two or more years later. There were other instances where young women had been offered a place in Queen's at the age of seventeen as a result of successful Senior Certificate examinations, but their parents refused them permission to come to university unless a place in Riddel Hall was secured. They returned to school for a further year to complete the Advanced Senior Certificate. In 1959 accommodation was stretched to seventy-two places including the two students who 'slept out' in number 1 Mount Pleasant, the avenue adjacent to the Hall.

The availability of county scholarships played a part in enabling students from less privileged backgrounds to attend university. This financial assistance may also have been a factor in the increasing number of female students. By 1957, 85 percent of Riddel students were 'of scholarship standing'. Miss Dawson argued that, as scholarships were now much more commonplace than in the past, low fees in the Hall were serving the purpose of subsidising the education authorities. This was not the original purpose of the Misses Riddel who aimed to 'assist suitable students who might otherwise have been unable to afford the amenities offered by the Hall'. From that year onwards a sum of £300 was allocated to fund the Eliza and Isabella Riddel Exhibitions of £30 each. The first student to benefit was from the Republic of Ireland, whose government did not fund higher, or until 1966, secondary education. The conditions were that the applicant had a satisfactory record, had no other scholarship and had a 'reasonable claim to assistance'.[7] In 1960 the Northern Ireland Government implemented the Anderson Committee's recommendation that all students accepted by a university should receive a local education authority grant.

In 1960 for a total of 3,570 students at Queen's there were places for only 221 students of both sexes in halls of residence, 151 in other hostels, 1,151 in lodgings, and the rest at home.[8] The long-term result of the University's investigation into the need for student accommodation was the construction of the Queen's Elms complex on the present Malone Road site to accommodate 800 students. In 1962 when the site was under construction, Miss Dawson prophetically told the governors:

> Looking a little beyond our own boundaries, we find again the old order yielding to the new... Prevailing winds here blow from the west. Who can yet say what wind of change will blow from that quarter in the future years? It seems likely that the Hall will be more closely integrated into the extra-curricular life of the university.

In 1967 Queen's joined UCCA (Universities' Central Council of Admission) system and a scheme of common application was also established in that year for all Queen's residential provision. Miss Dawson hoped that Riddel 'would fit into the general scheme of things' catering for 'students who prefer the old to the new, the smaller number to the mass, and even the segregation of the sexes'.[9]

From the 1950s onward university education was expanding throughout Europe. The old style of residential hall was becoming less financially viable and students were beginning to demand greater freedom than in the past. Miss Dawson kept the governors up to date with wider changes as she attended the annual conference of the Association of Wardens, Principals and Advisors each July. This was a forum for sharing experiences and discussing future developments for university residences. Miss Dawson visited many different types of hall each year under the auspices of this organisation. Problems of economy and expanding student numbers were common experiences for all wardens in the 1950s. In 1957 the conference delegates were told of the latest type of hall in Europe, residences where supervision was absent. The Warden was dismayed to find that

> it was assumed that students were fully-fledged adults and no provision was made for anything so old fashioned as a warden; there was no division of the sexes and no attempt at any collegiate atmosphere. The only unit seemed to be the floor and this was more from the cleaners' point of view than the students'... Residents ate in the restaurant on the ground floor or cooked their meals upstairs if they preferred... I enjoyed the discussion which followed but came away feeling that we were luckier in Belfast than we, perhaps, fully appreciated.[10]

At the conference the view was put forward that the increase in numbers was 'no justification for the diluting of the traditional life of Halls', and the solution should be that they be reserved for 'a student aristocracy which should be selected on academic merit. In that way character could be trained with academic ability'. Miss Dawson pointed out to the governors that this form of elitism had never been promoted by the management of Riddel Hall where 'we have tried, rather, to strike a balance between those who appeared most to need what we have to offer and those who might be expected to make the best contribution to community life'.[11]

In 1968 Miss Dawson visited Queen Margaret Hall, Glasgow, which was hosting the conference of the Association of Wardens, Principals and Advisors. (This was one of the institutions Miss Duffin had contacted to share information on rules, terms and conditions of staff etc. in the 1930s.) Queen Margaret's had been transformed from the original Hall, a 'small segregated unit in an adapted house', into a 'large tower building forming part of a complex of residences for men and women'. The Warden was retiring in 1969 to be replaced by 'a man administrator'. Miss Dawson feared that the way things were going conventional halls with 'anything as ridiculously archaic as a Warden' would be a thing of the past and non-catering study blocks 'would be the pattern for the foreseeable future'.[12]

Throughout the last twenty-five years of the Hall's existence financial problems were an increasing cause for concern to the Warden and governors. From the beginning of her time in office Miss Dawson was against raising students' fees unless all other avenues had been explored. 'One wonders if the present generation of students is not enjoying more than their share of the Miss Riddels' bounty but on the other hand one hesitates to raise fees to the point where our places might not be in such demand as at present.'[13]

Fees had been raised in the summer term of 1952 by 10 shillings a week for a single room and 7s 6d for a place in shared rooms. Miss Dawson saw the 'derationing of meat' in 1953 as a mixed blessing; it provided some relief for Miss Boyd in planning meals, but it was 'unfortunate that it will have quite the opposite effect on the monthly bills'.[14] Miss Dawson pointed out to the governors that the unusual credit balance at the end of 1954 'was achieved by a Crippsian austerity due to what I now believe was a mistaken conviction on my part that anything was preferable to raising fees again'. In retrospect she felt that 'watching every penny destroys the community spirit in a place like this. It leads to a ranging of residents and management in opposing camps and to a highly infectious grumbling on both sides, out of proportion to the grievance'.[15]

Former students remember Riddel's management as being 'penny pinching', very keen on thrift and operating a 'make do and mend' policy. In the early 1950s fees were lagging behind the increasing costs and the annual expenditure was higher than income. As a result of this deficit and considering that an increased proportion of students were in receipt of scholarships the Permanent Committee felt justified in raising fees in 1958 to £120 per thirty-week session. The quantity of food at lunch, and on Sundays, must still have been rather meagre as students

Girl studying wrapped in a rug. The rooms were not warm!
PRONI (D/3119/5/7)

suggested replacing the sweet course by steamed pudding. They filled the gap by eating 'white bread, which satisfied the appetite for only a short time'. One student remembers being served a single sardine in a pancake, and another remarked that 'sausages would have been a meal'.[16]

Every former student, with one exception, remembers the cold in the Hall. In the 1950s, Thelma Hutchison said, 'on a winter day you came in from outside and the cold in the Hall hit you'. Bree Sawh recalled the rush to the library after the evening meal to get closest to the fire:

> We all fought for that place. I would go early in the mornings to get the seat. It was a big room with tables; we sat with our rugs wrapped round our legs. There was an old fashioned servants' bell in the wall beside the fire, and we rang the bell when we wanted more coal. Mary or Lily would come in with a coalscuttle full. It was a different world, a different era.

Students from the 1930s to the early 1960s remembered the rugs that they had to bring with them to the Hall; one recalled that her mother had made her a dressing gown from the same material. Margaret Mitchell said that in the depth of winter the girls wrapped hot water bottles inside the rugs to keep themselves warm.

Sandra McMaster remembered her sister bringing coal from home to augment her allowance. Elizabeth Lyons, who came to the Hall in 1948, had complained so bitterly to kind friends about being cold that their son, who worked on a farm,

> arrived with a load of wood in a Land Rover and dumped it at the front, not quite at the door. Miss Dawson was not very impressed. She said 'This must be shared.' Everyone took some wood, and then they brought it back to me. We had lots of wood. I put some extra in to the lower drawer of my chest of drawers. The wood was green, the drawer swelled, and I couldn't get the drawer open! [17]

Past students looked back with nostalgia to the days when they had coal fires in their rooms. Many students lit their fires only two or three evenings each week when they invited friends into their rooms; on other evenings they returned the visit. A domestic revolution occurred in 1954 when the coal fires were replaced by electric fires. This led to more comfortable rooms for students who could augment their weekly ration of fuel with sixpences put into the meters. In 1965 Mildred Proctor wrote that there were several sought-after bedrooms where the 'fire sticks' (i.e. the meter became stuck) and the lucky owners basked in unpaid-for heat. Others maintained that there was no dramatic change in temperature. The fires were 'two bars set into the fireplace' and Thelma Hutchison recalled that despite wearing multiple layers of clothing it was still difficult to keep warm. On one occasion she set her dressing gown on fire trying to keep warm. 'It was very healthy; we used to say that the germs died going from one to another.' Everyone remembered enjoying good health while staying in the Hall; the sick room was used infrequently.

Electric fires must have been a relief for the domestic staff who had had to clean out the fires in more than forty rooms each day. A side effect was that 'curtains and covers no longer dangle in coal buckets'. It was a mixed blessing, for the houseman 'freed of his coal heaving', took over the washing of the corridors. It was a blow for one of the domestics whose services were dispensed with as a result. Some years later Thelma Hutchison visited her younger sisters in the Hall. 'When I went in there was heat; I couldn't understand it!' Central heating was installed in the early 1960s.

Several strategies were employed to balance the Hall's finances. During vacations when students were absent from Riddel, conferences were held which brought in much-needed revenue. To cope with the ongoing increase in demand for residential places in the early 1950s the accommodation in Riddel Hall had been stretched from the original forty-two places to sixty-five. In 1951, only six freshers could be accommodated. Miss Dawson went so far as to move from her

Study bedroom *c.*1963. The rooms were shared by several girls
PRONI (D/3119/5/7)

own bedroom to a smaller room; her original large room was converted to make space for three students. The creation of more accommodation not only provided 'a few more heads over which to spread the ever-increasing general expenses' but also allowed some students from the waiting list to enter Riddel.[18] Because of Riddel's popularity the governors had considered extending the Hall to accommodate a further forty-five to sixty students. In 1955 it was estimated that this would cost approximately £60,000, which worked out at £1,395 per student place. There would also have to be an investment of £10,000 for furnishings etc. The Chairman of the Permanent Committee, Professor Newark, argued that because of high interest charges the Hall could not afford the extension.[19] A more limited project, which would add twenty places at a cost of £32,000 was not considered to be viable.[20] These projects were shelved indefinitely and the building officer's task dealt with minor repairs rather than large schemes.

The popularity of Riddel Hall continued throughout the early 1960s and past students committed themselves to raising money so that their daughters' generation would share in the advantages of communal life which had meant so much to them. In 1961-2 Miss Dawson updated the records of all 808 past residents. They were all contacted with appeals for financial assistance, however modest. The Silver Jubilee year of 1963 was devoted to a multitude of fund-raising activities in order to 'modernise the Hall'.

Past and present students have combined in the pursuit, not of happiness itself, but of the funds necessary to promote and maintain it. The quarry so tirelessly chased was, of course, the £25,000, target of the Jubilee Appeal. To nearly all of us, at the outset, it seemed a mythical figure, representative of the needs of the Hall, perhaps, but a Goliath beyond the power of our David's sling.[21]

The agenda for modernisation included the kitchen, rugs for the floor, and beds – most of which still had the original hair mattresses. Characteristically a poem was written in honour of the jubilee celebrations, in the usual turn of phrase.

> For fifty years a happy throng
> Of students has enjoyed its bliss.
> But its finances now are wrong,
> It soon will be quite penniless.
>
> Its costs are rising year by year,
> Inflation rears its ugly head.
> And, to the Governors, it's clear
> It's very nearly in the red.
>
> The rugs are worn, the curtains old
> (They've seen 800 students pass).
> But that's not half the troubles told,
> The heating system's done – alas!
>
> New central heating's 'de rigeur'.
> We shiver, on a wind-swept ridge,
> While (irony of being poor)
> We can't afford to buy a fridge.
>
> We try to keep our charges low
> And all our students are assisted
> From our Endowment Fund. We know
> That is as the Miss Riddels wished it.
>
> The Governors make a public call
> To everyone, to raise a new
> Endowment Fund to save the Hall,
> Twenty-five thousand pounds will do.
>
> Let not Miss Riddel's open hand
> Be followed by our tight closed fist.
> But let us show to all the land
> A truly fine Subscription List.

The proceedings began in 1962 with formers students organising a very successful bridge drive and various coffee parties. The most important events planned for 1963 were a jumble sale, and the 'select' Jubilee Ball on 9 November for which a single ticket would cost 35 shillings. The 'great switch-on' of an efficient central heating system at a projected cost of £6,000 was planned for that evening. Every student's room had at least one radiator and all the public rooms had one or two extra. Miss Dawson announced 'We have, at last, proper heating. What a difference that has made!'[22] A memorial service to the Misses Riddel in Rosemary Street Presbyterian Church and a Grand Fête were both to be held in June. A cookery book was produced with recipes contributed by previous students. By October 1963 £10,000 had been raised and the fund 'was by no means closed'.[23] The final sum was almost £20,000 and as a result Riddel was able to remain open for a further ten years.[24] The benefits of the Jubilee year were both financial and social. The editorial of the *Jubilee Chronicle* pointed out, that 'In working together with fellow Riddel folks of other generations many of us have made new friends and all of us have renewed that corporate spirit which so bound us together when we were in residence in the Hall'.

The 1960s were a time of ideological change.[25] Traditional hierarchical relationships were called into question; a marked decline in deference resulted in an atmosphere of anarchy.

In May 1968 events in Paris and in Britain 'inspired hope of an alliance between students and young workers'. Students occupied their universities and demanded a 'more democratic relationship between students and teachers'. The more radical challenged 'the authoritarian knowledge factory', which they believed served the interests of military and capitalist systems. There was widespread reaction against American involvement in Vietnam and the Peace Movement attracted a substantial following.

Traditional gender roles were no longer accepted without question during the 'swinging sixties'. Young women who dreamed of being guerrilla fighters resented being sent to make the tea for 'budding revolutionaries' and only permitted to type anti-authoritarian leaflets. Ideas about women's liberation began to travel internationally. The American women's movements, in drawing attention to the limited opportunities for women in all walks of life, found resonance in many western countries. As Sheila Rowbotham expresses it:

> Arguments for rights, claims within society as it was, were converging with the idea of liberation which came from a new left vision of social transformation. Not just a transfer of political power or economic ownership but the democratisation of all relationships in society seemed possible in the late 1960s.

Another social revolution occurred in the 1960s as traditional sexual moral standards became more relaxed. The contraceptive pill first became available in 1961. The *Readers' Digest* prophesised 'one vast, all-pervading sexological spree', but more than a decade later 63 percent of British women did not have sex before marriage. In Northern Ireland it still remained daring to speak out in public about sex and contraception. Contraception was difficult to obtain for young unmarried girls, and the social pressure to get married lost little of its influence for many decades. Nevertheless, as Juliet Mitchell pointed out, because of the availability of widespread and reliable contraception child-bearing had become 'an option'. For the first time motherhood was made 'totally voluntary'; taking the pill resulted in 'a complete disassociation of sexual from reproductive experience'.

Professor Alwyn Williams, Secretary to the Academic Council, Pro-Vice-Chancellor of Queen's University and governor of Riddel Hall in the 1960s, saw similar changes occurring in Northern Ireland. Amongst some students, 'there was a sense of disrespect which I fully understood, that students felt they had to strip the mystique from structured authority, but there was another foundation to this which I disapproved of, because it was becoming loutish in parts'. The President of the National Union of Students from 1966 to 1968, Geoff Martin, found that

> there was a desire among students to enquire more deeply, and a greater degree of hostility to established values and institutions. Careerism, which was frowned upon, was also an element based on the need for people to succeed their own qualities, and on the basis that 51 percent of the vote actually meant something. There was no feeling of consensus – 51 per cent meant you won, 49 per cent meant that you lost.[26]

A former Riddel student, Honor Gray, remembered that as early as 1959:

> Rag Day was completely out of control. Students went into businesses, It was like 'trick or treat'– 'if you don't give us money in our collection boxes we will...' – and went in and out of schools laughing at the kids and disrupting classes. Some men students took a mini and lifted it over a metal fence and set it in a front garden. This was all in one day; the pieces had to be picked up afterwards. A lot of shop windows were decorated for the event. It was a typical Rag. Students sold *Pro Tanta Quid* magazines and collected money. The parade passed the hospital in Shaftsbury Square, and the nurses came out. It ended at the bombsite downtown where the University of Ulster Art College is now.

The Warden lost her enthusiasm for the tradition as years went by and students' stunts became more radical. The night before Rag Day in May 1961 there must have been some rather rowdy behaviour. Miss Dawson told the Permanent Committee that

Making fudge for the Jubilee Fête 1963
M. Gowdy

she would like to make a protest about the liberties taken by certain of the men students during the night prior to Rag Day. She thought it reasonable to ask that Halls should be declared out of bounds on this occasion, or that Rag Day should be confined to the actual day. The tradition was growing that the night before Rag Day was a time when students were exempt from penalty and free of all responsibility for their behaviour. They were not under the control of the Student Representative Committee and wore no identity discs.[27]

By complaining to the Chairman of the governors Miss Dawson was addressing Professor Newark, Secretary to the Academic Council, which had the ultimate authority in disciplinary matters. Unruly behaviour by students continued, and in March 1966 D.G. Neill, Professor Newark's successor, wrote to the President of the Students' Representative Council reminding them, 'as in previous years, that both Riddel Hall and Aquinas Hall are *private* premises. They are not part of the university. The... invasion of these Halls or their grounds will constitute a serious breach of the regulations governing Students' Day'.[28] The following year this message, which must have fallen on deaf ears, was reiterated in stronger terms.

Throughout the 1960s students' antics on Rag Day, while raising large sums of money for charity, became increasingly outrageous, daring and unpopular with the general public. For example in 1964 'the citizens of Belfast were perturbed by the sight of six-foot high black letters "PTQ" painted on the dome of the City Hall'. *PTQ,* the student publication containing risqué jokes which was sold to raise money, attracted a steady stream of complaints from 'enraged letter writers'.[29]

In 1964 the Senate decided to allow a beer bar in the new Students' Union and Malone Sports Pavilion. The decision precipitated numerous protests from churches, presbyteries and temperance societies, of which the Senate took note, but carried on regardless.[30]

There were inequalities in society which needed to be addressed. The Northern Ireland Civil Rights Movement gained momentum. From 1968 onward a campaign of protests and marches was supported by many students and some staff. Many people, 'not only nationalists' felt that there were 'genuine grievances to be redressed'. In October 1968 about 3,000 marchers including twenty university staff converged on the City Hall to stage a three-hour peaceful protest. This subsequently led to the founding of the political pressure group, the People's Democracy, which 'accepted a six-point reform programme broadly in line with Civil Rights demands'. Although the People's Democracy had its origins in the Students' Union at Queen's it 'developed a life of its own beyond the university'.[31]

All these changes had an effect on Queen's students who no longer accepted that the University should have parental authority over them. In early 1969 the Committee of Deans met with the Students' Representative Council of the Students' Union. At this meeting the students 'requested that Queen's should cease acting *in loco parentis*'. The response was that 'as a general principle, the Deans supported the view that the concept of *in loco parentis* is no longer valid'.[32] The following year the age of majority in the United Kingdom was reduced from twenty-one to eighteen. For the first time the great majority of Queen's students had reached adulthood before entering the University. It was inevitable that Riddel residents should share the beliefs pervading the wider student body.

18

The Final Decades

Miss Dawson, when looking back over the old records, felt Miss Duffin's remarks remained evergreen. Miss Duffin had written in 1915, 'it was clear that if residents valued their comfort they intended to lose none of their liberties'. Fifty years later her protégée found the remark 'equally applicable to-day. If, from time to time, I think I notice a new trend among students, I have only to read Miss Duffin's reports to discover it is not new after all'.[1] She had herself as a young student signed a protest about the quality of the lunches.

> I am sure that I was often enough a heretic but there was in my nature and upbringing a good deal that subsequently if not then responded to this influence and, looking back now, after 25 years in office, I feel sure that I was in the tradition. If not so exacting on myself or my flock, I still wanted to set and require good standards in this house.[2]

Miss Dawson concluded sadly that the honourable traditions espoused by Miss Duffin were no longer accepted by the majority of students in the early 1970s. She tried to comfort herself. 'Wardens must be prepared to move with the time and not allow themselves to become fossilised, even if they feel that the movement is at times retrograde.'[3] Miss Dawson's inability to follow her own advice possibly contributed to the demise of Riddel Hall.

While students in the 1950s and even in the early 1960s had challenged traditions seen as outdated, they largely accepted Miss Dawson's authority and enjoyed the communal life offered by Riddel Hall. As Bree Sawh said, 'We gave honour where honour was due; we never challenged her. Whatever the rules were we went with them, and that created harmony'. Even if Miss Dawson appeared unreasonable students believed 'she was within her rights, in all fairness, it was her role'. Several women resident in the Hall in the late 1950s and early 1960s felt that theirs was the last generation to accept authority unquestioningly.

In 1969 the *RHOSA Chronicle*'s regular 'Riddel Hall News' update began with the statement: 'Despite all the student riots, Riddel Hall is still standing'. The edition included an article describing an anonymous student's perception of life in the 1960s addressed to the previous generations of Riddel girls. It was entitled 'You don't know how lucky you are'.

> How many RHOSA mothers have said this to their student daughters? But do they realise what they are saying? Today, when student revolution is sweeping the world and governments shake in their shoes at the mention of a student protest, I'd like to put in a plea for us poor students... We were born into a world that has gone mad and we're simply involved in a search for sanity. If we're guilty of anything it's that we are still crazy enough to be idealistic. We can no longer accept a world divided into black and white or orange and green, with the appropriate colour on top. Starving children leap at us from every paper we open and the caption underneath tells us that we are responsible. We feel guilty yet helpless. We have been taught that our neighbour should be loved and that all human beings deserve equal respect. We simply want to put these things into practice. Truth, to us, is not an abstract idea for discussion; it is something we have to live out. Much has happened in Queen's over the last year that has given the word student a bitter taste. I am neither defending nor criticising – I am simply trying to explain. We are trapped behind the label 'student' – wondering what this strange word means. We have been educated to think for ourselves and to criticise – yet when we apply our talents to the society we live in, the results are terrifying. We too are afraid of the extremist elements – both in our society and in our university. We recognise that extremism in any form is dangerous and that a punch-up on the streets of our city creates nothing but fear and bitterness. Yet we are also deeply concerned about the sickness of a society that creates such extremes... We have been asking for leadership from those we respected. None came and so we have been forced to become the leaders. We have been forced to take a stand. I can't explain why we care so much or why we feel responsible. It's a heavy burden to carry – but no one seems willing to take it from us. Caring has led to

crucifixion before now. We know that we have come to university to learn. We are here to prepare ourselves for the place we shall take in society, yet this is no longer as simple as it was. The student of today is compelled to ask the question – 'In what sort of a society shall I be taking my place?' We have more freedom than our parents ever had. The possibilities open to us are bigger, the whole world lies before us – but so too do its sorrows. I don't know if this makes us luckier than our parents – but I have a feeling that it demands more of us.

Riddel Hall is an example of the way in which traditional power structures were dismantled in wider society. Its wardens saw the Hall as a large family where every one knew their place and things ran smoothly. It became increasingly apparent in the late 1960s that the traditional regime could not adapt to irreversible cultural changes. Even in the 1950s a small, but increasing number of students moved into flats after a couple of years. Thelma Hutchison thought of doing the same but her 'parents would not have countenanced it'; anyway, the routine of the Hall was convenient. A decade later many parents did not have the same level of authority over their daughters. Students' attitudes towards authority were changing and the 1960s was an increasingly difficult time for Miss Dawson. In 1966 she told the governors:

'A chill wind coming from the west'; Miss Dawson's view of the new Halls of Residence being built by the University at Beechlands, Malone Road, seen over her rockery at Riddel
Riddel Hall Archive

One is dealing with much more adult and more independent students. When they have realised this fully and are less on guard over new-won rights, it will be pleasanter all round... Now that the young people's revolt has been recognised in the home and victory conceded, another noticeable change has come about. Whereas the student was formerly often glad to escape from the straightjacket of home to the comparative freedom of the Hall, the trouble is now to keep her from returning home too regularly.[4]

The 'News of the Hall' for 1965 pointed out that there was a 'strong first year student drive to dispense with Hall life altogether'; they preferred to travel from home or take a flat. To keep pace with this new liberty in the home Miss Dawson decided in 1967 that students should have their own door-keys. 'I don't expect that this will alter our way of life but the psychological effect may be significant.'[5] This move would have seemed inconceivable to earlier generations of students.

When the University's accommodation service became centralised in 1967 the students themselves filled in the request form, entering their requirements and preferences. This marked the official demise of parental authority over students. Typically Miss Dawson saw potential problems with this change.

It is interesting, from my point of view, that whereas the old application form for Hall residence had the signature of the parent or guardian, the new form does not. What, then, is the warden's responsibility towards parents and how far should parents be consulted in cases of student discipline or other problems when, perhaps, the student concerned expresses the wish that her parents be not informed? I'm glad to say that as yet these are purely academic questions here but they indicate that more and more the student must be prepared to be the master of her own ship.

By the late 1960s Riddel was becoming less popular among students. In the academic year 1966-7 the Hall had its biggest ever turnover of students with forty-four changes in a comparatively short time.[6] Miss Dawson decried the situation.

It used to be the rule here that students who were lucky enough to get in were very glad to be able to keep their places till the end of their university course. In recent years there has been a noticeable change in attitude among the younger students. To stay in one hall for all of your course is no longer regarded as being loyal to a particular community but just as being stick-in-the-mud and students come up with the idea of sampling different ways of life and of staying one or two years only.[7]

The new attitudes were not simply a consequence of social diversity amongst the student body. Riddel Hall residents continued to be overwhelmingly middle-class, grammar school educated young women who had been prefects, if not head girls.

They were also active in extra curricular activities such as sports, drama, debating and literary societies as well as the Scripture Union. They were members of their congregations' youth clubs, sang in church choirs and very often were involved in Sunday school teaching.

Nevertheless, the close-knit family atmosphere of Riddel was becoming increasingly eroded. In the 1968-9 academic year the desire for autonomy and informality coupled with staff shortages led to its residents becoming 'do-it-yourselfers'. Students made their own breakfast on Sundays, and the serving of lunch on weekdays was discontinued. A rota of students answered the door and phone from 5 p.m. onward.[8] Miss Dawson admitted that this new regime seemed popular, as the number of returning students was high.[9] Several students who had not placed Riddel Hall as first or even second preference on their application forms must have been pleasantly surprised by life in the Hall, as they returned there for subsequent years.

As the 1960s gave way to the 1970s Miss Dawson began to lose all hope. The last three years of the Hall's existence, at least in the official record, appear to have been characterised by an inevitable and terminal decline. Students no longer accepted her 'parental' authority and the old familial community seemed to be deteriorating before her eyes.

The Hall had once been 'a body on its own which governed itself and looked after all the different facets of such an establishment'. The House Committee was central to its smooth running although, 'of course Miss Dawson was in the chair at these meetings'. The falling numbers of students willing to participate in the House Committee by the late 1960s contributed to its declining influence. In the context of house politics (where only students who had been resident for a year or more could vote) the short-term nature of students' residence must have been very disruptive. It is easy to see how depressing this was for Miss Dawson who remembered the way the committee once played a role in developing a sense of community. Bree Sawh pointed out that during her time in the Hall 'if there were any conflicts within the house, the House Committee discussed them. They played a very important part in preserving the harmony of the place'.

In the heyday of Riddel, house meetings were attended by the entire student body. Sub-committees organised hockey or tennis matches, the Entertainment Committee was in charge of the annual dance and the hops, the Library Committee enthusiastically chose new books and periodicals. It is significant that despite very careful maintenance of records in general the House Minute Book from 1964 onwards is missing. A book listing all House Committee members begun in 1924 has entries up to 1967; 1966 seems to have been a rather lean year with only a President and a Secretary named and no members listed.

The library
N. Duffin

Seetar Seeterram, a Trinidadian student, spent six years in Riddel Hall and was Head of House during this period. Private correspondence between her and Miss Dawson paints a more cheerful picture.

> How are you? With regards to feeling positively ancient – on the contrary – you are very young – for age should be judged by one's attitudes to change, and no one can say otherwise of you – on this subject – on the whole we appreciated your exercising of caution in changing the house rules for example, for change is not the criterion, but a change for the better.[10]

By 1971 house meetings struggled to attract any participants. Attendance put individuals 'at risk of election to one or other committee and that in turn leads to further chores'. The beleaguered Miss Dawson reported sardonically, 'better not to join the establishment, so that one can without compunction drop an iron, burn out a kettle or flood the laundry floor and go off, leaving the joy of discovery to another! Macauley put it in a nutshell – "The business of everybody is the business of nobody"'.[11]

In 1972 she told the Permanent Committee she was 'perturbed by the general lack of will to accept or implement regulation of any sort', even when rules were 'propounded by students themselves and passed, without dissent, at a house meeting'. Gladys Williamson (1970-73) was Head of House in 1973. Her perception of the role was that 'it was mostly a Public Relations job making sure that all the first year students were integrated, looking out for them, dealing with problems within the rooms – people who did not get on were moved – making sure the kitchens ran OK, making sure everything worked'. In the past these tasks would have been performed by the Matron.

The counselling and disciplinary duties of the House Committee were also a relic of the past. Miss Dawson believed that the committee suffered from the same inevitable decline as did the Hall in general. In 1973 she told the governors that 'the student committees were notable only for a masterly inactivity'. The following year the behaviour of two members of the House Committee was deemed to be unacceptable by the Warden and she told the governors that she 'wished to ask them to withdraw'. They agreed that the students should be given a week's notice to leave the Hall.[12]

Even the standards of tidiness demanded by Miss Dawson for students' rooms were a contentious issue. Gone were the days when Miss Boyd felt it was her place to 'scribble' in the dust on students' desktops. In 1970 the Warden had a delegation of 'mostly first year' students 'asserting their right to live as they chose in their own rooms'. Miss Dawson explained to the governors that the cleaners had not been able 'to get round their allocation of rooms because of the untidiness of certain students which gave them extra work'. She insisted on her right to require a minimum standard. This 'storm in a teacup' appeared to have blown over for the time being'.[13]

The increasing use of alcohol may have played a part in the decreasing formality of social events. Very few 'former students remember any alcohol being brought into the Hall in the 1950s or even the early 1960s'.[14] One recalled that if 'you had wanted to have a drink, you would have had to go somewhere else. There was no alcohol in Riddel, none at the formals'.[15] In 1960 the Riddel formal turned into what Miss Dawson called an 'unattractive and undignified occasion',[16] and problems with the dance continued in subsequent years. Miss Dawson told the Permanent Committee that 'several uninvited guests had partaken of supper' at the event held in December 1969. She thought 'it would be a good idea to drop this function for a session and substitute a Christmas supper for the whole house, perhaps also for RHOSA'.[17] Maybe Miss Dawson felt that she could rely on the support of old friends and colleagues when faced by a large number of students in a social situation where she was not in control.

In February 1972 the minutes of the Permanent Committee recorded there was 'no further interest in a hall dance'. In December the following year the 'dance which the students had proposed had to be cancelled because of lack of support from the residents'. A Christmas dinner had been put on in its place. Nevertheless, in 1973 there was a ball 'with a Grecian theme'. This was the last elegant event to be held in Riddel Hall. Miss Dawson appears to have been most enthusiastic, as Gladys Williamson recalls,

> We said could we do that – get all dressed up and bring partners? And the warden had replied, 'well, of course... you can have the run of the whole downstairs, whatever you want' and the Old Students came in and did all the catering. The entire dining room was set out with food, the lounge was cleared of furniture for the dance, we had some sort of band. I thought it was gorgeous; we all came down the stairs in our big dresses.

In 1972 Riddel Hall became 'mixed' not only in the more cosmopolitan sense, but also in the peculiar Northern Ireland sense. The governors had expressed different opinions on the advisability of this change, which was first discussed at the 1970 Annual General Meeting. One member thought that while there was sufficient demand from Protestant students, 'it would be hard to show grounds for wishing to change the conditions of the bequest'. The clerk of the Presbyterian General Assembly, the Reverend Jack Weir also thought 'it would be difficult to satisfy the courts merely on the grounds of a changing climate of opinion'. Mr Nicholas Duffin, with a great degree of foresight, 'wondered whether, in the event of the Northern Ireland government bringing in an anti-discrimination act, our memorandum might not offend against its terms'.[18]

By June 1971 the governors were agreed that the Memorandum of Association should be changed and that Mr Donald Murray, a senior counsel, should be engaged to deal with the issue 'even if this meant additional expense'. The case was heard in February 1972. Mr Justice McGonigal 'made an order permitting the deletion of the word "Protestant" from the relevant clauses in the articles but had not allowed the plea for deletion of "female"'.[19] The limiting words 'Protestant' and 'female' in the original Memorandum had both become unacceptable in early 1972. Miss Dawson argued that

> the Miss Riddels wished to do something to help students and if they qualified their foundation by 'women' and 'Protestant', it was because this was a category for which no one else was doing anything, at that time. It has always surprised me that because we were founded for Protestants, it should be assumed that we were, ergo, anti-Catholic. We were founded for women. Is it to be presumed that we are, therefore, anti-men? The second presumption seems to be as relevant as the first, which, nevertheless, everywhere tarnishes our reputation in the university and sets us apart.[20]

The sweeping staircase at Riddel. The telephone was situated under the stairs
PRONI (D/3119/5/7)

The opening up of the Hall to Catholic students did not lead to a rise in applications. In June 1972 only thirty-one students in total had registered. In the academic year 1972-3 Miss Dawson found:

> It was something of a surprise to me that the change in our Memorandum so quickly resulted in a quite well-mixed house and it is a very hopeful augury for the future that the mixing has apparently made no whit of difference to the atmosphere and has caused, so far as I can see, not so much as a ripple in our domestic pond.[21]

The same cannot be said for an article in *Gown*, written by Kathleen McKay on 24 October 1972, entitled 'It's All So Nice', which scathingly analysed several types of accommodation provided for Queen's students. The author argued that 'having available accommodation might be the key to the fostering of those attitudes which enable us to sink into comfortable bourgeois complacency never seeking to question values, organisation of the very existence of certain types of establishment'.

Riddel Hall

From the tall imposing blocks of Queen's Elms one can see the magnificently situated Riddel Hall. A rather grand mansion, it stands removed from the rest of the world, a relic of bygone years. One wonders if it produces people to match. Standing in spacious tree covered ground, equipped with tennis court, hockey field, and the usual amenities, it is an indomitable fortress.

Endowed by two 'staunchly bigoted' Unitarian sisters, it equips 70 girls for what seems to be a narrow and secluded life.

The size of the house could present some administration problems, so it is run by a House Committee with meetings once a month. The library which is well stocked is also run by a committee. There is no choice in meals and they are all taken at the same time. Each girl has to perform door duty at least once a month in the manner of concierges at old-fashioned hotels (to make sure only the right people get in). The boarding school manner of life is augmented by the numerous pictures of wardens resplendidly [sic] lining the walls: the old fashioned furniture adding to the effect. The long cheerless corridors seem cold and unfriendly at first, but most of the girls seemed happy, accepting the values proffered and questioning little.

High turnover

It has a high (over 50%) number of returning students and these are obviously satisfied, as 'Riddel has all the amenities any student would wish to have', yet one girl having been there for four years seemed to sum up the life at Riddel: 'Guests are out by 11.00 p.m.; the rules say so... of course we could keep guests in if we really wished to, but nobody wants to'. She was 22 years old. Perhaps that is the whole danger of such places; the unquestioning acceptance of rules. The strict Protestant only rule was abolished last year but it will be a long time before the sexually rigid standards are relaxed.

Miss Dawson drew this article to the attention of the Permanent Committee at their next meeting. They felt that it was 'up to the students to write a letter of protest for publication in the next issue'. The Warden said that the students had 'indeed been indignant at the inaccuracies in the account and at the image given to the Hall'. The student who had been 'misquoted' in the article had made a verbal protest to the editor, who appeared to shirk responsibility by saying that 'he published what his reporter laid on his table'. The Permanent Committee agreed that it would be best for them to maintain a dignified silence or 'take no notice'.[22]

Gladys Williamson distinctly remembers this incident. 'It stirred us all up; ten or fifteen of us went down to complain.' Thirty years on she pointed out the injustice of the article's assertion that the building was a relic of the past and so were those who inhabited it.

That really, really, annoyed us. If you look at the building of Queen's, an old building, are you going to say the people who go there have old ideas? Or Oxford, Cambridge, St Andrews or any of them? It prepares women for a narrow and secluded life? We just thought it was so insulting to us. If you thought of those two women, from a wealthy background; they could have done anything with their money, they could have bought themselves houses, clothes, anything – but they took it upon themselves to do something for women students, pretty decent, a huge place, and the best of everything in it; not just built shabbily or anything like that. We thought it was dreadful and about ten of us went down to *Gown* offices and really protested.

The following week *Gown* published 'a sort of a slight apology'. The student quoted in the article was also annoyed at the way the reporter portrayed her. 'She had been tired and was very offhand with him.' The *Gown* reporter went

to Aquinas next and they likened us to them, said it was a similar set up etc. Of course the girls there were just as mad, though I don't think they went down to the Union the same way as we did... The editor was apologetic but felt he had got a good story – 'see you are all roused up'. We said '*No*. We don't like the way you portrayed us, it is a brilliant place'.

J. Humbert Craig *Leenane*. This painting was acquired *c.*1930 and was hung in the drawing room
© J.Humbert Craig 2005 Queen's University Belfast

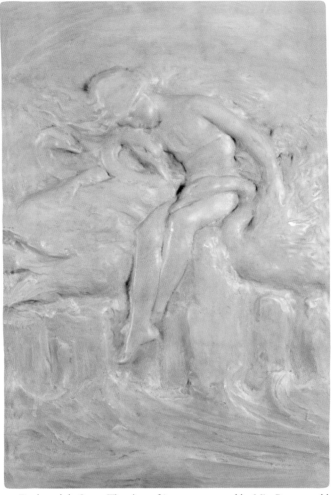

S. Rosamond Praeger *Finola and the Swans*. The plaster frieze was presented by Miss Praeger and hung in the library
© S. Rosamond Praeger 2005 Queen's University Belfast

The protesters invited the 'guys up to proper dinner to see what it is really like'.

> One of the guys did come up afterwards and I think he did feel differently about it. We took him to see the lounge – it was a fabulous room, we had chintz sofas, a TV, the fire was lit, and proper pictures on the wall – not just prints – water colours and oil paintings. There was this other wonderful plaque by Rosamond Praeger, and the wood panelling. Why would you want to knock this? And yet it has been adapted for life, it is here in the trendy wonderful seventies. We are working here, and we love it, it is fantastic and it is fun.[23]

Gladys Williamson thought that the reporter was rather embarrassed and that *Gown* printed a retraction the following week; however, she has not kept it and she and her friends did not buy the publication again. She felt 'that the harm had been done'. Indeed the Riddel students thought the attitude of the young men in the *Gown* office was distinctly anti-feminist.

> These guys were so laid back – so what's the problem girlies – that type of attitude. We said we don't like it, we felt we were standing up for women. Don't you dare speak to women like that! Are you are trying to say that because women all live together in one big place that we have to have men in all the time? Their whole attitude was wrong to us; we were women there for an education. This was a hall of residence, in which we were very privileged to be – it was just wrong.

There was thus a fundamental difference in opinion here. The article suggested that the Riddel girls were bound by old-fashioned rules and attitudes, but their view was it was the men of *Gown* who were behind the times. Women were asserting the right to education and career opportunities on equal terms with men and demanding the right to choose independence from men in the social sphere.

The adverse publicity had its effect. Having defended Riddel so strongly, the students came to feel more attached to it. Gladys Williamson recalls that they said from their hearts, 'No! You are wrong, this is a great place to be'. The repressive image created by the article was unfair. At the time students were able to have parties in their rooms, and frequently did so. There was no problem about this as long as the hostess told her neighbours in advance and showed consideration as far as noise was concerned. The girls also invited young men into their rooms as long as they left by 11 p.m.; this was not, however, rigorously policed. It was a place where the 'normal student activities took place'.

In interviews with past students of earlier decades the subject of bringing boyfriends back to the Hall was raised only once. One ex-student recalled that in her time – the late 1950s – it was only the very odd one who would have considered bringing a boyfriend back 'after a dance or something... it just wasn't done. That was the society in which we lived. It was before the days of the pill. When the pill came in, things would have been different. Then, permission was not required for anything'. As Bree Sawh pointed out 'the introduction of the pill changed the whole social structure of society'. In those days parents wanted to know if Riddel Hall would provide a safe, protective environment for daughters; now, parents would ask whether the Hall would give them the opportunity to experience unbounded freedom.

Miss Dawson felt that it was hypocritical to pretend that visiting hours were limited when in reality she had no real control over the comings and goings of guests. The Permanent Committee thought that it was important to enforce the regulations and 'promised support for the warden if she required persistent offenders to withdraw from the Hall'.[24] With up to seventy residents it was difficult for Miss Dawson to ensure that all non-residents left by the appointed time. In 1973 the students asked the Permanent Committee that the 'present limits on visiting hours at the Hall' be removed. Their argument was 'that there was no way of enforcing a limitation, which was in fact being ignored by some students'. The committee refused, arguing that 'students agreed to a package deal when they accepted a Hall place and could not opt out of a regulation when it pinched them personally'. For persistent non-cooperation in this matter a student was to forfeit her place.[25]

Miss Dawson was torn between reluctantly accepting that for present-day students 'the individual has superseded the community; each must be free to do her own thing', and her desire to live up to Miss Duffin's legacy. She quoted the final words of Miss Duffin's Chronicle: 'my dearest wish for the future of Riddel Hall is that it may play its part in helping students to have a right standard of values'.[26] The heart of the problem as Miss Dawson saw it was that while Miss Duffin approved of freedom of thought, conscience and opportunity, her concept was heavily overlaid with thought of duty. '"Trouth and honour, fredom and curteisye" as Chaucer had it. She would have understood the thought process, which moved Burke to pronounce: "Freedom is the cure of anarchy"'. The present Warden felt that freedom was no longer associated with taking up responsibilities or with dedication to duty:

> But today this statement seems to be the very reverse of the truth. The 'uncharted freedom' so eagerly sought by today's young people leaves ageing wardens perhaps too ready to shake their heads and raise admonitory fingers, too apt to agree with Burns that 'Freedom and whiskey gang thegither'.[27]

The Warden was concerned about the way she should present herself to the students. She wrote a Latin phrase on some scrap paper left in the records: '*justus esto et non metui*', which she translated as 'be honest/or upright/or merciful rather than one to be feared'. Like Miss Duffin she did not desire to be a despot feared by the girls, but wished to lead by example, hoping that if she trusted them to behave in an honourable and ladylike way they would do so. This may have worked in the 1890s in Cheltenham Ladies' College, and to a degree in Riddel until the 1950s, but not the 1970s.

Nevertheless, during her time in Riddel Hall Gladys Williamson found Miss Dawson to be a very capable Warden, competent, and a great believer in manners and politeness.

> I think she was very good at her job. She did not seem a totally caring person, but if there was a problem, and one went to her to explain it, she would be very understanding and sympathetic. She was like a lot of people who have done a job for a long, long time; she was good at it. If one knew the right words and the right way to handle her she was fine... Miss Mills, the deputy warden, was a bit more 'laid back'. I just remember seeing her about.

Miss Dawson could rally round in a crisis. In the early 1970s two students had to face the death of their parents and Miss Dawson rose to the occasion. 'She was brilliant, she had a wonderful way of saying just the right thing, and being so mannerly about it, and so in control.'[28] The role played by Miss Mills seems to have been a very minor one compared to that of her predecessor, Miss Boyd,

Constance Bradshaw *Landscape with Farmhouse*. This painting was acquired *c.*1930 for the sum of eight guineas. It was hung in the front hall of Riddel (see photograph page 169)
Queen's University Belfast

whom the students thought of as a second mother. The live-in domestic servants of the past are remembered by past students with affection, and many of them stayed in the Hall for years. By the late 1960s there were sporadic shortages of domestics. Lily Gaston's successors either stayed only a short time, or were unsuitable; others did not wish to live in the Hall, and in the early 1970s they were replaced by part-time domestic help. The governors were becoming increasingly concerned about the difficulties in recruitment and retention of affordable staff.

> The governors are conscious of the fact that they depend heavily on a conscientious and loyal staff who have been with the Hall for a long time and who give devoted service for small financial recompense. This position could quickly change and indeed must change within the next few years when the present warden retires and the gardener and the houseman, who has done a lot of repair work and redecoration and has recently had a coronary, are no longer fit to carry on. There can be little doubt that there will then be a very substantial increase in costs.[29]

Changes such as these, combined with different student lifestyles, led to the need for the governors to look to the future. Although Miss Dawson could not explain how or why things went wrong, the 1973 household 'never properly cohered'. Other problems included,

> illicit borrowing and abuse of Hall property, petty pilfering upstairs, noisy late visitors, an unwillingness to comply with even the simplest regulation for communal living, these things kept us in a state of irritation which prevented us from achieving our usual happy family atmosphere. We had among our numbers one or two problem children and one who was seriously mentally disturbed and who became an ever increasing burden until she was asked to withdraw at the end of the second term.[30]

This account indicates that Miss Dawson still drew on the analogy of the family to make sense of relationships within Riddel Hall, but for most of the students, this idea, like Riddel's other traditions, was an anachronism. By 1973 the Hall was, Miss Dawson observed sadly, 'at the bottom of the popularity pole'. Even though it took fourteen Stranmillis College students, there were only fifty-six students in residence. Every year fewer young women put Riddel down as their first choice at the centralised accommodation service. While trying to identify the reasons for this decline in popularity Miss Dawson wrote,

> Today, institutions are out, age is not honourable, segregation is ridiculous and anything remotely suggesting privilege or class, anathema. I have said before that buildings have a way of determining what goes on in them and certainly

our building and our setting have played a dominant role in our way of life. I do not doubt that the young girl of today has no trouble in accepting our persistent and prevailing image, namely a rather superior, high-minded, well-behaved sort of place.[31]

She was also aware that students from Northern Ireland, as a consequence of the 'Troubles', student grants and the UCCA system, were increasingly likely to 'go elsewhere in the UK for their higher education'. Nevertheless, some 'Riddelites' still loved the Hall, accepted the Warden's values, and were very happy there. In Miss Dawson's opinion the old community spirit, so characteristic of the Hall in the past, and central to the experience of old students, had disappeared. However, Gladys Williamson believed there was a really good community atmosphere: it was a very happy place.

The records of the Hall include the following letter written by students, dated only 30 October, addressed 'to whom it may concern' and concluding with PUBLISH OR BE DAMNED. Mention of the Ulster Workers Council strike dates it as 1974. It demonstrates the strength of feeling the authors had and their appreciation of the Hall.

With reference to the Student Handbook's Guide to accommodation, we would like to express our resentment at the gross inaccuracies stated concerning Riddel Hall. Contrary to popular belief it is not purely a Protestant Hall. In the past years Riddel has befriended Jews, Buddhists, Roman Catholics, Atheists, Vegetarians and even Stranmillis girls. It is also rumoured that there are a few Prods lurking about!! Yes, Riddel is a beautiful building, set in spacious landscaped gardens, with a wonderful view of Alanbrook and Livingstone.[32] (What a view!*!) As regards 'restrictions', the rules are made by the student body itself for the benefit and consideration of everyone. And, believe it or not, we can even have male, yes, MALE visitors in our rooms. Further libellous statements were made concerning food. The food is NOT spartan, in fact, the contrary. At least our food is cooked properly – Elms take note. No deaths from food poisonings have been reported yet! In fact our food is so popular it has even been stolen!! (Have Elms taken note??) We would also like to point out to the student population that Riddel ate while the rest of the campus starved during the UWC strike. As a final word Riddel boasts many facilities viz: laundry rooms, several kitchens for student use, as well as a hairdressing room and a well stocked library. On the recreational side, there is a large common room, a record library and a table tennis room, while outside we have a secluded tennis court (anyone for tennis?*!!), and a hockey pitch/jungle. Before you all rush to move in here – TOO LATE! – the Hall is full, and there is a waiting list.
Yours (ANYTIME!*?*!),
'The young ladies' of Riddel Hall.

This letter is especially poignant, as the Hall closed at the end of the next academic year. Miss Dawson's report recorded that there had been a much greater demand for places at the beginning of the new academic year, and all seventy places were filled. However, only forty-two of these were Queen's University students: the others were students at Stranmillis College and the Ulster Polytechnic (now University of Ulster). Unfortunately, the mixed population did not 'immediately settle down in peace and harmony together'.

> Each year the difficulties over double rooms increases. In addition, over the years most of the room keys have gone missing and new students do not feel able to trust other residents any more. In the end we had to have new keys cut for our mortise locks, to restore confidence and enable the house to settle... I was interested in this reaction to a security problem. My generation of students would have set about getting rid of the anti-social members for a means to protect individual property, which would seem to point to the demise of the ideal of a community. More and more, life here is centred on the individual rooms upstairs and the common rooms are half deserted.[33]

External security had also become an issue for the first time. In 1969, a young man 'of student age had been seen upstairs, unaccompanied, one afternoon'. Several students later found that sums of money and pieces of jewellery were missing. The House Committee thought that this could be the first of many such incidents and recommended that the front door should be kept locked.[34] Other male intruders entered the Hall on two occasions early in 1970, although nothing was reported missing. Students began to realise that as Gladys Williamson recalled, 'anything could have happened'. The front door had been locked and, as students took it in turns to answer the bell, the intruder must have known the name of a student to say he was going to her room. Miss Dawson reiterated the necessity of keeping the front door locked.[35]

19

The End of 'Ould Daecency'

The effects of financial measures instigated in the early 1960s were successful only in the short term. By 1971 the governors admitted that 'the apparent strength' of the Hall's finances had to be attributed to 'once-for-all economies introduced by the warden'. These included cutting out weekday lunches and weekend meals, which permitted the replacement of full-time by part-time staff, reduction in pension provision, reorganisation of the garden so that it could be managed by a retired gardener on a part-time basis and the postponement of redecoration and renewal. 'These have had the effect of delaying but not eliminating the impact of rising costs.' The impending retirement of key members of staff including Miss Dawson and the gardener was a cause for serious concern; the houseman had had two heart attacks and Miss Mills had been absent owing to family responsibilities. Replacements of the same dedication and calibre would be difficult or probably impossible to find. The Permanent Committee found that 'the possibilities of holding expenditure in check have now been exhausted, and that the financial position could in the present inflationary situation rapidly deteriorate'.

In the short term the assets of the Endowment could maintain the Hall. Investment income was received every year from stocks and shares purchased by the Permanent Committee over the sixty years of the Hall's existence. Examples include the Quebec Central Railway, British Transport, Bass Charrington, Equities Investment Fund for Charities, Gallagher's Tobacco Ltd and War Stock. In 1970 the year's income from these sources was £2,230 and in the last year of Riddel's life as a hall of residence it had risen to £3,513. The importance of the Misses Riddel's decision to endow the Hall as well as providing finance for its construction cannot be overemphasised. It was argued that *prudence and good management demand that the governors should be able to take whatever steps seem appropriate to ensure that the main object of providing a residence for students and staff can be carried out.*

The Jubilee Fund, which stood at £16,000 in 1970, was used to pay for new equipment required for the Hall. But this source of income fell in years to come as many donors had covenanted sums of money for a period of seven years only.[1] In the financial year 1964-5 income from the fund had been £1,597. Several women wrote to Miss Dawson in the early 1970s apologising for not renewing their covenanted donations because they had retired or because of other commitments. The Jubilee Fund significantly declined in the next decade. By 1975 the income from the appeal including investments made from the proceeds in ICI, Charifund, NI Electricity and London County had fallen to just under £525. In 1970 the auditors reported that Riddel's income had gone up by 'about £100'; however expenses had risen by £1,000.

In 1970 it was necessary to raise the term fee from £50 to £65 per student. Subsequently fees were subject to an annual increase until in the 1974-5 session the fee was £90. The annual income from students was £10,926 for the 1970-71 session and £15,930 in 1974-5. The early 1970s was a time when prices for all goods and services rose abruptly due to rising oil prices. Rising costs and the effect of inflation meant that real income was declining. When coupled with Riddel's faltering appeal to students from the late 1960s onward, management's financial policies proved ultimately to be a failure.

There were other reasons for the financial difficulties. The large building had not been designed with economy in mind and heating bills were a perennial problem. Maintenance of the Hall which was sixty years old was urgently required; for example on a day of high wind and lashing rain a maintenance officer found some of the rooms to be 'practically awash'. He stated that very little could be done with the present window frames and recommended that one or two of the worst examples should be replaced.[2] The cost of replacing all the windows, which would eventually become necessary, was beyond the capacity of the Hall's financial resources.

A winter view of Riddel Hall and its grounds, showing their extent
Riddel Hall Archive

The problems were compounded by the loss of revenue from conferences, which had brought in substantial sums of money in the past. This source of income could no longer be relied upon by the late 1960s because organisers were opting to use the new student halls, which had been built with conferences in mind. Riddel's rooms were too few in number and too small in size for the larger conventions of the time.[3]

The rates bill was a major drain on the Hall's income and many Permanent Committees had unsuccessfully attempted to gain exemption from this expense. In 1970 the Queen's Elms Halls had been granted exemption on the grounds that they were university premises.[4] Riddel Hall was private property and its liability for rates made it increasingly difficult for the Hall to maintain parity with the Elms when it came to setting fees. The rates bill was the largest single invoice received by the Hall. In 1969-70 the payment due was £1,946. This had dramatically risen to £5,109 in the 1974-5 session.

The governors believed that the 'natural approach' to resolving Riddel's problems would be to 'work out some scheme with the university'.[5] Several schemes had been considered in the early 1950s to extend the Hall but they had been shelved because of the cost. In October 1970 a sub-committee of the governors and Miss Dawson met with representatives of the University to discuss the possibility of building accommodation for postgraduate students on the site of the hockey pitch.[6] Miss Dawson agreed that the 'ample green space' would be ideal for married students with children and the proposed accommodation would be used all year round rather than the less economical 30-week year of the Hall.[7] The *raison d'être* of the Hall would be fulfilled; the University would be charged a 'peppercorn rent' and in return would maintain the grounds. However the governors 'might be reluctant to split up the land and perhaps diminish the value of the whole by the development of the part'.[8] The Memorandum of Association limiting residence to female students and teachers would have to be changed to admit the spouses of married postgraduate students.

The ten acres of ground, which had once been seen as an asset, was rapidly becoming an expensive liability.[9] The hockey pitch 'was not much used' for its original purpose and was no longer maintained. Miss Dawson had 'from time to time' given permission to men from the new Alanbrooke and Sinton Halls to play football on Sunday afternoons. However by 1971 groups of men 'came, as of right, whenever they chose'. One Sunday in February two groups arrived at the same time and one of them set up a game on the front lawn. Members of the public 'were in the habit of exercising their dogs in the Hall grounds'. As in the case of footballers, a concession had been made and then abused. A 'well-defined dog pad now ran all the way along the grass verge bordering the avenue and paw-marks, etc., were everywhere in the garden'.[10] In 1971 the head gardener estimated the annual cost of maintaining the gardens at £2,500. The hockey field and wood were valued at £22,000 (rental value £1,800) and £1,000 (rental value £50) respectively. The governors thought it unlikely that Queen's would agree to lease the grounds in their present condition.

A meeting of the Permanent Committee on 11 November 1970 considered investigating the legal position if the 'governors were to seek to wind up the corporation'. Other avenues were to be explored before such a drastic move was made. The Chairman, Professor Norman Cuthbert, thought it was time for the Board of Governors to 'consider whether to investigate the possibilities of complete integration with the university'. The long-awaited exemption from rates would be a consequence of this move.

In 1971 Mr Nicholas Duffin recommended that an approach should be made to the University 'at a higher level' to clarify the Hall's relationship to Queen's if the limiting word 'Protestant' were removed from the Memorandum. Riddel Hall was the only body associated with the University where any religious test was exercised. In 1972 the Protestant exclusivity of the Hall ended, thus eliminating any hindrance to a closer relationship between Riddel and the University.[11]

In May 1972 the governors applied to the courts for remission of rates, but the application was refused. This was a serious blow since the rates arrears was now £1,377. An appeal was lodged against this decision. But worse was to come. The appeal was heard eventually in March 1974 and 'dismissed with costs to the respondent'. Riddel Hall was defined as being residential, rather than 'an establishment providing direct teaching'. Other Queen's Halls were also 'soon to be rated'. The governors reluctantly decided to 'let the matter rest'.[12]

This disappointment further pushed the governors toward full integration with the University.[13] By December 1973 various sub-committees of the governors and the University had come to the conclusion that Queen's should purchase the 'whole property', the only problem being that 'it was not easy to find the capital sum for such a large investment'.[14] Negotiations with the Ministry of Education were commenced in the hope that the cost of purchasing the Hall would be met by the government. In March 1974 no formal offer had been received from the University and the Chairman thought it would be reasonable to limit their approach to Queen's to one year. The committee 'thought it would without a doubt sell very well on the open market'. Rising costs, including 'giant leaps in the cost of electricity etc.', caused difficulties when setting fees for the following year. At least one member of the committee made the unpalatable suggestion that the students could be dispensed with for a while, but 'the committee rejected any thought of maintaining the Hall for a time without residents'.[15]

In September 1974 an Extraordinary General Meeting was held to consider the current and future financial position of the Hall and the Trust. It gave powers to the Permanent Committee to conduct negotiations for the disposal of Trust property and to consider how the objects of the Trust could best be carried out. It concluded that as provision had been made in the Memorandum of Association for the dissolution of the Trust, it was possible for the Board of Governors to dissolve itself and sell its assets to the University as an appropriate institution with similar objects to the Corporation.[16]

It was decided at the meeting that the Articles of Association could be altered 'in such a way as to make the University the main trustee, with possibly a small number of added members to the present Board'. The University would be bound by the present Memorandum of Association. 'It would have full control over the land, buildings, and investments, with the obligation to use the income and property of the Trust for the provision and maintaining of residences for women students of the University.'[17]

In November 1974 the University's report on the viability of Riddel Hall as a university-administered centre of residence concluded there was little demand for accommodation of the type currently provided by the Hall, and that the University could not hope to manage the Hall profitably as a conventional hall of residence. It was thought that, by spending over £20,000, the University could operate the Hall as a self-catering unit, but a subsidy from other areas of accommodation would be necessary if a deficit were to be avoided. A modernisation scheme costing over £70,000 (or £800 per resident), could provide accommodation for 90 students but all rents in university accommodation would have to be increased by £6.00 per annum to subsidise the scheme. If the University Grants Commission insisted on the University repaying the cost of purchase of the Hall from rents, no scheme to use it for residential accommodation would be viable.[18]

Negotiations between the governors and the University continued throughout the winter of 1974-5. The University was promised finance from the Ministry of Education and the parties eventually agreed a sum of £232,000 as the property's value. The University did not believe that the existing building could be adapted for modern students' needs at a viable cost, and they intended to lease it to the Arts Council of Northern Ireland for the time being.[19] It was decided that modern purpose-built halls should be built using the assets of the Riddel Hall Corporation 'as far as possible in the way intended by the original bequest'.[20] The governors and the University agreed a rental value of the property for the period between the sale of the Hall and the end of term at £17,000.[21] On 12 March, with funding secured, it was agreed that the legal documents would be signed on 17 April, although the location of a new Riddel hall of residence had not been finally decided.[22] The Chairman of the Board of Governors, Professor Cuthbert and appropriately, Nicholas Duffin, Managing Director of John Riddel and Son Ltd, ordinary governor, representative of the Riddel family and relative of Miss Ruth Duffin, signed the conveyance on behalf of the Board.[23]

By the time of the May meeting of the Permanent Committee the sale was completed. Members had been informed and the minutes record that 'no comment had been received'. The Hall's staff were to be given notice of termination of employment as it would close at the end of June. Miss Dawson had provided a 'farewell dinner' for the students, which was held on 12 May. The students had made a 'little presentation' to the Warden on this occasion.[24]

In her final annual report Miss Dawson wrote:

> I spent a good many years here trying to uphold what my old warden always called 'proper values and right standards' until I finally realised that I was condemning myself to the fighting of endless rearguard actions, doomed in advance to failure, at the same time giving to the Hall the image of being the last bastion of what might be called 'ould daecency'.

It is significant that 'ould daecency' was the term Miss Duffin used to describe the generosity of the Misses Riddel. We can see from Miss Dawson's words that Miss Duffin was her life-long mentor and that she had run the Hall in the tradition which her 'old warden' had established. She also recognised, with deep regret, that times had changed and the Hall in its original form was no longer viable.

The opening of new Riddel Hall by Miss Molly Duffin. Nicholas Duffin is second from right.
The comparison between this building and the original Riddel Hall can be seen
Riddel Hall Archive

Students were 'stunned' when they heard that the Hall was closing down. They felt that perhaps something more could have been done. 'It was a shame.' Miss Dawson had to inform the Old Students' Association that the Hall was closing for students at the end of the academic year.

> Miss Dawson then went on to speak about how the changing social pattern had affected life in the Hall in recent times. It was an age of moving out of the big family house into a smaller apartment more easily managed with a minimum of service. The time had come for Riddel to do the same.

At the last meeting of RHOSA to be held in Riddel Hall before it ceased to be a hall of residence for female students more than fifty members attended. On this 'memorable, if sad occasion' the Chairman, Dr Bartley, one of the first Riddel students, said that she was glad that the good weather would ensure that 'everyone could take away a pleasant memory of the grounds even if the process of dissolution had already begun in the Hall'. They were also able to purchase items of the Hall's furniture, which were auctioned at the end of the meeting. Many students took this opportunity to take away memories of their first home away from home.[25]

The 1976 *RHOSA Chronicle* included an article entitled 'The Last Term'.

If readers imagine that this final term must have been sad beyond measure and poignant in the extreme, they are wrong. Energies were required for other things. The students had their exams to think of and also arrangements to make for their accommodation in the new session. Governors and warden had arrangements to make for the great evacuation which was so soon to come... Compensations there were, of course. One remembers the many bouquets from the silent majority of departing students at last rendered vocal, the kindness of Governors, and many helping hands – those of Mary (Irwin) Logan and Enid (Roulston) Trotter in particular, the many funny contretemps which occasioned the good laugh, the return of many an old student not seen since her graduation and above all the constant support of the staff.

The anonymous author was probably Miss Dawson. She handed the keys over to Kenneth Jamieson, Director of the Arts Council on Monday 4 August 1975, just over sixty years after the Hall had been first declared ready for residents by the builders.

In November 1976 the site for the new Riddel Hall at Beechlands, Queen's Elms estate was approved by the University Senate, and it was agreed that there should be a Riddel Hall advisory management committee that would be consulted on 'non-routine matters'. This body included one of the relatives of the late Misses Eliza and Isabella Riddel or former governors, a person nominated by Riddel Hall Old Students' Association and one nominated by the Queen's University Women Graduates' Association. There was to be a Warden 'or similar person preferably drawn from the staff of the university in any residential accommodation that the university may provide under the terms of the primary trust'. Residential bursaries would still be available for qualified students.[26]

The new Hall was built to provide accommodation for fifty-nine students, in the form of self-catering units for six students. The official opening was performed in October 1979 by Miss Molly Duffin, the youngest sister of Ruth Duffin. The new trust deed made it possible to cater for both men and women. Nicholas Duffin pointed out that 'Riddel Hall is still very active behind the scenes, and will soon be ready to enter the next phase of its history'.[27] A past student, who had also been a governor, expressed the feelings of all. There is nothing to add except regret that the experience of such a 'belle epoch' is no longer desired by, or available to, students.

Riddel Hall is dead – long live the new Riddel to which we look forward, eagerly and anxiously. Whatever the future holds for its successor, Riddel Hall will be remembered for its wonderful achievements during sixty years of life (1915-75). It welcomed in new students each year – girls at one of the most important stages in their development, straight from school, often gauche and immature. They were absorbed into a community imbued with the spirit of friendship, trust and responsibility. It was an enriching and a maturing experience. No wonder we look back to our days at Riddel as some of the best we have known.[28]

E. Murray

POSTSCRIPT

During the summer of 2004 while the final draft of this account of Riddel Hall was being written the new Riddel Halls were demolished as part of the accommodation renovation programme of Queen's University.

James Allen, *Riddel Hall* 1988
When the Hall closed as a hall of residence, the Arts Council of Northern Ireland rented the building
from Queen's. At that time the Belfast Print Workshop was based in the old kitchens where this
picture of Riddel was produced

EPILOGUE

RIDDEL HALL: AFTER THE LADIES

by Marcus Patton

When I started work with the newly formed Hearth Housing Association in 1978 I was told that I would be setting up office in either the Crown Bar or Riddel Hall. The Crown, recently acquired by the National Trust who had no immediate plans for its upper floors, and Riddel Hall, taken over by the Arts Council but not being used to full capacity. Sir Charles Brett was Hearth's chairman and had strong connections with both the other bodies. No members of Hearth's committee were teetotal objectors to holding committee meetings in snugs at the Crown, but as it turned out it was to the Ladies' Hall that Hearth moved.

At that time the Arts Council under the benevolent leadership of Kenneth Jamieson was using Riddel not as mere offices but also as rehearsal space, art gallery and sculpture park, and there was a variety of peripheral organisations like Hearth and the Ulster Architectural Heritage Society who made use of the remaining rooms in the large building. At half-past ten every morning the gong was sounded and people in the offices above decanted down to the common room to discuss the day's events and plans. Literature officers chatted to their counterparts in the visual arts, and writers, painters and musicians joined in the debates. As a mere architect, but one with a strong interest in the arts, I found this mixture heady and fascinating.

For the rest of the day, the common room might be used by visiting artists, as rehearsal space before their performances with the Ulster Orchestra, running through pieces accompanied by the Arts Council's grand piano, or it might be used for seminars of artists or local authority arts committees. The former library was the main meeting room where the Arts Council's committee and its various sub-committees deliberated. The previous dining room was the schools gallery, showing the best work in art from children around the province. A stream of children was bussed in to see the exhibitions.

In those days most of the Arts Council's officers were practising artists in their field, as were many of the committee members. While that might have led to some criticism of favouritism or amateurishness, it also made the building seem like a real centre for the arts, with a sense of enthusiasm and bonhomie. Michael Longley, Brian Ferran, Brian Ballard and Philip Hammond were only some of the well-known artists who had daytime jobs in Riddel. The booming singing voice of the writer John Morrow could be heard echoing up the back stairs as he made his way back to his office, while Ciaran Carson seemed to spend much time in his office practising his traditional flute. The Arts Council was a regular purchaser of paintings at local exhibitions, and while much of the collection was stored in a locked room on the ground floor or distributed on loan to other buildings, many works were hung on the capacious walls of Riddel.

The Endhouse Print Workshop, subsequently the Belfast Print Workshop, was based in the kitchens of Riddel Hall from 1977 to 2003; visual artists were literally producing work in the building under the watchful eyes of Jim Allen and his wife Sophie Aghajanian. For a while Cherith McKinstry had a painting studio in the attic. The print workshop's annual Christmas show in the hall and common room saw the building leap into life with holly and ivy drawn from the greenery of the grounds, a blazing log fire in the great fireplace, and the smell of mulled wine and mince pies.

Until the move to their own rehearsal and office space at the former Elmwood Church, the Ulster Orchestra's administration was based in Riddel, as was that of the Studio Opera Group, and later Opera Northern Ireland. Theatrical companies benefited from the expertise of other staff members who helped with grants and stored an array of spotlights along the back corridor between productions.

At first the grounds were well maintained, the lawns kept trim and the extraordinary bank of laurel hedge at the front drive cut neatly to waist height and kept free of weeds. A pair of wonderful flowering cherry trees shed pink petals every spring over the steps alongside the tennis court, and a large hawthorn dominated the front lawns like an ancient fairy tree. Younger members of the Arts Council staff used the tennis court in the summer, and the cinder path around the grounds was lined with sculptures commissioned or purchased by the Arts Council (the best loved probably being the bronze shepherd and sheep that now stands in more urban surroundings at the Waterfront Hall). Further down the slopes towards the Vice-Chancellor's lake was a massive tree used as a swing, the ground beneath it worn bare from generations of children's feet starting and stopping their pendulations. The vegetable garden still had an impressive clump of rhubarb, and the orchard gave abundant apples.

Gradually the grounds became overgrown. Billy Burns worked hard to revive them when he became the building's caretaker, but a single gardener was hard pressed to keep the gardens under control, let alone bring a semblance of order to the rampant ivy and weeds of the further reaches. Rumours of Queen's University's intention to build in the grounds, and that the Arts Council was to leave the building, undermined confidence in undertaking any major work or maintenance that would bear long-term fruit. When trees fell across the path they rotted away *in situ*, and paths began to disappear under encroaching grass. The car park was extended towards the former hockey pitch. The University put greenhouses on the tennis courts. Lorries left vicious tyre marks on the verge of the drive.

When the Arts Council moved out to Riddel's Catholic counterpart, Aquinas Hall (now known as MacNeice House), a few subsidiary organisations like the Northern Ireland Museums Council, the Print Workshop and Hearth were left rattling about in the otherwise empty building, but no doubt we helped to discourage the vandalism that might have homed in on a completely abandoned property. Eventually we moved to new premises, and Queen's University began to put the building to new uses. It is presently a useful temporary home to departments whose own premises are being refurbished.

The first such department was the School of Music. For a year Riddel was full of the sound of pianos being practised, the library became a store for percussion instruments, and orchestras and choirs rehearsed in cramped conditions in the common room. But there was some interaction between these musicians and the artists in the print workshop, so the building was lively again. Before the new Sonic Arts Centre was established in Cloreen Park its electronic equipment, that bridges the gap between music and science, was set up in Riddel. Since that time, Queen's has put more investment into the building, but it is still seeking its new permanent role. It is to be hoped that its value is now fully appreciated, and that the University will find a long-term use for the Hall which exploits to the full the dignified and spacious surroundings of the foundation of the Misses Riddel.

Marcus Patton

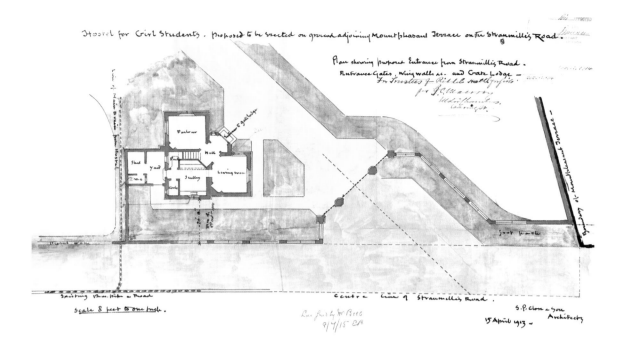

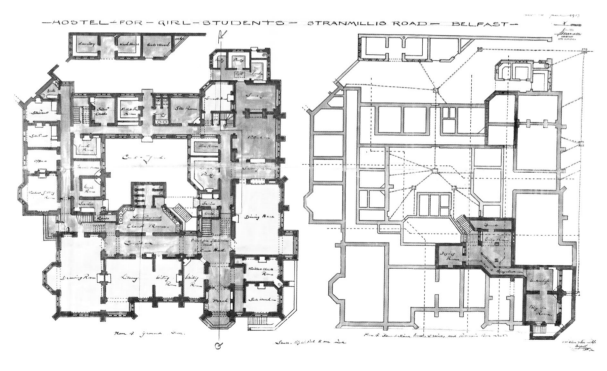

Original plans of Riddel Hall, dated 1913 and signed S.P. Close. The upper plan is of the gate lodge and the angled entrance from Stranmillis Road; lower left is of the ground floor, showing main rooms; lower right shows the basement and foundations
Belfast City Council, Building Control

APPENDIX

ARCHITECT AND BUILDING

by Marcus Patton

The long career of William Henry Lynn started very much in the shadow of Charles Lanyon, his original employer. Lanyon was the head of the firm and the architect known to clients, but there seems little doubt that Lynn provided many of the drawings and designs for buildings that went out under Lanyon's name. This was recognised when the firm became first Lanyon & Lynn, and then Lanyon Lynn & Lanyon.

Lanyon seems to have had strongly classical taste: the Italian Renaissance was the inspiration for many of his buildings such as Crumlin Road gaol and the Belfast Custom House. When it came to the design of Queen's University's main building (1845-49) the style of the Oxford and Cambridge colleges was the obvious source to use, linking the new red brick university with its more distinguished predecessors, and hoping that some of the glamour would rub off in the process. But it was Lynn who was more at home with the Gothic style, and almost certainly his designs that gave detail to the well loved 'Lanyon building'. The Old Library building alongside it, designed in the 1860s to look like a collegiate chapel, was Lynn's work using the newly fashionable Venetian Gothic style that John Ruskin had popularised. The use of stripey brickwork and stone is quite jazzy compared to the more straightforward Gothic of the Lanyon building, and it is particularly remarkable in that having started the building in the middle of Queen Victoria's reign, Lynn extended it nearly fifty years later with hardly a dropped stitch in the fabric.

Finished in 1913, the Old Library extension was one of Lynn's last buildings. His very last was Riddel Hall, completed only months before his death at the age of 87; the work was supervised by the firm of S.P. Close. (In fact, the drawings lodged with the Council for byelaw approval were all signed by Close, and the rather crude penwork is very different from Lynn's immaculate draughtsmanship.) The contrast between the exuberance of the Library and the austerity of the Hall is not therefore due to his age, and must have reflected the sober (or cautious) brief of the clients. The young ladies were not to be indulged with any fripperies but housed in a serious somewhat Scottish building in red brick and Dumfries sandstone. The mullioned and transomed windows and plain stone-coped shouldered gables, with simple buttressing between bays, refer to the collegiate tradition again, but there is no unnecessary ornament. The plan is broken up by sections that are recessed or set forward from the main block, and there is a first floor oriel window over the entrance porch. The roofline is enlivened by tall chimneys and the square attic turret which rises over one of the back staircases. In certain lights the building can look quite grim, but when warmed by sunlight and the caresses of Virginia creeper and wisteria that have grown up along its front elevation, Riddel is still dignified and also very welcoming.

No one likes to see a new building blocking their view, and it must have been quite disturbing to the residents of the exclusive cul-de-sac of Mount Pleasant when the three stories of Riddel were reared up to their south. Suitably softened by trees over the years, it has settled into its grounds, and the rear of Riddel itself enjoys handsome views over Mount Pleasant, and in particular the early Victorian Summerhill at the end of the street.

The visitor enters through a pillared gateway set at an angle to the Stranmillis Road. Just inside on the south side is a two-storey brick and stone gate lodge, built to an L-shaped plan in a style similar to the main building, but slightly less formal. The drive winds up through the entrance pillars, rising slightly to come to rest in front of the Hall. A narrower path follows round the sides of the building. The grounds were laid out with lawns to the front, the hockey pitch beyond hidden below a terrace, a sunken garden on the west, tennis court on the east, and the vegetable garden and orchard behind a wall to the north. Further west a wooded area falls towards the lake of what is now the Vice-Chancellor's grounds.

A view of the lake *c.*1975
N. Duffin

The plan of the building is simple, with the rooms arranged round an internal courtyard. The front porch with its unglazed openings, and the main communal rooms are ranged along the south-facing front elevation. The kitchens are on the east range, and still retain their large sinks and white-glazed walls, while on the back range are stores and larders. The outbuilding in the courtyard included a laundry and wash-house. On the upper floors were large bedrooms providing very comfortable accommodation for the young ladies, while the back attic housed the sick bay with a number of bedrooms isolated from the main life of the Hall.

Inside, red quarry tiles provide a sensible durable finish to the hall floor, the dadoes are timber panelled and the staircases of stone with metal balustrading and plain timber handrails. The hall fireplace is of creamy sandstone and contains a bronze plaque in memory of the Riddel sisters. All this is very reminiscent of another educational building by Lynn, Campbell College, which he completed in 1894; the same building contractors, Henry Laverty & Son, were responsible for both buildings.

Riddel Hall is not a spectacular piece of architecture – it never set out to be anything other than a decent solid and comfortable residence for young ladies whose sights were set on intellectual and perhaps athletic challenges. However it represents qualities of modest determination and care that are rare in modern buildings, and if properly maintained will give pleasure to many generations to come.

Marcus Patton

NOTES

Chapter 1. A Riddel Hall Chronicle

1 A poem written for the Jubilee Appeal in 1963.

2 J. Sangster, 'Telling our stories: feminist debates and the use of oral history', in *Women's History Review*, Vol. 3, no. 1 (1994), p. 5.

3 *Census of Ireland 1881*, part ii, *General Report*, HC 1882 lxxvi; *Census of Ireland 1901*, part ii, *General Report*, HC 1902 cxxix; *Census of Ireland 1911*, part ii, *General Report*, HC 1912-13 cxviii.

4 Mary E. Daly, *Women and work in Ireland* (Dundalk, 1997), pp 34-5; Myrtle Hill, *Women in Ireland: a century of change* (Belfast, 2003), pp 44-47.

5 Jane Lewis, *Women in Britain since 1945* (Oxford, 1992), pp 74-87.

6 Hill, *Women in Ireland*, p. 137.

7 Ibid.

8 Ibid., p. 177, quoting from a statement issued by the Northern Ireland Women's Rights Movement in 1975.

Chapter 2. Pioneering Women

1 M. Luddy, *Women in Ireland, 1800-1918: a documentary history* (Cork, 1995), p. 90; M. Vicinus, *Independent women: work and community for single women, 1850-1920* (London, 1985), pp 4-5.

2 E. Olafson-Hellerstein, L.P. Hume and K. Offen (eds), *Victorian women: a documentary account of women's lives in nineteenth-century England, France and the United States* (Stanford, 1995), p. 3.

3 L. Duffin, 'Prisoners of progress: women and evolution', in S. Delamont and L. Duffin (eds), *The nineteenth-century woman: her cultural and physical world* (London, 1978), p. 68.

4 C. Bolt, *The women's movements in the United States and Britain from the 1790s to the 1920s* (Hemel Hempstead, 1993), p. 162.

5 J. Kamm, *How different from us: a biography of Miss Buss and Miss Beale* (London, 1958), p. 96.

6 Maria Luddy, 'Isabella M.S. Tod', in Mary Cullen and Maria Luddy (eds), *Women, power and consciousness* (Dublin, 1995), p. 201.

7 *Victoria College Magazine*, July 1893.

8 *Belfast Health Journal*, Vol. 1 no. 3, April 1893, p. 37.

9 Isabella M.S. Tod, 'On the education of girls of the middle classes' (London, 1874), quoted in Luddy, *Women in Ireland*, p. 110.

10 A. Jordan, 'Opening up the gates of learning: The Belfast Ladies' Institute, 1867-97' in J. Holmes and D. Urquhart (eds), *Coming into the light: the work, politics and religion of women in Ulster, 1840-1940* (Belfast, 1994), pp 33-57.

11 Ibid., p. 38.

12 A. Jordan, *Margaret Byers, pioneer of women's education and founder of Victoria College* (Belfast, nd, 1992?), p. 13.

13 *Northern Whig*, 25 August 1875.

14 Luddy, *Women in Ireland*, p. 137.

15 Obituary of Anne Jellicoe in Journal of the Women's Education Union, 8 (1880). Quoted in Luddy, *Women in Ireland*, p. 137.

16 Rita McWilliams-Tullberg, *Women at Cambridge: a men's university, though of a mixed type* (London, 1975), p. 106.

17 *Northern Whig*, 26 August 1874.

18 *The Witness*, 16 Oct. 1874.

19 D.H. Akenson, *The Irish educational experiment: the national system of education in the nineteenth century* (London, 1970), p. 349.

20 Luddy, 'Isabella M.S. Tod', pp 201-2.

21 Quoted in T.W. Moody and J.C. Beckett, *Queen's, Belfast 1845-1949: the history of a university*, Vol. I (London, 1959), p. 277.

22 Moody and Beckett, *Queen's, Belfast*, Vol. I, p. 286

23 Brian Walker and Alf McCreary, *Degrees of excellence: the story of Queen's, Belfast 1845-1995* (Belfast, 1994), p. 32.

24 *Victoria College Magazine*, May 1891.

Chapter 3. Students and Suffragettes

1 Brian Walker and Alf McCreary, *Degrees of excellence: the story of Queen's, Belfast 1845-1995* (Belfast, 1994), p. 33.

2 *Census of Ireland 1911*, HC 1912-13, cxviii.

3 T.W. Moody and J.C. Beckett, *Queen's, Belfast 1845-1949: the history of a university*, Vol. II (London, 1959), pp 455-6.

4 *Queen's University Belfast, Calendar* 1915-16, p. 42.

5 *QCB*, Vol. XV, no. 2, Jan. 1914, pp 12-14.

6 As her Christian name is not given it is not possible to know if she was one of two Misses Thompson who entered Riddel Hall the following academic year.

7 *QCB*, Vol. XV, no. 2, Jan. 1914, p. 3.

8 This was the term used by the Duke of Abercorn at the graduation ceremony of the

first nine women to receive degrees from the Royal University of Ireland in 1884. M. Hill and V. Pollock, *Women of Ireland: image and experience c.1880-1920* (Belfast, 1993), p. 123.

9   *QUB Calendar* 1915-16.

10 Report of the Standing Committee of the Convocation of Queen's University Belfast, 18 April 1910.

Chapter 4. The Founding of Riddel Hall

1   Quotations from Miss Duffin's Chronicle are printed in italics. Subsequent references to the Chronicle have not been footnoted.

2   M. Hilton and P. Hirsch (eds), *Practical visionaries: women, education and social progress 1790-1930*, (Harlow, 2000), p. 40.

3   Alison Jordan, *Who cared? Charity in Victorian and Edwardian Belfast* (Belfast, nd, 1993?), p. 20.

4   Historical pamphlet describing the firm of Riddels Limited, published in 1935, Belfast Central Library.

5   Ibid., p. 10.

6   C. Dyhouse, *No distinction of sex? Women in British universities, 1870-1939* (London, 1995), pp 98-9.

7   The Senate as constituted in 1908 had a quota of two places for women, one for a graduate, Mrs May Hutton and the other a crown appointee, Mrs Margaret Byers, who died in 1912. She had been granted this position due to her services to women's education. Eliza Riddel (even though she was eighty-four years old at the time) was her replacement and qualified in the same way.

8   Dyhouse, *No distinction of sex?*, pp 91-4.

9   See *Hutchinson's Belfast and the Province of Ulster Street Directory, 1904.*

10 Brian Walker and Alf McCreary, *Degrees of excellence: the story of Queen's, Belfast, 1845-1995* (Belfast, 1994), pp 39-40.

11 *QCB*, Vol. XVII, no. 2, p. 17.

12 *Memorandum and Articles of Association of the Incorporated Governors of the Riddel Hall, Belfast*. Pamphlet, June 1913.

13 *Belfast Evening Telegraph*, 17 Jan. 1915.

14 T.W. Moody and J.C. Beckett, *Queen's, Belfast 1845-1949: the history of a university*, Vol. I, (London, 1959), pp 434-8.

15 Walker and McCreary, *Degrees of excellence*, p. 63.

Chapter 5. Miss Ruth Duffin

1   Adrian Rice, 'The lonely rebellion of William Drennan' in G. Dawe and J.W. Foster (eds),

The poet's place: Ulster literature and society (Belfast, 1991), pp 82-3.

2   Dorothy Gharbaoui, 'The Duffins', *Ulster Tatler* (1970), p. 31.

3   Riddel Hall Chronicle QUB Archive; Diaries of Ruth Duffin 1895-1901 PRONI D/2109/17/2-4; 1900-05 PRONI D/2109/6/5; Miscellaneous Duffin family correspondence 1895-7 PRONI D/2109/6/4-6.

4   J. Kamm, *How different from us: a biography of Miss Buss and Miss Beale* (London, 1958), p. 52.

5   M. Vicinus, *Independent women: work and community for single women, 1850-1920* (London, 1985), p. 172.

6   Kamm, *How different from us: a biography of Miss Buss and Miss Beale*, pp 54-5.

7   Diary of Ruth Duffin, 5 July 1898.

8   Kamm, *How different from us: a biography of Miss Buss and Miss Beale*, pp 115-6.

9   M. Hilton and P. Hirsch (eds), *Practical visionaries: women, education and social progress 1790-1930* (Harlow, 2000), p. 40.

10 Vicinus, *Independent women*, p. 166.

11 *Census of Ireland 1901*, HC 1902 lxxvi; *Census of Ireland 1911*, HC 1912-13 cxvi, p. 37.

12 *Victoria College Belfast, Centenary 1859-1959*; Newman, K. *Dictionary of Ulster biography* (Belfast, 1993), p. 83. Bea Grimshaw was born in 1870 and lived until 1953. The cousins do not appear to have kept in close contact.

13 Diary of Ruth Duffin, 14 July 1898.

14 Kamm, *How different from us: a biography of Miss Buss and Miss Beale*, p. 176.

15 Miscellaneous Duffin family correspondence Ruth to Maria, 19 May 1895, PRONI D/2109/6/4-6.

16 Quoted in Kamm, *How different from us: a biography of Miss Buss and Miss Beale*, p. 117.

Chapter 6. Early Days

1   Riddel Hall Archive, QUB.

2   C. Dyhouse, *No distinction of sex? Women in British universities 1870-1939* (London, 1995), p. 106.

3   Obituary of Miss Florence Irwin, March 1966 in Riddel Hall Archive, QUB.

4   Letter of appreciation on the death of Miss Florence Irwin 5 March 1966 in Riddel Hall Archive, QUB.

5   Minute Book of Incorporated Governors of Riddel Hall (IGRH), 13 June 1913, p. 41.

6   *Ulster Year Book* 1925.

Chapter 7. Contentious Issues

1   President's Address printed in Riddel Hall Old Students' Association *RHOSA Chronicle*, 1964, p. 10.

2   M. Vicinus, *Independent women: work and community for single women 1850-1920* (London, 1995), p. 147.

3   President's Address in *RHOSA Chronicle*, 1964, pp 10-11.

4   P. Tinkler, 'Refinement and respectable consumption: the acceptable face of women's smoking in Britain 1918-70', in *Gender and History*, Vol. 15, no. 2 (2003), pp 342-60.

5   These rules are not dated but are an early edition, PRONI D/3119/5/13.

6   Miss Duffin quoting from the minute book of the early House Committee, which has not survived; it must not have been kept with the rest of Miss Duffin's records which are all available.

7   *QCB*, Vol. XIX, no. 1, Feb. 1918.

8   Margaret Byers and her late husband had been missionaries to China in the 1850s.

9   *Annual Report of the President of Queen's College Belfast*, HC 1890, p. 77.

10 Letter by 'Paterfamilias' to *Belfast Telegraph*, November 1921.

11 M. Hill, *Women in Ireland: a century of change* (Belfast, 2003), p. 97.

12 Letter by 'Bystander' to *Belfast Telegraph*, November 1921.

Chapter 8. Warden and Matron

1   *The Spectator*, 21 June 1930, p. 1004

2   Personal correspondence between Annie Roden and Molly Dawson 1968.

3   Warden's report to governors' meeting 27 Nov. 1968.

4   *Belfast Telegraph*, 11 Feb. 1958.

5   J. Purvis, *A history of women's education in England* (Milton Keynes, 1991), p. 19.

6   Ibid., p. 118.

7   A. Woollacott, 'Maternalism, professionalism and industrial supervisors in World War I Britain', in *Women's History Review*, Vol. 3, no. 1, 1994.

8   This is included in Miss Duffin's first draft of her Chronicle written in a notebook.

9   Testimonial written by J.E. Lane-Claypon, Dean of the Household and Social Science Department, King's College for Women, London, 6 June 1923.

10 Letter from Miss Drennan to Miss Duffin applying for the post, 11 Jan. 1924.

11 Letter from Miss D.L. Hooke, D. Litt, Headmistress of St George's School, 19 Jan. 1924.

12 Minute Book Incorporated Governors of Riddel Hall, 1 Feb. 1924, p. 167.

13 CV sent to Miss Duffin by Miss Roper.

14 Reference for Miss Boyd written by Maude Herdman JP, Commandant of Strabane Auxiliary Hospital.

15 Letter from Madeline Boyd to Ruth Duffin, 6 Feb. 1934.

16 Reference for Miss Boyd written by Olive Herdman, Strabane, 12 March 1934.

17 Poem written in honour of Miss Boyd's twenty-first year in Riddel in *RHOSA Chronicle*, 1956.

18 Moira Strawbridge, recollections.

19 Elizabeth Mills/Smiley, recollections.

Chapter 9. In Loco Parentis

1   T.W. Moody and J.C. Beckett, *Queen's, Belfast 1845-1945: the history of a university* Vol. II, (London, 1959), p. 518.

2   *Frav-lio-Queen's*, No.2, May 1926, p. 7.

3   Moody and Beckett, *Queen's, Belfast*, Vol. II, p. 518.

4   *Ulster Year Book* 1921 and 1935.

5   The student's name and personal details are not included here for reasons of confidentiality.

6   Warden's annual report to general meeting, 1935.

7   Queen's University Women Graduates' Association Annual Report 1946 and Enid Roulston's student record.

8   On one occasion in the late 1930s the boot boy was stealing biscuits and in the late 1950s a student stole some money.

9   M. Vicinus, *Independent women: work and community for single women, 1850-1920* (London, 1985), p. 146.

10 Records of Riddel Hall, PRONI D/3119/3/2.

11 Letter from Margaret Mills to Ruth Duffin, 29 April 1940.

12 As student records are confidential personal name shave been omitted.

13 Letter from parent of Riddel Hall students, 24 April 1940.

14 Letter contained in student's record, Riddel Hall Archive, QUB.

15 Ibid.

16 This is discussed in more detail in Chapter 12.

17 Letter contained in student's record, Riddel Hall Archive, QUB.

18 Minute Book Incorporated Governors of Riddel Hall, 14 April 1926, p. 213.

19 B. Walker and A. McCreary, *Degrees of excellence: the story of Queen's, Belfast* (Belfast, 1994), p. 76.

20 Letter to Miss Duffin from Prof. Savory, 29 April 1929.

21 Letter to Miss Duffin from Prof. R. Galland, 15 Sept. 1926.

22 Letter in Mlle Mouzat's staff record, Riddel Hall Archive, QUB.

Chapter 10. A Vision of Culture

1 Warden's address to house meeting, Oct. 1929.
2 Warden's annual report to general meeting, 1924-5.
3 Tinkler, P. 'Refinement and respectable consumption: the acceptable face of women's smoking in Britain 1918-70', in *Gender and History*, Vol. 15, no. 2, 2003, p. 355.
4 Minute Book Riddel Hall House Committee, 9 May 1935.
5 Recollection of Moira Strawbridge.
6 Warden's address to house meeting, Oct. 1928.
7 Ibid., Oct. 1930.
8 This was probably the Drawing Room Circle, a women's literary entertainment group founded in Belfast in 1926.
9 No author's name is included.
10 Warden's address to house meeting, Oct. 1933.
11 Ibid., Oct. 1929.
12 Ibid.
13 Minute Book Incorporated Governors of Riddel Hall (MB IG RH), 9 April 1924.
14 MB IG RH, 10 Nov. 1937.
15 Warden's address to house meeting, Oct. 1930

Chapter 11. Citizenship

1 Warden's address to house meeting, Oct. 1931.
2 For Miss Beale's philosophical ideals on education see S. Raitt, *May Sinclair: a modern Victorian* (Oxford, 2000); J. Kamm, *How different from us: a biography of Miss Buss and Miss Beale* (London, 1958), pp 51-64.
3 Warden's report to general meeting, 1942.
4 Warden's address to house meeting, Oct. 1928.
5 Ibid., May 1933.
6 Warden's address to House Committee, Oct. 1928.
7 Warden's address to house meeting, Oct. 1926.
8 Warden's report to general meeting, Nov. 1933 and an article on Ruth Duffin and her family by Lisa Duffin in *RHOSA Chronicle*, 1988-9.
9 Father O'Flynn is associated with Irish folklore and ballads.
10 Warden's address to house meeting, Oct. 1928.
11 Ibid., Oct. 1925.
12 Bishop Creighton was a nineteenth-century Cambridge historian and Bishop of London.
13 Warden's address to House Committee, Oct. 1938.
14 Information on Deutscher Akademischer Austauschdienst website. The service was reformed in 1950 and still operates today.

15 Letter from Ruth Mayer, Mannheim, to Miss Duffin, 22 July 1938.
16 A. Owings, *Frauen: German women recall the Third Reich* (London, 1993), pp xxxiii-v.
17 Letter from Jemima Paul to Miss Duffin, 6 May 1935.
18 Minute Book Incorporated Governors of Riddel Hall, May 1938.
19 Warden's address to house meeting, Oct. 1938.
20 Ibid.
21 One of several letters written by Gudrun Weiler to Miss Duffin preserved in her student record, Riddel Hall Archive QUB.

Chapter 12. The War Years

1 Minute Book Incorporated Governors of Riddel Hall (MB IG RH), 11 June 1941.
2 Minute Book Riddel Hall House Committee (MB RH HC), Oct. 1939.
3 These letters are available in PRONI D/3119/2/8.
4 Letter from Isobel Coleman to Miss Duffin, 27 Sept. 1940.
5 MB IG RH, 14 April 1943.
6 Ibid., 12 Jan. 1944.
7 PRONI Education Leaflet 2, 'The Belfast Blitz'.
8 Warden's report to general meeting, 1941.
9 MB RH HC, Jan. 1941.
10 Warden's report to general meeting, 1941.
11 MB IG RH, Oct. 1941.
12 Warden's report to General Committee, 1942-3.
13 Letter from 'very much annoyed' mother to Miss Duffin, 7 July 1942. The student's name has been omitted.
14 MB IG RH, 9 June 1943.
15 Ibid., 13 May 1942.
16 Ibid., May 1942.
17 Ibid., 13 Jan. 1943. The papers were *The Times, Times Literary Supplement, Manchester Guardian, The Scotsman, Glasgow Herald, Irish Times.*
18 MB IG RH, 10 March 1943.
19 MB RH HC, May 1943.
20 MB IG RH, 30 June 1943.
21 Undated newspaper column in Riddel Hall Archive – likely date is July 1943.

Chapter 13. Miss Joyce Power Steele

1 Reference written for Miss Power Steele by R.W. Ditchburn Trinity College Dublin, (TCD) Physics Department, 11 May 1934.
2 Reference written for Miss Power Steele by the Principal of Alexandra College, Dublin, 8 March 1934.

3   Reference written for Miss Power Steele by J.V. Harcourt MA, Headmistress of Runton Hill School, 27 March 1938.

4   Ibid.

5   Reference written for Miss Power Steele by R.W. Ditchburn, 11 March 1934.

6   Report of Permanent Committee on Miss J. Power Steele.

7   Curriculum vitae of Miss Power Steele.

8   Letter from Miss Power Steele to Miss Duffin, 5 Nov. 1940.

9   Minute Book Incorporated Governors of Riddel Hall (MB IG RH), 12 Nov. 1941.

10 Telephone interview with Miss Power Steele, Nov. 2003.

11 Decisions on which students should leave the Hall to create vacancies, letter writing, taking minutes etc. were done by both women. In June 1943 the minutes of the Permanent Committee were written by Miss Power Steele. She had also been responsible for the analysis of the waiting list.

12 Typescript memories of Riddel Hall 1944-7, Mrs M.J. Faris (née Campbell).

13 Warden's report to General Committee, 1943-4. Miss Power Steele appears to have wrestled with the wording of this tribute, which appears only in her first hand-written draft.

14 MB IG RH, 13 Oct. 1943-11 April 1944.

15 Minute Book Riddel Hall House Committee (MB RH HC), Oct. 1941.

16 Reminiscence of Mollie McGeown.

17 MB RH HC, Oct. 1943.

18 MB IG RH, 13 Oct. 1943.

19 Omitted from Warden's address to Permanent Committee 1943-4.

20 Typescript memories of Riddel Hall 1944-7, Mrs M.J. Faris (née Campbell).

21 Telephone interview with Miss Power Steele, Nov. 2003.

22 Typescript memories of Riddel Hall 1944-7, Mrs M.J. Faris (née Campbell).

23 MB IG RH, 10 May 1944.

24 Ibid., 14 Oct. 1945.

25 Ibid., 10 Oct. 1945.

26 Telephone interview with Miss Power Steele, Nov. 2003.

27 Warden's address to general meeting, Oct. 1943.

28 Telephone interview with Miss Power Steele, Nov. 2003.

29 MB RH HC, 7 Oct. 1943.

30 Warden's address to general meeting, Oct. 1943.

31 Ibid.

32 Ibid., Oct. 1944.

33 Ibid., 1946-7.

34 Ibid., 1945-6.

35 Telephone interview with Miss Power Steele, Nov. 2003.

36 Ibid.

37 MB RH HC 1943-6, particularly Oct. 1946.

38 Warden's report to general meeting, 1947-8.

39 Telephone interview with Miss Power Steele.

40 MB RH HC, 15 May 1947.

41 Ibid., 13 Oct.1947.

Chapter 14. Miss Dawson

1   Miss Dawson's letter of application for the post of Warden of Riddel Hall, 14 July 1947.

2   Letter from Molly Dawson to Miss Duffin, from Yverden, Switzerland, 3 Jan. 1934 in Miss Dawson's student record.

3   J. Purvis, *A history of women's education in England* (Milton Keynes, 1991), p. 120.

4   Letter from Molly Dawson to Miss Duffin, from Swanage, 1935 in Miss Dawson's student record.

5   Miss Dawson's letter of application.

6   Testimonial of M. Morris, Senior Mistress of Holme Valley Girls' School, 11 July 1947.

7   Miss Dawson's letter of application.

8   Testimonial of K.R. Brain, Headmaster of Holme Valley Girls' School, 4 July 1947.

9   Testimonial of M. Morris, Senior Mistress of Holme Valley Girls' School, 11 July 1947.

10 Warden's report to AGM, 1974.

11 Minute Book Riddel Hall House Committee (MB RH HC), 8 Oct. 1963.

12 Warden's report to general meeting, Nov. 1968.

13 In March 1966 when she was eighty-nine years old, despite failing eyesight, Miss Duffin wrote an obituary for the first Matron of the Hall, which she sent to Miss Dawson. 'I think we should have some little memorial notice of Florence Irwin in the next number (RHOSA Chronicle), but am not satisfied with the enclosed, so if you can add to it or improve on it or get some old student to write something, please don't hesitate.' (Ruth Duffin to Molly Dawson, 5 March 1966).

14 Warden's report to governors' meeting, Nov. 1968.

15 With the exception of thirteen students these women identified themselves as British and have been placed in the category of English by their addresses and schools.

16 Warden's report to general meeting, Nov. 1956.

17 MB RH HC, 6 Oct. 1958.

18 Warden's report to AGM, Oct. 1962.

Chapter 15. A Story-Book Existence

1   Minute Book Riddel Hall House Committee, (MB RH HC), May 1950.
2   Ibid., Oct. 1951.
3   Ibid., Oct. 1961.
4   In May 1948 Miss Dawson told the house that as the tennis courts at Cherryvale were now open on Sundays it 'was not necessary to play tennis at Riddel on Sundays'.
5   Margaret Goodwin was a member of that year's House Committee. All the old students interviewed for this research remember being called Miss.
6   Warden's report to general meeting, Nov. 1953.
7   *RHOSA Chronicle*, 1955.

Chapter 16. Demands for Change

1   Miniute Book Riddel Hall House Committee, (MB RH HC), Oct. 1949.
2   Ibid., 10 Oct. 1954. Two other proposals were discussed at the extraordinary meeting, the first being that medical students be given a refund of 1s 8d per day for lunches in the Royal Victoria Hospital instead of the current one shilling. Even more controversially, it was requested that male friends could be invited into students' rooms at the weekend. Both requests were granted.
3   Minute Book Incorporated Governors of Riddel Hall (MB IG RH), 11 Oct. 1954.
4   MB RH HC, 18 Oct. 1954.
5   Ibid., 24 April 1961.
6   *RHOSA Chronicle*, 1966.
7   Warden's report to general meeting, Nov. 1965.
8   MB RH HC, Oct. 1948.
9   Ibid., Oct. 1951.
10 Ibid., 6 Oct. 1958.
11 Warden's report to general meeting, Nov. 1951.
12 MB RH HC, 6 May 1957. Interviews with contemporary students were also integrated into the narrative.

Chapter 17. Changed Times

1   T.W. Moody and J.C. Beckett, *Queen's, Belfast 1845-1945: the history of a university* Vol. II (London, 1959), p. 533.
2   Prior to this Act the fee-paying grammar schools were the only form of post-primary school education available. Around 70 percent of grammar school pupils continued to come from middle-class backgrounds.
3   *Ulster Year Book*, 1950.
4   J. Lewis, *Women in Britain since 1945* (Oxford, 1992), p. 87.

5   *Census of Population of Northern Ireland 1951, General Report*, table 15, p. 21.
6   Myrtle Hill, *Women in Ireland: A Century of Change,* (Belfast, 2003), p. 128.
7   These scholarships are still available to Queen's students. Warden's report to general meeting, Nov. 1958.
8   Brian Walker and Alf McCreary, *Degrees of excellence: the story of Queen's, Belfast 1845-1995* (Belfast, 1994), p. 115.
9   Warden's report, Nov. 1966.
10 Ibid., Nov. 1957.
11 Ibid.
12 Ibid., Nov. 1968.
13 Ibid., Nov. 1952.
14 Ibid., Nov. 1953.
15 Ibid., Nov. 1955.
16 Reminiscences of Susan Wallace and Thelma Hutchison.
17 Reminiscence of Elizabeth Lyons.
18 Warden's report, Nov. 1952.
19 Minute Book Incorporated Governors of Riddel Hall, (MB IG RH), 17 Jan. 1956.
20 MB IG RH, 13 March 1956.
21 Riddel Hall, Belfast, *Jubilee Chronicle 1913-63*, p. 4.
22 Ibid., p. 5.
23 Miniute Book Riddel Hall House Committee, (MB RH HC), 8 Oct. 1963.
24 Riddel Hall Old Students' Association *RHOSA Chronicle*, 1976.
25 This and the following paragraphs are based on S. Rowbotham, *A century of women: the history of women in Britain and the United States,* (London, 1997), pp 345-94.
26 Both statements are quoted in Walker and McCreary, *Degrees of excellence*, p. 147.
27 MB IG RH, 9 May 1961.
28 Letter from D.J. Neill to the President of Students' Representative Council, 7 March 1966, included in MB IG RH.
29 Walker and McCreary, *Degrees of excellence*, p. 125.
30 Ibid., p. 125.
31 Ibid., p. 148.
32 Academic Council Minutes 1968-9, p. 140. My thanks to Prof. Leslie Clarkson for this information.

Chapter 18. The Final Decades

1   Warden's report, Nov. 1965.
2   Ibid., Nov. 1972.
3   Miss Duffin wrote this in 1944 when the students were going bare legged to breakfast in

the summer term and she had to accept this due to the unavailability of silk in wartime.

4 Warden's report, Nov. 1966.

5 Ibid., Nov. 1967.

6 In 1951 there was room for only six first-year students at Riddel.

7 Warden's report, Nov. 1966.

8 These tasks were previously done by the domestic servants, with the exception of one hour each evening before dinner when the girl who chose the evening's poem answered the telephone. Many students who were in the Hall during Lily's twenty-six-year career recall her extremely loud voice which reverberated along the tiled corridors, 'like an intercom' yelling 'Miss... there's a gentleman on the phone. He says he's your father!'

9 Warden's report, Nov. 1969.

10 Letter preserved in Seetar Seeterram's student file, Riddel Hall Archive QUB.

11 Warden's report, Nov. 1971.

12 Minute Book Incorporated Governors of Riddel Hall (MB IG RH), 12 Nov. 1974. Details of the unacceptable behaviour are not given.

13 MB IG RH.

14 It is not mentioned by Miss Dawson until 1972.

15 Reminiscence of Thelma Hutchison.

16 Minute Book Riddel Hall House Committee, 6 Oct. 1961.

17 MB IG RH, 10 Dec. 1969.

18 AGM IG RH, 26 Nov. 1970.

19 Minutes of the Permanent Committee, 14 March 1972.

20 Warden's report, Nov. 1970.

21 Ibid., Nov. 1972.

22 Minutes of the Permanent Committee, 14 Nov. 1972.

23 Reminiscence of Gladys Williamson.

24 MB IG RH, 18 Jan. 1972.

25 Ibid., 13 Nov. 1973.

26 Warden's report, Nov. 1971.

27 Ibid., Nov. 1972.

28 Reminiscence of Gladys Williamson.

29 Letter to R.N.C. Watts, solicitor to Riddel Hall, from the governors dated 6 Jan. 1971.

30 Warden's report, Nov. 1973.

31 Ibid.

32 These were two of the eleven storey tower blocks of Queen's Elms Halls.

33 Warden's report to general meeting, 1974.

34 MB IG RH, 13 May 1969.

35 Ibid., 10 Feb. 1970.

Chapter 19. The End of 'Ould Daecency'

1 Minute Book Incorporated Governors of Riddel Hall (MB IG RH) AGM, 26 Nov. 1970.

2 Ibid., 14 March 1972.

3 Warden's report to general meeting, Nov. 1968.

4 MB IG RH, 26 Nov. 1970.

5 Letter to R.N.C. Watts, solicitor to Riddel Hall, from the governors, dated 6 Jan. 1971.

6 MB IG RH, 13 Oct. 1970.

7 Warden's report to Permanent Committee, 1969-70.

8 MB IG RH, 11 Nov. 1970.

9 Ibid., 13 Jan. 1971.

10 Ibid., 10 Feb. 1971.

11 Letter to R.N.C. Watts, solicitor to Riddel Hall, from the governors, dated 6 Jan. 1971.

12 MB IG RH, 12 March 1974.

13 Ibid., 16 May 1972.

14 Ibid., 11 Dec. 1973.

15 Ibid., 12 March 1974.

16 Minutes Extraordinary General Meeting IG RH, 24 Sept. 1974.

17 Letter from Norman Cuthbert, Chairman of IG RH to Vice-Chancellor QUB, 1 Oct. 1974.

18 Document signed by Mr D.H. Wilson, Assistant Secretary, Queen's University, 13 Nov. 1974.

19 MB IG RH, 22 April 1975.

20 Letter from Sir Arthur Vick, Vice-Chancellor of QUB to Nicholas Duffin (governor of Riddel Hall and a relation of the Riddel sisters, Managing Director of John Riddel and Son Ltd), 28 Oct. 1975.

21 Minutes of Extraordinary General Meeting IG RH, 28 Feb. 1975.

22 MB IG RH, 12 March 1975.

23 Ibid., 22 April 1975.

24 Minutes of Permanent Committee, 13 May 1975.

25 Minute Book RHOSA, 26 Oct. 1974.

26 (Undated,?1975) Trust deed included in the Permanent Committee's records.

27 *RHOSA Chronicle*, 1976, p. 28.

28 Ibid., pp 25-7. The article was unsigned. The author was perhaps Eileen O. Bartley President of RHOSA and one of the first students in the Hall. She maintained a high profile connection throughout the sixty-year life of Riddel Hall.

BIBLIOGRAPHY

BOOKS

Akenson, Donald Harman. *The Irish Educational Experiment: The National System of Education in the Nineteenth Century* (London, 1970)

Alexander, Sally. *Becoming a Woman and Other Essays in Nineteenth and Twentieth Century Feminist History* (London, 1994)

Bolt, Christine. *The Women's Movements; In the United States and Britain from the 1790s to the 1920s* (Hemel Hempstead, 1993)

Braybon, Gail. *Women Workers in The First World War: The British Experience* (London, 1981)

Budge, Ian and Cornelius O'Leary. *Belfast, Approach to Crisis: A Study of Belfast Politics 1613-1970)* (London, 1973)

Cullen, Mary (ed.). *Girls Don't Do Honours: Irish Women in Education in the Nineteenth and Twentieth Centuries* (Dublin, 1987)

Cullen, Mary and Maria Luddy. *Women, Power and Consciousness in Nineteenth Century Ireland* (Dublin, 1995)

Cullen-Owens, Rosemary. *Smashing Times; A History of the Irish Women's Suffrage Movement 1889-1922* (Dublin, 1995)

Daly, Mary E. *Women and Work in Ireland* (Dundalk, 1997)

Duffin, Lorna and Sarah Delamont. (ed.). *The Nineteenth Century Woman; Her Cultural and Physical World* (London, 1978)

Dyhouse, Carol. *Girls growing up in Late Victorian and Edwardian England* (London, 1981)

No Distinction of Sex? Women in British Universities, 1870-1939 (London, 1993)

Gribbon, Sybil. *Edwardian Belfast: A Social Profile* (Belfast, 1982).

Hill, Myrtle. *Women in Ireland; A Century of Change* (Belfast, 2003)

Hilton, Mary and Pam. Hirsch, *Practical Visionaries: Women, Education and Social Progress 1790-1930* (Harlow, 2000)

Jordan, Alison. *Who Cared? Charity in Victorian and Edwardian Belfast* (Belfast, n.d.) *Margaret Byers, pioneer of women's education and founder of Victoria College* (Belfast, n.d.)

Kamm, Josephine. *How Different from Us: A Biography of Miss Buss and Miss Beale* (London, 1958)

Lewis, Jane. *Women in Britain since 1945* (Oxford, 1992)

Luddy, Maria. *Women in Ireland, 1800-1918: A Documentary History* (Cork, 1995) *Women and Philanthropy in Nineteenth Century Ireland* (Cambridge, 1995).

Moody, T.W. and J.C. Beckett, *Queen's Belfast 1845-1949: The History of a University* (London, 1959)

McWilliams-Tullberg, Rita. *Women at Cambridge, A Men's University – Though of a Mixed Type* (London, 1975)

Newmann, Kate. *Dictionary of Ulster Biography* (Belfast, 1993)

Olafson-Hellerstein, L.P. Hume, and K. Offen, *Victorian Women: A Documentary Account of Women's Lives in Nineteenth-Century England, France and the United States* (Stanford, 1995).

Owings, A., *Frauen: German women recall the Third Reich* (London, 1993).

Owings, Alison. *Frauen; German Women Recall the Third Reich* (London, 1993)

Raitt, Suzanne. *May Sinclair; A Modern Victorian* (Oxford, 2000)

Rowbotham, Sheila. *A Century of Women: The History of Women in Britain and the United States* (London, 1997)

Vicinus, Martha. *Independent Women; Work and Community for Single Women, 1850-1920* (London, 1985)

Victoria College, Belfast, Centenary 1859-1959

Walker, Brian and Alf McCreary. *Degrees of Excellence; The Story of Queen's, Belfast, 1845-1995* (Belfast, 1994)

Ulster Year Book 1925

Ulster Year Book 1950

ARTICLES

Jordan, Alison. 'Opening Up The Gates of Learning; The Belfast Ladies' Institute, 1867-97', in Janice Holmes and Diane Urquhart (eds), *Coming into the Light; The Work, Politics and Religion of Women in Ulster 1840-1940* (Belfast, 1994), pp 33-57

Luddy, Maria. 'Isabella M.S. Tod', in L.M. Cullen and M. Luddy, *Women, Power and Consciousness* (Dublin, 1995), pp 197-230

Sangster, J. 'Telling our Stories: Feminist debates and the use of oral history' in W*omen's History Review* Vol. 3 no. 1 (1994), pp 5-28

Tinkler, P. 'Refinement and Respectable Consumption: The Acceptable Face of Women's Smoking in Britain 1918-70, in *Gender and History,* Vol. 15 no. 2 (2003), pp 342-60

Woollacott, A. 'Maternalism, Professionalism and Industrial Welfare Supervisors in World War I Britain', in *Women's History Review* Vol. 3 no. 1 (1994), pp 29-56

Obituary of Anne Jellicoe in *Journal of the Women's Education Union*, 8 (1880)

PARLIAMENTARY PAPERS

Census of Ireland for the Year 1901, H.C. 1902 [Cd.1123] lxxvi; *Census of Ireland for the Year 1911*, H.C. 1912-13 [Cd. 6051-X] cxvi p. 37.

Census of Ireland for the years 1891 and 1901 and 1911. Irish Data Base Dept. E.S.H, QUB.

Census of Northern Ireland 1961 Table xxv terminal education age.

HC Reports of Commissioners 1914 xxvi pp 288 and 369 HC 1890 xxx p. 77

Medical Acts Commission on Women in Medicine, Minutes of Evidence, HC 1882 [Cd.3259] xxix.

Report of the Commissioners of Intermediate Education Board (Ireland) 1892, HC 1893-4 [Cd.7040] xxvii.

Evidence of Mrs. Byers to the Intermediate Education Commissioners 1899. HC 1899 [Cd.9512] xxiii.

Census of Northern Ireland 1951

ARCHIVAL SOURCES

BELFAST NEWSPAPER LIBRARY

Northern Whig, 25 Aug. 1874.
Northern Whig, 26 Aug. 1874.
Northern Whig, 14 Sept. 1915
The Witness, 16 Oct. 1874.
Belfast Evening Telegraph, 17 Jan. 1915
Belfast Evening Telegraph, 1 Jan. 1915
Belfast Telegraph, 22 Oct. 1921.
Belfast Newsletter, 31 Oct. 1964

QUEEN'S UNIVERSITY BELFAST

QUB Calendar 1908-9, 1909-10, 1914-15, 1915-6.
Academic Council Minutes 1968-9, p. 140.
QCB, Vol. XII no. 8, June 1911; Vol. XV no. 2, Jan. 1914; Vol. XIX no. 1, Feb. 1918.
Frav-lio-Queen's no. 2, May 1926.
Ulster Year Book 1921 and 1935.
Ulster Yearbook 1925, Ministry of Finance Report, p. 115.
Hutchinson's *Belfast and the Province of Ulster Street Directory.*
The British Medical Journal 24 Jan. 1925, p. 144.
Calendar of Queen's College Belfast 1913-4.
QUB Alumni magazine, Spring 1998.
Queen's Women Graduates' Association Annual Reports.

BELFAST CENTRAL LIBRARY

Historical Pamphlet describing the firm of Riddel's Limited, published in 1935.

PUBLIC RECORDS OFFICE OF NORTHERN IRELAND

Diaries of Ruth Duffin 1895-1901 PRONI D/2109/17/2-4; 1900-1905 PRONI D/2109/6/5.
Miscellaneous Duffin family correspondence 1895-7 PRONI D/2109/6/4-6.
Duffin, Riddel and Musgrave family trees.
Riddel Hall Rules undated early edition PRONI D/3119/5/13.
Box of Records of Riddel Hall PRONI D/3119/3/2.
Wills of Samuel Riddel 1904; Eliza Riddel, 14 March 1924; and Isabella Riddel 29 Dec. 1918
     PRONI.
PRONI Education Leaflet 2, 'The Belfast Blitz'.

RIDDEL HALL ARCHIVE

Riddel Hall Chronicle, written by Ruth Duffin on her retirement as Warden in 1944.
Miss Duffin's notebook (handwritten draft for the Riddel Hall Chronicle).
Minute Books of the Incorporated Governors of Riddel Hall 1913-76.
Minute Books of the Permanent Committee 1955-63, 1963-70 1970-76.
Warden's report to the Annual General Meetings 1916-76.
Warden's report to the governors' Meetings 1916-76.
Warden's addresses to the house meetings 1926-41.

Minute Books of the Riddel Hall House Committee 1921- 65.

Riddel Hall House Committee members 1924-67.

Incorporated Governors of Riddel Hall wages and salaries books.

Incorporated Governors of Riddel Hall accounts ledgers 1913-76.

Incorporated Governors of Riddel Hall cash receipts.

Incorporated Governors of Riddel Hall register of members 1913-1975.

Incorporated Governors of Riddel Hall record of attendances at general meetings 1925-1975.

Minute Book of the Riddel Hall Jubilee Appeal Committee 1961-63.

Jubilee Fund ledger 1962-76.

Riddel Hall library catalogue.

Riddel Hall Old Students' Association minute books 1934-1997

Riddel Hall Old Students' Association Chronicle 1951-93.

Obituary of Miss Florence Irwin cut from undated unidentified newspaper clipping ? early March 1966.

Letter of appreciation on the death of Miss Florence Irwin 5 March 1966.

Article in 'Tatler Woman' entitled 'The Duffins' by Dorothy Gharbaoui, in *The Ulster Tatler*, no date. ?early 1970s. p. 31.

Queen's University of Belfast, Centenary Celebrations 1949.

Miss Dawson's letter of application for the post of warden of Riddel Hall 14 July 1947.

Testimonial of M. Morris, senior mistress of Holme Valley Girls' School, 11 July 1947 (Miss Dawson).

Testimonial of K.R. Brain, headmaster of Holme Valley Girls' School, 4 July 1947 (Miss Dawson).

'As I was walking down Stranmillis Road; Riddel Revisited', in *Gown*, 22 Nov. 1957.

Prospectus of Riddel Hall 1934.

Typescript memories of Riddel Hall 1944-7 M.J. Faris née Campbell.

Riddel Hall, Belfast *Jubilee Chronicle 1913-63*, p. 5.

Letter from D.J. Neill to President of SRC 7 March 1966.

Letter to R.N.C. Watts, solicitor to Riddel Hall, from the governors dated 6 Jan. 1971.

Letter from Norman Cuthbert, Chairman of IGRH to Vice-Chancellor QUB 1 Oct. 1974.

Letter from Arthur Vick, Vice-Chancellor of QUB to Nicholas Duffin 28 Oct. 1975.

Architects' draft plans for QUB loan financed students' residence 1971.

(undated ?1975) Trust deed included in the Permanent Committee's records.

Individual student records 1915-75.

RHOSA Chronicles.

Queens' Women Graduates Association Annual Reports.

Miscellaneous correspondence.

INTERVIEWS WITH AUTHOR

Summer and autumn 2003

Rhoda Acheson, Dorothy Campbell, Lesley Crozier, Helen Gallagher, Gina Martin, Honor Gray, Kathleen Heron, Thelma Hutchinson, Elizabeth Lyons, Margaret Lyons, Joey McCausland, Molly McGeown, Rosemary McIlroy, Sandra McMaster, Diana Martin, Nessie Maybin, Elizabeth Mills, Margaret Mitchell, Betty Nicholl, Bree Sawh, Elizabeth Small, Moira Strawbridge, Susan Wallace, Gladys Williamson, Eleanor Wilson

Miss Joyce Power Steele

GLOSSARY

AGM	Annual General Meeting
ARP	Air Raid Protection
ATS	Auxiliary Territorial Service
BLI	Belfast Ladies' Institute
BCSW	Belfast Council for Social Welfare
IG RH	Incorporated Governors of Riddel Hall
IWSF	Irish Women's Suffrage Federation
MB RH HC	Minute Book Riddel Hall House Committee
NIWRM	Northern Ireland Women's Rights Movement
PRONI	Public Record Office of Northern Ireland
QCB	Queen's College Belfast
QUB	Queen's University Belfast
QWGA	Queen's Women Graduates' Association
RHOSA	Riddel Hall Old Students' Association
SRC	Students' Representative Council
TCD	Trinity College Dublin
VAD	Voluntary Aid Detachment
WEU	Women's Education Union
WSH	Women Students' Hall
WSPU	Women's Social and Political Union
UCCA	Universities' Central Council of Admission
YWCA	Young Women's Christian Association

INDEX